Napoleon's Eagle Standards

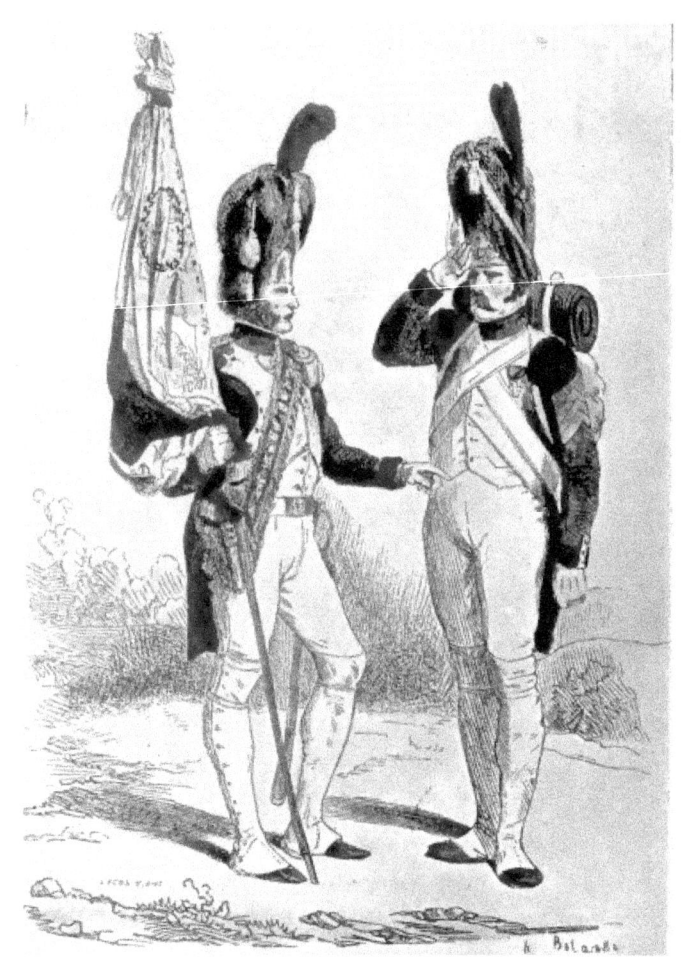

PORTE-AIGLE, IMPERIAL GUARD,
AND GRENADIER SERGEANT IN PARADE UNIFORM

Napoleon's Eagle Standards
The Story of the Creation, Defence and Loss of the Regimental Eagles of the French Army of the First Empire

Edward Fraser

Napoleon's Eagle Standards
The Story of the Creation, Defence and Loss of the Regimental Eagles of the French Army of the First Empire
by Edward Fraser

First published under the title
The War Drama of the Eagles

Leonaur is an imprint
of Oakpast Ltd

Copyright in this form © 2014 Oakpast Ltd

ISBN: 978-1-78282-431-2 (hardcover)
ISBN: 978-1-78282-432-9 (softcover)

http://www.leonaur.com

Publisher's Notes

The views expressed in this book are not necessarily those of the publisher.

Contents

Preface	9
Napoleon Adopts the Eagle of Caesar	11
The Day of the Presentation on the Field Of Mars	20

IN THE FIRST CAMPAIGN:

Under Fire With Marshal Ney	45
On the Field of Austerlitz	66

IN THE SECOND CAMPAIGN:

Jena and the Triumph of Berlin	83
The "Eagle-Guard"	118
Before the Enemy at Aspern and Wagram	127
"The Eagle With the Golden Wreath" in London	137
Other Eagles in England From Battlefields of Spain	153
After Moscow: How the Eagles Faced Their Fate	166
That Terrible Midnight at the Invalides	201
The Eagles of the Last Army	218

AT WATERLOO:

"Ave Caesar! Morituri te Salutant!"	237
After the Downfall	274

These Eagles to you shall ever be your rallying-point. Swear to sacrifice your lives in their defence; to maintain them by your courage ever in the path of victory.—On the day of the Presentation on the Field of Mars.

The soldier who loses his Eagle loses his Honour and his All!
                       Address to the 4th of the Line after Austerlitz.

The loss of an Eagle is an affront to the reputation of its regiment for which neither victory nor the glory acquired on a hundred fields can make amends.
                  55th Bulletin of the Grand Army: 1807.

                                                Napoleon.

Preface

This book breaks fresh ground in a field of romantic and widespread interest; one that should prove attractive, associated as it is with the ever-fascinating subject of Napoleon. Incidentally, indeed, it may also help to throw a new sidelight on certain characteristics of Napoleon as a soldier.

I venture to hope at the same time that it will arouse interest further as offering independent testimony to the valour of our own soldiers, the Old British Army which, under Wellington, defeated on the battlefield the veterans of the Eagles whose feats of heroism and hardihood are described in the book. Magnificent as were the acts of fine daring and heroic endurance of the men whom Wellington led to victory, no less stirring and deserving of admiration were the deeds of chivalrous valour and stern fortitude done for the honour of Napoleon's Eagles by the gallant soldiers who faced them and proved indeed foemen worthy of their steel. All who hold in regard cool, self-sacrificing bravery and steadfast courage in adversity and peril will find no lack of instances in the stories of what the warriors of the Eagles dared and underwent for the name and fame of the Great Captain.

The record of Napoleon's Eagles in war has never before been set forth, and the centenary year of Badajoz and Salamanca and the Moscow Campaign seems to offer a befitting occasion for its appearance.

The world, indeed, is in the midst of a cycle of Napoleonic centenaries. Our own centenary memories of Talavera—the victory of which Wellington said, in later years, that if his Allies had done their part, "it would have been as great a battle as Waterloo"—of Busaco ridge and Torres Vedras, of heroic Barrosa and desperate Albuhera,—these are only just behind us. Immediately ahead lie the centenaries of yet greater events. In less than a twelvemonth hence England will mark the centenary of Vittoria, Wellington's decisive day in Spain, the crowning triumph of the Peninsular War; and yet more than that in its import and sequel for Europe. It was the news of Vittoria that, in July 1813, decided Napoleon's father-in-law to throw Austria's sword into the balance against the Man of Destiny, compelling Napoleon, with what remained of the Grand Army, to stand at bay for the "Battle of the Nations" on the Marchfeldt before Leipsic. Within six months from then, the world, in like manner, will recall the Farewell of Fontainebleau, and Elba; and finally, in the year after that, the British Empire will commemorate the epoch-making centenary of the greatest of all British triumphs in arms on land—

> *Of that fierce field where last the Eagles swooped,*
> *Where our Great Master wielded Britain's sword,*
> *And the Dark Soul the world could not subdue,*
> *Bowed to thy fortune, Prince of Waterloo!*

—the triple-event, indeed, of Waterloo, the *Bellerophon*, St. Helena.

The stories told here exist indeed, even in France, only in more or less fragmentary form, scattered broadcast amongst the memoirs left by the men of the Napoleonic time. They have not before been brought together within the covers of a book.

I have utilised, in addition to the personal memoirs of Napoleon's officers, French regimental records, bulletins, and despatches (noted in my List of Authorities), other official military documents, contemporary newspapers, both British and foreign, and information kindly placed at my disposal by the authorities of Chelsea Royal Hospital and the Royal United Service Institution, and by friends abroad.

Edward Fraser.

CHAPTER 1

Napoleon Adopts the Eagle of Caesar

Napoleon Bonaparte became Emperor, "by Divine Will and the Constitution of the French Republic"—Imperator and hereditary Caesar of the Republic—on Friday, May 18, 1804. Three weeks later it was publicly announced in the *Moniteur* that the Eagle had been adopted as the heraldic cognisance of the new *régime* in France.

Its selection for the State armorial bearing of the Empire was one of Napoleon's first acts. That the Roman *lictor's* axe and fasces surmounted by the red Phrygian cap, with its traditions of revolution, which had supplanted the *Fleur-de-Lis* of the monarchy, and had served as the official badge on the standards of the Republic and the Consulate, should continue under the Imperial *régime*, was obviously impossible. But what distinctive emblem should be adopted in its stead?

Napoleon had the question debated in his presence at the first *séance* of the Imperial Council of State. He had, it would seem, not made up his mind in regard to it. At any rate, a few days before the meeting of the Council, he had directed a Committee to draw up a statement and offer suggestions.

The matter was brought forward at the first meeting of the Imperial Council, held at the Château of Saint-Cloud on Tuesday, June 12, 1804, after a preliminary discussion on the arrangements for the Coronation, when and where it should be held, and what was to be the form of ceremonial. The Coronation, all agreed at the outset, must take place in the current year. Rheims, Aix-la-Chapelle, and Paris, in turn, were suggested as suitable places for the ceremony, Paris being finally decided on; the scene of the event to be the Champ de Mars. Napoleon himself proposed the Champs de Mars, with a threefold ceremony there—the taking of the constitutional oath, the actual coronation, the presentation of the Emperor to the assembled people.

A brief discussion followed on the form of the Coronation ceremony, whether it should be accompanied by religious rites. It was put forward that, as Charlemagne had received his authority from the Pope, might not the Pope now be induced to visit Paris and personally crown the Emperor? Napoleon, intervening in the discussion, made a strong point of the necessity of some kind of religious service on the occasion. He did not care much, he cynically remarked, what religion was selected; only it must be in accordance with the views of the majority of the nation.

It would be impossible to do without some sort of religious observance. In all nations, said he, Ceremonies of State were accompanied by religious services. As to asking the Pope to take part, from his point of view, at the moment, the attendance of a Papal legate would be preferable. If the Pope himself came to Paris, his presence would assuredly tend to relegate the Emperor to a secondary position: "*Tout le monde me laisserait pour courir voir le Pape!*" The matter, however, as the discussion proceeded, seemed to present so many difficulties, that the Council, after declaring themselves generally against having any religious ceremony at all, decided to leave the question for further consideration.

On that the Council turned to deal with the selection of the heraldic insignia and official badge of the Empire.

Senator Crétet, on behalf of the special Committee appointed by Napoleon to prepare a statement for the Council, presented his report. The Committee, he said, had decided unanimously to recommend the Cock, the historic national emblem of Ancient Gaul, as the most fitting cognisance for Imperial France. Should that not find favour with the Council, either the Eagle, the Lion, or the Elephant, in the opinion of the Committee, might well be adopted. Individual members of the Committee, added Crétet, had further suggested the Aegis of Minerva, or some flower like the *Fleur-de-Lis*, an Oak-tree, or an Ear of Corn.

Miot, one of the members of the Council, rose as Crétet sat down, and protested against the re-introduction of the *Fleur-de-Lis*. That, he said, was imbecility. He proposed a figure of the Emperor seated on his throne as the best possible badge for the French Empire.

He was not seconded, however, and Napoleon interposed abruptly to set aside the Committee's suggestion of reviving the Gallic Cock. He dismissed that notion with a contemptuous sneer. "Bah," he exclaimed, "the Cock belongs to the farmyard! It is far too feeble a creature!" ("*Le Coq est de basse cour. C'est un animal trop faible!*") Napoleon spoke rapidly and vivaciously. He had not yet, in those early days, acquired the impressive Imperial style that he afterwards affected. "His language at these earlier Council meetings was still impregnated with his original Jacobin style; he spoke frequently, spontaneously, familiarly; monologued at the top of his voice (*avec des éclats de voix*); apostrophised frequently, appearing at times as though overcome with nervousness, now almost in tears, now breaking out in a frenzy of passion, unrestrainedly emphasising his personal likes and dislikes."

Count Ségur, Imperial Grand Master of the Ceremonies, suggested the Lion as the most suitable emblem: "*parcequ'il vaincra le Léopard*," he explained.

Councillor Laumond proposed the adoption of the Elephant instead; with for a motto "*Mole et Mente*" The Elephant had a great vogue at that day among European heraldic authorities as being pre-eminently a royal beast. There was a widely prevalent belief, on the authority of old writers on natural history, that an Elephant could not be made to bow its knees. Further, too, the elephant typified resistless strength as well as magnanimity. And had not Caesar himself once placed the effigy of the Elephant on the Roman coinage? Nobody else at the Council, however, seemed to care for the Elephant.

Councillor Simon objected to Ségur's proposition, on the score that the Lion was essentially an aggressive beast.

Cambacérès, ex-Consul and Arch-Chancellor of the Empire, suggested a swarm of Bees as the most suitable national emblem. It would represent the actual situation of France, he explained—a republic with a presiding chief.

Councillor Lacuèe supported Cambacérès. The Bee, he added, was the more suitable, in that it possessed a sting as well as being a maker of honey.

Cambacérès remarked that he favoured the idea of the Bee as typifying peaceful industry rather than offensive power.

The other members took no interest in the idea of the Bee, and after some discursive talk the Council fell back on the Committee's original suggestion of the historic Gallic Cock. The general voice favoured the adoption of the Cock, and they unanimously voted for it.

That, however, would not do for Napoleon. He sharply refused once more to hear of the Cock in any circumstances. He had for some minutes sat silent, listening to the discussion until the vote was taken. On that he rose and banned the Cock absolutely and finally. He exclaimed:

> The Cock is quite too weak a creature. A thing like that cannot possibly be the cognisance of an Empire such as France. You must make your choice between the Eagle, the Elephant, and the Lion!

The Eagle, however, did not commend itself to the Council. That emblem, it was pointed out by several members, had been already adopted by other European nations. For France, such being the case, the Eagle would not be sufficiently distinctive. The German Empire had the Eagle for its cognisance. So had Austria. So had Prussia. So had Poland even—the White Eagle of the *Jagellons*. The Council was plainly not attracted by the Eagle.

Lebrun, the other ex-Consul, Arch-Treasurer of the Empire, now put in a word again for the *Fleur-de-Lis*. It had been, he said, the national emblem of France under all the previous dynasties. The *Fleur-de-Lis*, declared Lebrun, was the real historic emblem of France, and he proposed that it should be adopted for the Empire.

Nobody, though, supported him, one member, Councillor Regnaud, condemning the idea of the *Fleur-de-Lis* as utterly out of date. "The nation," added Regnaud, with a sneer, "will neither go back to the cult of the Lilies nor to the religion of Rome!"

At that point Napoleon lost patience. Interposing to close the discussion, he curtly bade the Council to cease from wasting time. They must decide on the Lion for the Imperial Emblem. His preference was for the figure of a Lion, lying over the map of France, with one paw stretched out across the Rhine: "*Il faut prendre un Lion, s'étendu sur la carte de France, la patte prête à dépasser le Rhin.*" Napoleon proposed in addition, by way of motto, beneath the Lion-figure, these defiant words: "*Malheur à qui me cherche!*"

No more was said on the subject after that. The Council submitted forthwith to Napoleon's dictation, and, as it would appear, without taking any formal vote, passed to the remaining business of the day: the inscription on the new coinage and certain amendments to the Criminal Code.

But even then, as it befell, the decision as to the national emblem was not conclusive. Napoleon changed his mind about the Lion shortly after the Council had broken up. The Lion as the designated cognisance of the French Empire did not last twenty-four hours. Napoleon himself, on the report of the Council meeting being presented for his signature, definitely rejected the Lion. He cancelled his own proposition with a stroke of his pen. With his own hand the Emperor struck out the words "*Lion couchant*," with the reference to the map of France and the Rhine, writing over the erasure, "*Un Aigle éployé*"—an Eagle with extended wings. So Napoleon independently settled the matter.

Napoleon, as it would appear, in making his ultimate choice of the Eagle, had this in his mind. Charlemagne was ever in his thoughts at that time as his own destined exemplar. The Eagle of Charlemagne, it was now borne in upon his mind irresistibly, had a pre-eminent claim to be recalled and become the national heraldic badge for the new Frankish Empire of the West, as having been the traditional emblem of Imperial authority in the ancient Frankish Empire, the prototype and historic predecessor of the Empire of which he was head. Said Napoleon, indeed, in justifying his final adoption of the Eagle: "*Elle affirme la dignité Impériale et rappelait Charlemagne.*"

A commission to design the new Imperial Eagle "after that of Charlemagne" was forthwith given to Isabey (the elder Isabey—Jean Baptiste), "*Peintre et Dessinateur du Cabinet de l'Empereur*," whose reputation was at that moment at its zenith. The artist, however, had no Carlovingian model to draw from, and nobody, it would appear, could give him any advice. He had to depict "*Un Aigle éployé*"—a spread-Eagle. Discarding heraldic conventionalism, he produced the Napoleonic Eagle of history; an Eagle *au naturel*, shown in the act of taking wing. The idea of it Isabey took from a sketch he himself had made nine years before, in the Monastery of the Certosa of Milan, of an eagle sculptured on one of the tombs of the Visconti.

Following on his adoption of the Eagle for the cognisance of the Empire at large, Napoleon announced that the Eagle would in future be the battle-standard of the Army. He had, though, as to that Eagle, yet another thought in his mind. For his soldiers he desired the French Eagle to represent the military standard of Ancient Rome, the historic emblem of Caesar's legionaries, with its resplendent traditions of world-wide victory. That intention, furthermore, Napoleon went out of his way to emphasise significantly through the place and moment that he chose for the promulgation of the Army Order appointing the Eagle of the Caesars as the battle-standard of the French Empire. The Imperial rescript was dated from the Camp of the "Army of the Ocean" at Boulogne; from amidst the vast array of soldiers mustered there for the threatened invasion of England.

At the same time Isabey's design for one Eagle would suffice as a model for the other. It sufficiently suggested the Roman type. Like Charlemagne, had not Napoleon led his army across the Alps? like Caesar, was he not about to lead it across the Straits?

The Eagle with wings outspread, as on the Imperial Seal, will be at the head of the standard-staves, as was the practice in the Roman army—(*placèe au sommet du bâton, telle que la portaient les Romains*). The flag will be attached at the same distance beneath the Eagle, as was the Labarum.

So Napoleon wrote in his preliminary instructions from Boulogne to Marshal Berthier, Head of the *Etat-Major* of the "Army of England," at that moment on duty at the War Office in Paris.

The Eagle, Napoleon directed, was of itself to constitute the standard: "*Essentiellement constituer l'étendard*," were Napoleon's words. He set a secondary value on the flag which the Eagle surmounted. The flag to Napoleon was a subsidiary adjunct.

Flags, of course, would come and go. They could be renewed, he wrote, as might be necessary, at any time; every two years, or oftener. The Eagle, on the other hand, was to be a permanency. It was to be for all time the standard of its corps: also, to add still further to its sacrosanct nature and *éclat*, every Eagle would be received only from the hands of the Emperor.[1]

Every battalion of Foot and Squadron of Horse was to have its Eagle, which, on parade and before the enemy under fire, would be in the special charge of the battalion or squadron sergeant-major, with an escort of picked veteran soldiers; "men who had distinguished themselves on the battlefield in at least two combats."

Exceptional care, Napoleon laid down, was to be taken by regimental commanders that no harm should befall the Eagle. In the event of accident happening to it, a special report was to be made

---

1. "The Eagle for each standard," said Napoleon, going into details with Berthier, "must be made 'strong and light'—'*Il convient de la rendre a la fois solide et légère*.'"
"An Eagle looking to its left, with wings half expanded, and with its talons grasping a thunderbolt, as in the old Roman standard," was the approved design: the bird measuring eight inches from head to feet, and in the spread of its wings from tip to tip, nine and a half inches. Below the thunderbolt, as base and support, was a tablet of brass, three inches square; bearing in raised figures the number of the regiment. The weight of the whole the Eagle was to be of copper, gilded over was just three and a half pounds avoirdupois, and a stout oaken staff was provided, eight feet long and painted *bleu impérial*, to which the silken regimental colour was attached; the flag being thirty-five inches along the staff and thirty-three lengthwise, in the fly.

direct to the Emperor. Should it unfortunately happen that the Eagle was lost in battle, the regiment concerned would have to prove to the Emperor's satisfaction that there had been no default. No new Eagle would be granted in place of one lost until the regiment in question had atoned for the slur on its character by either achieving "*éclatante*" distinction in the field, by some exceptionally brilliant feat of arms, or by presenting the Emperor with an enemy's standard "taken by its own valour."

The silken tricolour flag, as has been said, was in the eyes of Napoleon of subordinate account. It was to be considered merely as a set-off to the Eagle, as merely "*l'ornement de l'Aigle*" The Eagle, and the Eagle only, must be the object of the soldier's devotion. Napoleon paid little regard to the flag, beyond as being of use for displaying the record of a regiment's war career. He would have liked indeed, as it would seem, to substitute another flag altogether, and went so far as to have designs for a green regimental flag submitted to him.[2]

Prudence, however, forbade its introduction, and directions were issued that the general pattern of tricolour standard in use under the Consulate should be retained, with minor alterations of detail in the design rendered necessary in consequence of the new constitution of the State.

The regimental flags would consist of a white diamond-shaped centre, with the corners of the flag alternately red and blue; according to the pattern authorised two years previously by Napoleon as First Consul. Thus the national colours would continue to be represented. For the Infantry, in the centre of each flag would be, on one side, the words "*Empire Français*," with the legend, inscribed in letters of gold, "*L'Empereur des Français au —^{e} Régiment d'Infanterie de Ligne*," which would take the place of the Republican inscription hitherto borne there; the number of each corps being inscribed in the blank space and in a laurel chaplet embroidered at each corner of the flag. For Cavalry the inscription ran: "*L'Empereur des Français au —^{e} Cuirassiers*," or "*au —^{e} Chasseurs*"; and so on for other corps, Artillery, Dragoons, and Hussars.

On the reverse, for corps of all arms, with the exception of the Guard, was emblazoned the motto "*Valeur et Discipline*," and beneath it the number of the battalion or squadron in each regiment.

Below the numbers was added any Inscription of Honour which

---

2. The drawings made and laid before Napoleon at Saint-Cloud are in existence, preserved among the archives of the Ministry of War in Paris.

had been granted to the corps, such as, in the case of one regiment,

"*Le 15ᵉ est couvert de la Gloire*"; in the case of another, "*Le Terrible 57ᵉ qui rien n'arrête*"; with others, "*Le Bon et Brave 28ᵉ*"; "*Le 75ᵉ arrive et bât l'Ennemi*"; "*J'étais tranquille, le brave 32ᵉ etait là*"; "*Il n'est pas possible d'être plus brave que le 63ᵉ*"; "*Brave 18ᵉ, je vous connais. L'Ennemi ne tiendra pas devant vous*"; and so on.

These were mostly quotations from "mentions in despatches" made by Napoleon in regard to regiments in his famous "Army of Italy," authorised by him, at first of his own initiative, and later as First Consul, to be recorded as Inscriptions of Honour on the regimental colours. The flags of other corps bore names of victories of note in which the regiments had taken part; as, for instance, "Rivoli," "Lodi," "Marengo."³

Napoleon overlooked nothing that might add to the prestige of his Eagles. Not only would he himself personally present its Eagle to each regiment, but, further, there would be at the outset a general presentation of Eagles in Paris to the whole Army, which would be made a State event of significance, and form an integral part of the ceremony of his Coronation.

On that Napoleon had insisted, in reply to a technical legal objection raised at one of the meetings of the Council of State. It was not to be a Parisian popular show.

He was ready, indeed, he said, to transfer the ceremony to Boulogne. "*Je rassemblerais deux cent mille hommes au camp. Là j'aurais une population couverte des blessures dont je serais sûr!*" He gave directions that the Presentation of the Eagles should take place on the Field of Mars

---

3. All armies, as a fact, owe to Napoleon the introduction of the practice of inscribing on the colours of a regiment the names of battles in which that regiment has won honour; nowadays an essential feature of the war-flags of all nations. It originated after Napoleon's first campaign as General Bonaparte, at the head of the Army of Italy; and, together with the inscriptions of quotations of passages from his despatches, was introduced by him as a device to aid in developing military spirit and a sense of *esprit de corps* among the soldiers. The Directory promptly censured the innovating young general for acting without having first referred the matter to Paris. They sent orders that all such inscriptions were to be forthwith deleted from the flags. Napoleon, however, refused to obey; and the regiments of his Army supported him. One and all protested against the removal of their titles to fame, the first appearance of which on their flags had been hailed with enthusiasm. In the result the Directory deemed it advisable to accept the situation; and after that, in turn, the flags of the regiments of the other Republican armies elsewhere were authorised to display similar decorations of their own. The practice in due course was adopted in the other armies of Europe.

in front of the Military School, on the same day as the Coronation, and should follow immediately after the religious service and his actual crowning and consecration by the Pope in Notre Dame.[4]

---

[4] The sending of an invitation to the Pope had been finally decided on in July, after a series of protracted discussions in the Imperial Council of State.

CHAPTER 2

The Day of the Presentation on the Field Of Mars

The Coronation, Napoleon first proposed, should take place in the chapel of the Invalides, on the historic day of the 18th *Brumaire* (November 9). Directly after it he would proceed in Imperial State, wearing his crown and robes, to the Field of Mars—the Champ de Mars, in front of the Military School, a stone's-throw away—there to administer the Military Oath of Allegiance to the army and distribute the Eagles at a grand review to be attended by representative deputations from every regiment of the army from all over the Empire, assembled in Paris for the occasion. It was found preferable, however, that the Coronation service should take place in the Cathedral of Notre Dame instead of at the Invalides; and at a later date.

Still, however, Napoleon held to his first idea of proceeding direct from the Coronation ceremony to the Field of Mars. He insisted that the presentation of the Eagles should follow as a joint ceremony immediately after his own consecration service. But there was Josephine to be considered. She was to accompany Napoleon throughout. The Empress, for her part, on hearing what was intended, declared herself physically incapable of bearing the strain of the double ceremony, and, in the result, Napoleon changed his original purpose at the eleventh hour. He consented to put off the presentation of the Eagles until the following morning.

That plan, in turn, had to be altered. On the very afternoon of the Coronation, on his return to the Tuileries from Notre Dame, Napoleon found himself compelled, in consequence of the Empress's state of nervous prostration after the fatiguing cathedral service, again to defer the ceremony of the presentation of the Eagles. The Emperor now fixed the following Wednesday, December 5, for the "*Fête des Aigles*," as the army spoke of it—three days from then. There was no further putting off after that.

The plans for the muster were drawn up on a *grandiose* and elaborate scale. They provided for an immense attendance under arms of, according to one account, eighty thousand men; to comprise the Imperial Guard, and the garrison of Paris, together with special detachments sent to Paris as representative deputations by every regiment and corps of the army, from all over the Empire. Over a thousand Eagles altogether were to be presented: two hundred and eighty to cavalry regiments; six hundred odd to infantry, artillery, and special corps; between forty and fifty to the Navy (one for the crew of every ship of the Line in commission); besides a hundred and eight to the departmental legions of the National Guard, the constitutional militia of Revolutionary France, which Napoleon, for reasons of policy, could not pass over. Every infantry battalion and cavalry squadron, and brigade (or battery) of artillery was to have its Eagle.

Each infantry deputation, from both the Imperial Guard and the Line, would comprise the colonel or regimental commander, four other officers, and ten *sous-officiers* and men from each of the three battalions that at that period made up a French regiment of Foot. In all, in addition to the regiments of the Imperial Guard, one hundred and twelve regiments of the Line were to be represented, together with thirty-one of Light Infantry, twelve of grenadiers, and one of foreign infantry. A deputation of fifteen officers and men was to represent each of the hundred and odd cavalry regiments of the Guard and Line; and smaller individual detachments would represent the various other arms and branches of the service appointed to receive Eagles. They would all pass before the Emperor and receive their Eagles from him personally, on behalf of their absent comrades, the six hundred thousand men who at that moment constituted the active field army of France. From every French ship of the Line in commission there would in like manner attend ten officers and men.

From far and near the detachments of soldiers and sailors converged on the capital, marching some of them hundreds of miles from the most distant frontier garrisons of the Empire, and being several weeks on the road. The deputations of the First Army Corps, for instance, part of which was stationed in Hanover, set off early in October; some of its soldiers, quartered by the Elbe, and with from four to five hundred miles of road before them, started in the last week of

September. The detachments from Italy and the Venetian frontier, for another instance, the deputations from the 1st of the Line, the 10th, the 52nd, and 101st of the Verona garrison, had over eight hundred miles to go, and started early in September.

Quite an army, indeed, was on the move along the highways of France during October and November; all heading for Paris, marching by day and being billeted in the towns and villages by night. A huge series of detachments came from the camp of the "Army of the Ocean" at Boulogne assembled for the invasion of England. Marshal Soult, the commander-in-chief at Boulogne, with Marshals Davout and Ney, preceded them, Admiral Bruix, in charge of the Boulogne "Invasion Flotilla" of gunboats and transports, accompanying Soult. The troops in Holland; the garrisons of the Rhine fortresses, such as Mayence and Strasburg, and of Metz; that of Bayonne on the Spanish frontier; troops at every place of arms and cantonment and regimental *dépôt* all over France—all sent their deputations; also every outlying camp, every naval port along the coast, from the Texel and Antwerp, Brest, Rochfort, and L'Orient round to Toulon, in the south.

Orders were given in every case that the detachments were each to bring the existing regimental colours, which, it was understood, were to be given up on parade in exchange for the Eagles.

A roomy expanse of level ground several acres in extent, an oblong-shaped area nearly three-quarters of a mile in length and six hundred yards across, the Field of Mars offered an ideal place for a showy military spectacle. Thousands of people could look on comfortably at the display from the turfed slopes of the twenty-feet-high embankment which skirted the Field of Mars on three sides, and had been fitted up by the municipality with rows of seats in closely set tiers. As many as three hundred thousand spectators, indeed, could on occasion be accommodated there.

The fourth side of the Champ de Mars was bounded by the *façade* of the *Ecole Militaire*—three great domed blocks of buildings connected together and affording a grand view of the scene for hundreds of privileged guests. The entire frontage of the Military School to the height of the first-floor windows was taken up for the Day of the Eagles parade by an immense grand-stand, constructed to form a series of pavilions for the accommodation of the great official personages invited; with, in the centre, in front of the lofty colonnaded portico, a magnificently decorated Imperial Pavilion, whence Napoleon and Josephine seated on their thrones would look on and receive the homage of the army.

The only thing that was unpropitious was the weather. It proved, as far as the weather went, an unfortunate change of date. The day of the Coronation, December 2—it was, by the way, Advent Sunday—had been cold and trying, with lowering clouds overhead, but dry. On the Monday, Napoleon's second choice, it was much the same out of doors; and on the Tuesday the weather kept fair. Then, however, it changed. During Tuesday afternoon the glass began to go down ominously and a chilly wind from the south-east set in. Towards ten at night rain and sleet in incessant showers began to fall—typical *Frimaire* weather, in keeping with the character of the "sleety month." "When it did not rain," says somebody, "it snowed, and between whiles it rained and snowed at the same time." That was what the weather was like when Wednesday morning broke; but in spite of it the Imperial programme was to be carried out in its entirety, and hundreds of thousands of intending spectators braved the discomfort and started early to get a good place for witnessing the historic display.

All Paris turned out early, prepared to sit out the day from eight in the morning until probably after four in the afternoon, packed in dense masses round the Champ de Mars.

The heavy firing of salvos of artillery soon after dawn, from a dozen points all over Paris, ushered in the day's doings. The whole city was already, as has been said, astir and in the streets, making its way to the Champ de Mars. Everywhere dark columns of cloaked soldiers, horse and foot, artillerymen without their guns, were tramping along through the slush and mud for their posts; some to take part on the route of the procession, which was to start from the Tuileries; most of them bound for the Field of Mars. Along the streets to be passed by the Imperial procession the houses were gaily decked out with festoons and branches of evergreens, or with coloured hangings and drapings. Oriental rugs of gorgeous hues and patterns, hired or borrowed for the Coronation week, hung from most of the windows; they were the favourite form of decoration. Here and there flags were seen, but it was not the fashion in Paris at that day to fly flags largely on days of public rejoicing.

At ten o'clock the cannon again thundered out an Imperial salute—a hundred and one guns. All knew what that was for, and there was a hush of expectation all over Paris. The guns meant that the Emperor had started; that the Imperial State procession had left the Tuileries. At that moment the chilly drizzle of sleet was still coming down, but the universal enthusiasm rose superior to the wet and cold. No weather could damp the anticipations of the excited Parisians over the Imperial spectacle.

On the Champ de Mars, as the guns began to fire, the soldiers—all long since in their places drawn up in closely massed columns, that ranged right round the parade ground on three sides—stripped off and rolled up their soaked cloaks, fixed bayonets, and stood to arms. Murat, Governor of Paris, commander-in-chief on the parade, took post in front of the Imperial Pavilion before the *Ecole Militaire*: a gorgeous figure in a bright blue velvet uniform coat, resplendently embroidered with gold, a lilac sash with crimson stripes round his waist; in scarlet breeches braided with gold, purple leather Hessians, trimmed and tasselled with gold, with gleaming gold spurs and sabre-scabbard; wearing a marshal's cocked hat with crimson ostrich-plumes, and mounted on a no less splendidly caparisoned charger, with leopard-skin and crimson and gold saddle-trappings. A brilliant *entourage* of staff officers and dandy *aides de camp*, daintily attired in pearl-grey uniforms, with silver lace, or in crimson and green and gold, clustered in rear of their chief.

Simultaneously, the massed bands of the Imperial Guard, who had been playing national airs and popular music at times during the past hour, formed to the front nearby.

For the time being, until after the Emperor should arrive and take his seat on the throne, the troops on parade, comprising the Army deputations to receive the Eagles, remained as they had been marshalled on arrival; arranged in a vast fan-shaped formation round three sides of the Champ de Mars. The entire Imperial Army of Napoleon stood represented within that space: Imperial Guard, and Line, Cavalry and Artillery; the sailors of the Navy; the National Guard,—the *mise en scène* presenting a tremendous impression of martial power, as all stood formed up in close order, in their full-dress review-uniforms, muskets held stiffly at the support, bayonets fixed.

The Imperial procession set off in full State, accompanied by much the same display of martial pomp that had attended the great Coronation progress to Notre Dame of three days before. It moved off in a pelting squall of sleet; but, almost immediately afterwards, as though Heaven would fain spare the show, within a few minutes of the start, the sleet and rain ceased and the weather unexpectedly improved.

Foremost of all, the mounted Mamelukes of the Guard came prancing by, radiant in Oriental garb, their curved scimitars drawn and gleaming; a hundred swarthy figures in scarlet *calpacks* swathed round with white turbans, garbed in vivid green *burnous*-cloaks well thrown back to display gold-embroidered scarlet jackets, bright straw-coloured sashes, and baggy scarlet trousers.

Their famous Horse-tail Standard headed the squadron. Eight hundred stalwart troopers of Napoleon's pet regiment, the corps whose uniform he always wore in camp, the *Chasseurs* of the Guard, followed immediately after the Mamelukes. An ideal *corps d'elite* they looked as they rode by, in their bristling busbies of dark fur topped with waving crimson and green plumes, dark green double-breasted jackets, and crimson breeches; with crimson *pelisses* hanging at the shoulder, fur-trimmed and barred with yellow braid in hussar style. These two corps led the van of the procession.

The first set of Imperial coaches, with six horses each and outriders, thereupon came by. They carried mostly State *magnificos* and *grandees* of exalted position at Court. Coach after coach went slowly past at a dignified pace: eight—nine—ten—eleven—conveyances, all spick and span with new gilding and varnish. The twelfth coach, beside which rode a bevy of smart equerries, held the Princesses of the Bonaparte family: five grown-up ladies and the little daughter of Princess Louis. It was rather a tight squeeze, for the five Imperial Highnesses were plump and bulky persons, and had to be wedged closely; they brought with them too, each lady, several yards of train, brocaded stuff with stiff edging of gilt-gimp, and thick purple and emerald green velvet mantling, which had all to be got in and kept from crumpling as much as possible!

What they said to one another has not been recorded—they were usually free-spoken women with comments for most things ready to their tongues, like other daughters of the Revolution. At any rate this is known. They were in white silk dresses, low necked, and, in spite of their close packing, shivered with the cold, which they felt bitterly. "We were all," related a lady of honour elsewhere in the procession, "thinly dressed, as for a heated ball-room, and had only thin Cashmere shawls to keep our shoulders warm with."

Then came more soldiers. The immediate escort of the Emperor now appeared. Sitting erect and stiff in their saddles, the *Carabiniers* rode up—the senior cavalry regiment of France—eight hundred picked horsemen uniformed in Imperial blue and crimson and gold, with helmets of burnished brass, over which nodded thick tufted crests of crimson wool. The officers, superb beings adorned with breastplates of gleaming brass, led the regiment. The *Carabiniers* claimed to be the only corps of the Napoleonic Army which could prove continuity with the Old Royal Army, if not indeed with the historic "*Maison du Roi*" itself, the Household Brigade of the monarchy, owing to a curious oversight at the Revolution through which the regiment had escaped dispersal.

Then came the Man of the Hour.

Napoleon now appeared, in his brand-new Imperial State coach. Eight noble bays drew it—with harness and trappings of red morocco leather studded with golden bees. A marvellous vehicle to look at was Napoleon's coach, gleaming all over with gilded carved work; its roof topped by a great golden crown, modelled "after that of Charlemagne," as people told one another, upheld by four glistening gilded eagles. The State coach sparkled all over, looking as if encrusted with gold; a gleaming mass of carved and gilded decorations, representing allegorical emblems, heraldic designs, and coats of arms in colour.

Napoleon's head coachman of the Consulate days, César, sat on the box, his fat form embedded in the centre of a luxurious hammercloth of scarlet velvet, spangled over with golden bees. Outriders in green and gold and walking footmen beside the horses added their part; also half a score of Pages of Honour, hanging on all round at the sides and back of the coach, in green velvet coats, gold laced down the seams, with green silk shoulder-knots, scarlet silk breeches and stockings, and white ostrich-plumes in their jaunty black velvet hats: most of the lads future officers of the Guard. At either side rode equerries and *officiers d'ordonnance*, in white and gold or pale blue and silver.

To the crowds that lined the streets the State coach was a sight of the day—the coach, for some, as much as the Emperor. All Paris, of course, had not been able to find room round the Field of Mars, spacious as the accommodation there was. The pavements all along the streets from the Tuileries were packed with a dense crowd, which pressed everywhere close up behind the double rows of *gendarmes* and Imperial Guardsmen keeping the processional route.

They shouted "*Vive l'Empereur!*" lustily, for all had a good view of Napoleon through the great glass windows of the coach; seated inside on the right, wearing his ostrich-feathered cap of semi-State, a gold embroidered purple velvet mantle, and the Grand Master's collar of the Legion of Honour, sparkling with costly gems.

Josephine, a slender figure in ermine cloak and white silk dress, sat on Napoleon's left, and on the front seats sat Joseph and Louis, side by side—the elder brother sleek and smiling, wrapped up in a poppy-red cloak as Grand Elector of the Empire; Louis Bonaparte wearing his blue velvet Constable's mantle over the brass breastplate of the colonel-in-chief of the *Carabiniers*, to which rank Napoleon had specially promoted Louis, with the idea of maintaining an old tradition of the Monarchy that the titular commander of the *Carabiniers* should always be a Prince of the Blood, "*Frère du Roi*"

Napoleon's Imperial Standard was borne immediately after the State coach; a crowned eagle heading the staff; the flag a silken tricolour, richly fringed with gold and bespangled with golden bees.

Four of the marshals, readily recognised by their scarlet ostrich-plumes and gold-tipped batons of command, attended the Standard, and, as Colonels-General of the Imperial Guard, led the Imperial Military Household, the "*Maison Militaire de l'Empereur.*" The four were: Davout, titular chief of the Grenadiers of the Guard; Soult, Colonel-General of the *Chasseurs*; Bessières, of the Heavy Cavalry; Mortier, of the Guard Artillery. Close behind them four other gorgeously brilliant officers of rank rode abreast, the Colonels-General of the Cavalry of the Army: St. Cyr, of the *Cuirassiers*, disdainful and sardonic of mien; stern Baraguay d'Hilliers, of the Dragoons; good-looking Junot, Colonel-General of the Hussars; and Napoleon's son-in-law, the chivalrous Eugène Beauharnais, Colonel-General of *Chasseurs*. A brilliant cavalcade of little less resplendent cavaliers, the Emperor's *aides de camp*, all of them generals of division or brigadiers, rounded up the group.

Another eye-surfeit of gleaming varnish, gilded carvings, and green liveries continued the pageant: twelve other State coaches, six-horsed like those in advance; carrying the personal suites of Napoleon and Josephine and the princesses, Court Chamberlains and similar gold-embroidered functionaries, ladies of the palace and "Officers of the Crown." The procession ended after them; the rear being brought up by the Mounted Grenadiers of the Guard, strapping troopers in huge bearskins soldiers picked for their height and bearing from the Cavalry of the Line—and the *Gendarmerie d'Elite*, who formed the Imperial palace-guard.

More than half the Imperial Guard—numbering, in 1804, ten thousand officers and men lined the streets under arms; detachments of Grenadiers and *Velites*, Foot-*Chasseurs*, Veterans of the Guard, Marines of the Guard. Through double rows of these, all standing with presented arms, the procession took its way, passing from the Tuileries Gardens, across the Place de Concorde and over the bridge there, to the Esplanade des Invalides. Yet another thundering Imperial salute from the twenty old cannons of the *Batterie Triomphale* greeted Napoleon at that point; while rows of old soldiers, the maimed veterans of Arcola and Rivoli and Marengo, shouted themselves hoarse, standing ranged in front of the Outer Court beside Napoleon's Venetian trophy, kept there temporarily, the Lion of St. Mark.

From the Invalides, by way of the Rue de Crenelle, it was not far to the Military School.

Withindoors at the *Ecole Militaire* a pause was made in the Governor's apartments, which had been sumptuously furnished for the occasion from the Imperial storerooms of the *Garde Meuble*. Napoleon here accepted a number of selected addresses from the military delegations. One of them was brought by the regimental deputation of the 4th Chasseurs stationed at Boulogne. It thanked the Emperor in advance for the new standard he was presenting to the corps, "trusting that the day is at hand when we shall be able to contribute towards consolidating the splendour of the Empire by planting our Eagle on the Tower of London."

The Emperor also received the congratulations of the Ambassadors and Diplomatic Corps. Ten hereditary German Princes of the Rhineland, visiting Paris for the Coronation, attended at the Military School to witness the Presentation of the Eagles; at their head the Prince-Bishop-Elector of Ratisbon, Arch-Chancellor of the German Empire, the Margrave of Baden, and the Princes of Hesse-Darmstadt and Hesse-Homburg. Napoleon and Josephine after that withdrew to assume their crowns and Imperial Regalia and pass outside to the two thrones prepared for them and standing side by side in the grand central pavilion in front.

The vast array of "guests of the Emperor," seated outside, had of course been long since in their places, awaiting the advent of their Majesties amid surroundings designed on a scale of lavish magnificence regardless of cost. On either hand pavilions and galleries and platforms, canopied and carpeted, draped and curtained and hung in crimson and gold, decorated with festoons and banners, and fenced with gilded balustrading, covered the whole length of the *façade* of the *Ecole Militaire* fronting the parade ground. In the centre stood the Imperial Pavilion, beneath a canopy of crimson silk supported by tall gilded columns. Side galleries draped, and under awnings led from it right and left to two other pavilions, at either end of the *façade*, similarly adorned in lavish gorgeousness.

Below the galleries extended long stands, sloping forward to the ground, draped in green and crimson, and packed with rows of seats five or six deep. Here, partly in the open, sat the provincial Coronation guests from the Departments: the local *prefects* and *sub-prefects*, *procurators*, magistrates and syndics, mayors and councillors, and other municipal functionaries, all in gala-day attire of every colour, plumes in their hats, and buttons and embroidery all over their coats. They made a many-hued show in the mass, seen from the parade ground. The higher State dignitaries had seats under the canopies of the galleries, and looked yet more decorative.

Seated in the pavilions on cushioned chairs were the ambassadors and foreign princes, the Senate, *corps legislatif,* and *tribunate*, High Court Judges in flowing robes of flame-coloured silk, and velvet-clad "Grand Officers of the Empire," in full-dress all. They looked imposing and magnificent, but most of them were shivering, with damp bodies and numbed fingers.

The sleet had stopped for the time, but after the all-night's downpour of rain and snow the seats everywhere were in a sad condition. Canopies and cushions, curtains, seats, carpets—everything had been drenched through and swamped during the night. The discomfort, however, was past helping and had to be borne. The Imperial Pavilion itself indeed had not escaped a wetting, and in parts it was in little better condition than the other places. "Only with the greatest diligence," describes one of the suite, "had it been possible to keep the thrones dry."

Napoleon's throne, with beside it the throne for Josephine, at a slightly lower elevation, stood at the front of the Imperial Pavilion. A gilt-framed crimson velvet Chair of State was provided for the Emperor, with a crowned eagle in gilt *stucco* perched on the back; made on the model of Dagobert's chair on which Napoleon had sat during the ceremony of the distribution of the Crosses of the Legion of Honour at Boulogne. As on that day, so now, trophies of captured battle-flags adorned the back of the Imperial dais, selected from the two hundred and odd standards taken in battle by the Armies of Italy and Egypt which Napoleon had led in person: trophies of Montenotte and Arcola, of Tagliamento and Lodi, of Rivoli and Castiglione; the red-and-white banner of the Knights of Malta; the green Horse-tail Standard of the Beys of Egypt; Austrian standards won by Napoleon at the crowning triumph of Marengo.

To right and left of the Emperor, on richly decorated chairs of ceremony, Joseph and Louis Bonaparte and the princesses were seated. The Imperial suites in attendance were grouped at the back together with a cluster of court *grandees*, filling most of the spacious platform behind the throne.

In the forefront, at the Emperor's right hand, stood a splendid galaxy of stalwart figures—the Marshals of the Empire. They stood forward prominently. For them that was the day of days. All must see on such a day the champion warriors of France, the renown of whose victories had filled the world! The whole eighteen were there—all except one. Marshal Brune alone was absent; on service out of France as Napoleon's Ambassador at Constantinople. The group was completed by the four "Honorary Marshals"—the veteran Kellermann, the victor of Valmy; Perignon; Serrurier; and Lefebvre.

Glance for one moment round the main group of thirteen, the chosen lieutenants of Napoleon the War Lord, as they stand beside their Chief, with, arrayed in front, the serried columns of the destined victors of Austerlitz. Next to the Emperor and the Eagles it is they who on this Day of the Eagles are the principal objects of interest to the general spectator.

Let the reader for one moment imagine himself on the Imperial Pavilion, with at his side a convenient friend who knows everybody, to point the marshals out.

That short, spare, low-browed, swarthy, Italian-faced man, with crafty, pitiless eyes, is Masséna—"*L'Enfant chéri de la Victoire*," as Napoleon himself hailed him on the battlefield; the very ablest undoubtedly of all the marshals. He knows it too. When the list of the marshals first came out, a friend called on Masséna to know if it was true that he was one, and to congratulate him. "Oh yes, thank you," replied Masséna in an icy tone, puckering up his dark face with a sour look, "I am one; *one of fourteen!*" He's Italian in blood and breeding, and in his tricky ways; every point about him: but he'd give his soul to be a Frenchman! "Massène" is what he is always trying to get people to call him.

And the airs and self-importance he assumes—though only like most of the others in that, indeed—ever since he became "*Monseigneur le Maréchal*" and has had the honour of being addressed as "*Mon Cousin*" by the Emperor! Just think of it! In the old days, behind the counter of that little olive-oil and dried-fruit shop up a narrow, smelly back street at Antibes, plain "Citoyen Andre" was good enough! Just look at that thin, pouting chest, gleaming all over with gold embroidery, with the broad crimson riband of the Legion of Honour slanting across it, and the aggressive tilt of his ostrich-plumed hat! Imagine all that being once upon a time just a cabin-boy on a Marseilles to Leghorn coaster, half-starved and sworn at and cuffed and kicked about by a curmudgeonly *padrone*! Then fancy it a sneaking smuggler, chevied about, and crouching along to keep out of carbine shot of the Nice *douaniers*! After that Sergeant Masséna of the late king's *Royal Italien* regiment of the Line! And so to the *bâton*.

They are most of them rather *tête montée* just now, with their exaltation spick and span on them, these *demi*-gods of war of ours! Just see them in the field, or on the march; away from the Emperor. They stalk ahead in solitary *grandeur*, each with his own *pas seul*, keeping the lesser creation at arms' length, wrapped up in his own dignified importance. Yet only six months since their lofty Excellencies were mere generals of division, "*Citoyen Général*" this or that, each one; just units among a hundred and twenty odd others! Nowadays, on the march, your marshal rides by himself, forty yards ahead of everybody; his staff have to tail off well in rear and keep back!

M. le Maréchal doesn't deign to open his lips, except to give an order. He lives by himself: nobody now is good enough to ask to dinner, except perhaps another marshal! No off-duty pleasantries nowadays; no more *bon camaraderie*; no more telling of Palais-Royal stories, as it used to be; no more cracking of jokes beside the bivouac fire. You might as well expect a bishop to have a game of marbles! Let a former brother-officer *tutoyer* a marshal! Poor fellow! Let him try, if he wants to know what a paralysing, rasping, cold-blooded snub is, to get a flattening backhander he'll remember as long as he wears the uniform.

That tall, bull-necked, heavy-featured man is Augereau; "*gros comme un tambour-major*"; absolutely fearless under fire, kind-hearted to those he takes a fancy to, they say, but ordinarily a coarse-tongued swashbuckler, with barrack-room manners. There too is Lannes, that keen-eyed, short man, holding his head as if he had a crick in his neck! He has one, a permanent one, the result of a bullet under the jaw from a British marine's musket in the trenches at Acre. A hot-tempered, fiery, devil-may-care fellow is Lannes; but as cold as ice on the battlefield when things look like going wrong! Among friends, chivalrous and generous-hearted to a degree, his men worship Lannes; "the Roland of the Grand Army," some call him.

That is Moncey: and that very tall and erect, dry, rather dense-looking, hawk-nosed marshal with the shaggy eyebrows, Mortier. Mark Bernadotte there, that shifty-eyed Gascon with a sharp nose and thick hair; of medium height,—nobody really trusts him. An ingrained Jacobin—strip his arm and you will find tattooed on it, indelibly, for life, "*Mort aux rois*"—and a schemer, Napoleon named him a marshal for political reasons mainly; although, no doubt, he has the same soldier-qualifications as the rest; has won a pitched battle or taken two fortresses.

A cunning, plausible fellow is Bernadotte; with ready smile and a smooth tongue. He calls everybody "*Mon ami*" whether he is talking to a brigadier or a bugler. "*Que diable fait il dans cette galèe?*" say a good many people of the commander of the First Army Corps. Over yonder stands Bessières, Murat's great friend; a gentlemanly enough fellow, but at times thick-headed, hardly of the mental calibre of his *confrères*. Yet Bessières is an ideal leader of Horse on the battlefield; as reckless as a lion at bay: you should see him head a charge sword in hand! One of Napoleon's pets is he and the only man in the army who sticks to his queue. Bessières flatly refused to cut it off when the order was given last June for everybody to copy "*Le petit tondu*" ("The little shorn one"), as the men call the Emperor, and it hangs half-way down his back.

That dark, sleek-faced, heavy-eyed man is Jourdan, commander-in-chief once of the Army of the Revolution. "The Anvil," some call him, he has been so often soundly beaten. But, all the same, he was too popular with the Army for Napoleon to pass him over. Jourdan it was who invented the conscription system. He started in life as a linen-draper at Grenoble. There is of course, too, Brune, who isn't here today: but he doesn't count for much. A minor-poet and a journalist was he once upon a time. He's another of the clever-tongued Jacobins the Emperor gave the baton to as a sop.

Look near the Emperor, at that neat athletic figure, of middle height: that is "Old Berthier." He is from ten to fifteen years older than most of the other marshals; or, in fact, than the Emperor himself. Berthier, in fact, is old enough to have been a captain in the Army of the *ancien régime*, and can remember how he first smelt powder fighting under Lafayette and Washington against the British in America. He was a staff officer when Napoleon first came to the *Ecole Militaire* here from Brienne, as a boy gentleman-cadet. A heaven-born chief of the Staff is Marshal Berthier, and the Emperor without him in a campaign would be like a man without his right hand. Every detail goes like clockwork with Berthier at the head of the *Etat-Major*.

You should see the two of them on campaign, working together in the *Quartier-Général*. Napoleon will be sprawling on his stomach at full length over a huge set of maps which cover, spread out, nearly the whole floor of the tent; an open pair of compasses in his hand, a box of pins with little paper flag-heads, red, blue, yellow, green, at one side, some of them already stuck over the map marking the positions of the different corps and of the enemy. He has the compasses set to scale, to mark off some seventeen to twenty miles, which means from twenty-two to twenty-five miles of road, taking into account the windings. To and fro he twists and turns the compasses like lightning and decides in an instant the marches for each column to arrive at the desired point, all timed exactly to the very day and hour with an astonishing certainty and precision.

He calls out his instructions in half a dozen words or so, sharply snapped out, for Berthier, who all the time is standing near, bending down at Napoleon's shoulder, notebook and pencil in hand, to take down. Old Berthier has a veritable instinct for understanding what the Emperor means. He can interpret the smallest grunt Napoleon makes. He can spin out three or four broken ejaculations into detailed orders for an Army Corps, all worked out with absolute clearness, in beautiful language. It is amazing how he does it, but he does do it. A staff officer, or else Bacler d'Albe, the Imperial Military Cartographer, the officer in charge of the maps, it may be, is all the while also kneeling by the pin-box, and has the pins of the right colour out and stuck in the maps as fast as the Emperor wants them.

The instant the Emperor is satisfied, Berthier is off, and with the secretaries at work in his own quarters drafting the orders. Then, before you know well where you are, a dozen *estafettes* are galloping all over the country with the orders—in the case of a very important order sometimes three or four staff officers each take a copy, to ride by different routes so as to minimise the risk of delay or capture. That is the working of Berthier's system, and there is not often a miscarriage or serious hitch in the delivery.

And mark Soult, the coming man of the marshals when he gets his chance; a wary old dog-fox for an enemy to tackle. A sergeant of infantry in the old "Royal Regiment" of former days, the old 13th of the Line, then a drill-instructor of Volunteers, now he is at the head of the army at Boulogne for the descent on England. Hardly even the Emperor knows more about tactics than Soult. Note how self-possessed and masterful he looks, so cold and impassive of demeanour. Those eyes that seem to pierce through you, those clear-cut aquiline features, that face like a mask of bronze, show the character of the man. You wouldn't think though, to see his fine soldier-like figure as he stands there, a warrior born to look at, that Soult is not only lame from a fall from his horse years ago, but has limped from his birth, from a club-foot.

That bald-headed marshal over there is Marshal Davout, a dashing subaltern of dragoons once in the Old Royal Army. A fine tactician for a hot place is Davout; and when the fight has been won, no leader so harsh and pitiless to the vanquished enemy. He wears spectacles on service: he can hardly see ten yards in front of his big nose. The ladies are very fond of Davout; he waltzes so nicely.

And that other there is Marshal Ney; "the Indefatigable" is the army's name for him. He never spares himself, nor the enemy, on the battlefield; but after the last shot there is no more generous victor than Marshal Ney. For sheer dogged pluck against odds, for simply marvellous intrepidity, the world cannot match Ney. Stalwart and square-shouldered, he carries himself with all the jaunty assurance of manner you would expect in perhaps the most dashing leader of hussars the Army of France has known. He is an Alsatian, born by the Rhine; a pleasant-faced man, with frank grey eyes, curly red hair over a broad open forehead. "Red Michael" is one of the soldiers' names for Ney; and there is not one of the marshals for whom his men would do more.

Such, if it may be permitted to describe them in this way, is something of what the marshals of Napoleon looked like on the day of the Eagle presentation on the Field of Mars. All eyes were turned on the marshals as they stood there beside Napoleon; a brilliant array of soldierly figures in their red ostrich-plumed cocked hats, richly laced uniforms, gleaming brass-bound sword-scabbards and high jack-boots with clanking brass spurs.

From the foot of the throne a grand staircase led down to the parade ground, widening out with a curving sweep to either side at the foot. It terminated there with, flanking the lower steps, two gilded statues, designed to represent, the one, "France granting Peace," the other, "France making War." From top to bottom of the stairs and extending at the foot to right and left along either side, stood in rows the colonels of the regiments on parade, together with the senior officers of the National Guard, all awaiting the Emperor's appearance on the throne. Each bore the new Eagle standard to be presented to his own corps. All were at their posts as the appointed moment neared, while at the same time Murat and his attendant cavalcade of brilliantly bedecked horsemen closed in and formed up in front, so as immediately to face Napoleon.

On either hand of Murat were ranked the massed bands of the Imperial Guard, flanked by two solid phalanxes of drummers, each a thousand strong. Nearby these were drawn up on horseback, on one side the officers of the Headquarters Staff at the War Office, on the other, the staff officers of the army corps of the marshals.

Napoleon and Josephine made their entry into the Grand Pavilion heralded by a procession, the bands of the Guard playing the Coronation March. Then, to the accompaniment of three successive shouts of "*Vive l'Empereur!*" from the soldiers—the formal greeting to Napoleon on parade, in accordance with army regulation—the Emperor seated himself on the throne. He was in full Imperial garb, wearing his Imperial mantle of rich crimson velvet studded with golden bees, and the Imperial crown, a golden laurel chaplet "after Charlemagne." In his right hand he bore the Imperial sceptre, a tall silver-gilt wand with an eagle surmounting it, also designed, as they said, "after Charlemagne."

Seating himself with Josephine at his side, in her State robes and with a magnificent crown of diamonds on her head, Napoleon gave the order for the proceedings to begin.

Murat, as Governor of Paris, in immediate command of the parade, raised his glittering marshal's baton. The bands of the Guard ceased playing abruptly. The next moment the two thousand infantry drums began to beat. It was the appointed signal for the detachments to advance and form up in front of the throne.

At once, at the first roll of the drums, the soldiers ranged round the ground began to move.

Wheeling some, counter-marching others, here rapidly doubling, there marking time —looking, indeed, for the moment, at first, in the mass, to the untrained eye of the non-military spectator like a swarming ant-heap in motion and inextricably intermingled—like magic all suddenly appeared in order, a series of columns, the heads of which, arrayed at regular intervals, were in unison converging concentrically towards the foot of the grand staircase in front of the throne. A dozen paces in rear of where Murat stood all halted as one man. There was a quick movement of bayonets as arms were shouldered; the action making a glint of flashing steel in spite of the dull grey light overhead.

Every sound was hushed as Napoleon rose to his feet. He faced the wide-spreading multitude and gazed silently over them for a moment; standing well forward where all might see him. Then he addressed the parade in strong vibrant tones which rang out clear and resonant over the whole assembly like a trumpet-note. In words that seemed to thrill with intensified energy he called on the soldiers before him, on behalf of themselves and their absent comrades, to take the oath of devotion to the Eagles. He began, his right arm outstretched with an impassioned gesture towards the Eagles, whose bearers held them stiffly erect, all glancing and gleaming like polished gold, the bright-hued silken flags unfurled:

> Soldiers! behold your standards! These Eagles to you shall ever be your rallying-point. Wherever your Emperor shall deem it needful for the defence of his throne and his people, there shall they be seen!

He paused. Then raising his right hand in the air with a swift strenuous movement Napoleon pronounced the oath:

> You swear to sacrifice your lives in their defence: to maintain them by your courage ever in the path of Victory! You swear it?

The vast gathering stood as though spellbound. For one instant all remained motionless and silent, held down as it were by overmastering emotion.

Then, all together, with one accord, the soldiers found their voices. With a thundering shout that seemed to shake the air, the Army made its response, answering back in one deep chorus:

"*Nous le jurons!*"—"We swear it!"

One and all enthusiastically re-echoed the words; while the colonels excitedly brandished and waved aloft the Eagles. In a frenzy of martial ardour the entire assembly, at the top of their voices, again and again declaimed, "We swear it! We swear it!" A wild pro-longed outburst of cheering followed, and exuberant shouts of "*Vive l'Empereur!*"

Before the cheering had abated, the drums broke in again. The sharp clash and rattle recalled all to order instantly. Again a dead silence fell over the great host, standing now with recovered arms.

Up once more went Murat's marshal's baton. The next moment the dense-set columns were standing stock-still like rows of statues, with arms at the shoulder.

Napoleon resumed his seat on the throne, and as he did so yet once more a wave of enthusiasm swept over the vast array. Redoubled shouts of "*Vive l'Empereur!*" burst wildly forth, the soldiers pulling off their hats or helmets, and hoisting them on the points of their bayonets, excitedly waving them, while they shouted themselves breathless.

Again the drums rolled, and again order was restored. And now the supreme act of the drama opened—the formal presentation of each Eagle to its own regimental deputation.

Forthwith the wide-fronted columns, breaking swiftly into quarter-column formation, began to move, section by section, in turn. Rapidly, and, as it almost seemed, automatically, they resumed their first formation, extending round the Field of Mars on three sides. From front to rear the quarter-columns took up a full mile and three-quarters. Ranked in close order, the long-drawn-out array of troops on that set off, to a stately march from the bands of the Guard, to pass along the front of the Military School, before the flanking pavilion, and galleries and stands. So, in due course, all in turn came opposite to the foot of the great stairway ascending to the throne.

Each section, as it came in front of the steps, made a pause. The colonels at the same moment were passing in file before Napoleon. Each in turn inclined the Eagle that he bore towards the Emperor. He held the staff at an angle of forty-five degrees—the regulation method of salute, in accordance with an Imperial order issued in the previous July, when the adoption of the Eagle as the Army standard was first announced. Napoleon on his side, with his ungloved right hand, just touched each Eagle. The colonels, then, saluting, turned, one after the other, to descend the stairs. At the foot of the stairway each delivered over the Eagle to the standard-bearer of his regiment, who, together with the deputation, was at the spot to receive it. (*See note following.*)

> Note:—One of the Eagles so presented by Napoleon on that afternoon is now at Madrid. It is a trophy that is absolutely unique. Upwards of a hundred and thirty of Napoleon's Eagles, the spoils of war, now decorate cathedrals, chapels, and arsenals in the capitals of Europe; but there is only one French naval Eagle now in existence, the trophy at Madrid; the Eagle of a line-of-battleship named the *Atlas*.

Every French line-of-battleship was represented on the Champ de Mars and received its Eagle. "*Tous les vaisseaux*," to quote the words of M. Le Brun, in his *Guerres Maritimes de France*, "*étaient gratifiés d'une aigle et d'un drapeau à leur nom, donnés par l'Empereur à son couronnement, ou avaient assisté et prêté serment des députations du port et de l'Armée Navale; chaque vaiaseau avait envoyé sa députation composée de trois officiers, trois officiers mariners, et quatre gabiers ou matelots.*"

The Eagle of the *Atlas* was received on the Field of Mars by the ship's deputation of three officers, three warrant officers, and four seamen, sent from Toulon, where the *Atlas* then was in harbour with Admiral Villeneuve's fleet, which Nelson was watching. The *Atlas* crossed the Atlantic in the Toulon fleet with Nelson in pursuit, returned to Europe, fought in the indecisive battle off Cape Finisterre in July 1805, and was so shattered in the fight, in which the ship only just escaped capture, that she was left behind for repairs at Ferrol when Villeneuve put to sea finally, to meet his fate at Trafalgar. The *Atlas* had to remain there and fell into the hands of the Spaniards in 1808, at the time of the national uprising against Napoleon. Thus the naval Eagle passed into Spanish possession.

The crew of the *Atlas* were taken by surprise, while the ship was in dock at Ferrol, by the Spanish regiment of Navarre in garrison there when the news of the Rising of May 2 at Madrid reached Galicia. They were trapped and pounced down upon. The ship was seized by a sudden assault, the officers and men being made prisoners to the provincial Junta, before they had a chance of concealing or making away with their Eagle.

In other cases elsewhere, undoubtedly, the naval Eagles were somehow disposed of surreptitiously.

It is very remarkable that not a single French naval Eagle came into British hands on board the thirty odd ships of the line which we captured between 1805 and 1814 during the war with Napoleon. At Trafalgar, according to a French officer on board the French flagship, the *Bucentaure*, they had one. Describing the approach of the Victory, at the outset of the battle, says the officer:

> A collision appeared inevitable. At that moment Villeneuve seized the Eagle of the *Bucentaure* and displayed it to the sailors who surrounded him. 'My friends,' he called out, 'I am going to throw this on board the English ship! We will go and fetch it back or die!' (*'Mes amis, je vais la jetter à bord du vaisseau Anglais! Nous irons la reprendre ou mourir!'*) Our seamen responded to these noble words by their acclamations.

Admiral Villeneuve, all the same, did not throw any Eagle on board the *Victory*; nor was one found in the *Bucentaure* during the forty-eight hours that the ship was in our possession after the battle, previous to her wreck in the storm at the entrance to Cadiz harbour. None too were found on board any of Nelson's other prizes. As to that, also, what was done with, or became of, the Eagles of the five battalions serving as marines in the French fleet at Trafalgar, officers and men of which were taken prisoners by us those of the 2nd of the Line, the 16th, 67th, 70th, and 79th?

At the Field of Mars all eyes were on the six hundred and fifty officers and men of the Naval Brigade as they marched round the arena to receive their Eagles. Soldiers everybody was familiar with. There was nothing particular about them which had not been seen before. But a French sailor was not often seen away from his port; and to Paris man-of-war's men were things quite new and strange. And, besides, were they not *"nos braves marins,"* who were going to clear the way for the "Invasion Flotilla" and the "Army of England"; to strike the blow that should sweep from the path of the Emperor *"ce terrible Nelson!"*

One and all gazed in wonder at the sailors: the captains in their long, swallow-tailed blue *coatees* barred with gold lace, white breeches, and high top-boots; the sprightly *"aspirants,"* or midshipmen, in cut-away jackets and little round hats with turned-up brims; the showy *"Marins de la Garde,"* wearing broad-topped *shakos* edged with yellow braid, over which tall red tufts nodded, red-cuffed and yellow-braided blue jackets, and blue trousers striped with yellow; the other sailors of the fleet in massed squads, in shiny black flat-brimmed hats, blue jackets studded with brass buttons, red waistcoats, red, white, and blue striped pantaloons, wide in the leg, *"a l'Anglaise,"* and shoes with round steel buckles. Such a sight the good people of Paris had never witnessed before, and they gazed at it rapturously with all their eyes, and shouted their loudest *"Vive la Marine!"*

There was too, in addition to the sailors, one Eagle deputation the strange appearance of which attracted special curiosity and interest that afternoon. Everybody gazed in wonder at a group of strapping-looking foreigners of all ages who marched along by themselves, got up as light infantrymen, with green tufted *shakos* and bright green uniforms. They belonged to one of the Emperor's newest creations; and were the Eagle escort of Napoleon's "Irish Legion." They had come to the Field of Mars to receive the only Eagle that Napoleon ever gave to a foreign regiment in his service, with a flag designed specially for them, of "Irish Green," as it was described, of silk, fringed with gold cord, inscribed on one side in letters on gold: "*Napoléon, Empereur des Français, à la Legion Irlandaise,*" and bearing on the other a golden harp, uncrowned, and the words "*L'Independance d'Irlande*."

Two ex-patriated men of good Irish family, refugees escaped from the penalty of treason under English law for their part in the Rising of '98, seven years before, headed the deputation; a Captain Tennant and a Captain William Corbet. In the ranks of the regiment the deputation represented marched other Irish refugees, who had shed English blood at Wexford and Enniscorthy; fugitives from political justice before that who had had a part in the attempted raids of Hoche and Humbert; "Wild Geese" who had made their flight overseas after the fiasco of 1803; and a sprinkling of French-born Irish, some of whom had worn the red coat of the old Irish Brigade in the Royal Army of France, grandsons of the men of Fontenoy.

Napoleon had enrolled his Irish Legion just a twelvemonth before, in view of a descent on Ireland from Brest simultaneously with the crossing of the Straits of Dover from Boulogne. At the request of those who first came forward to enlist, he had uniformed the corps in the "national" green, in place of the former red coat which had been the historic colour of the old French-Irish regiments ever since James the Second, under the Treaty of Limerick, carried over to France the remains of the army that had fought for him at the Boyne. The Eagle the Irish Legion received on the Field of Mars faced Wellington in Spain, and narrowly escaped falling into Blücher's hands in Germany in 1813. It was hidden away after Fontainebleau, and reappeared during the "Hundred Days," finally to disappear after Waterloo.

With the Eagles in their charge the regimental parties moved on. Passing in front of the stands and pavilions beyond, all wheeled there, to pass again round the arena of the Field of Mars, until they had reached their former stations, and halted, all ranged in the order in which they had taken post at their first arrival.

There remained after that the grand *finale*.

The March Past of the Eagle detachments before Napoleon now

came on, designed as the consummation of the day's doings.

In connection with that, however, there was an unfortunate incident. On the Field of Mars were displayed also the old army colours of the Consulate, which, as has been said, had been brought to Paris at the order of the War Minister by the regimental deputations. Paraded together with the new Eagles they helped to render the scene the more striking; but their presence led to an unforeseen complication, and in the end a deplorable *contretemps*.

The standard-bearers who had received the Eagles were each, in addition, still carrying the old regimental flag. They had to carry both. No instructions had been given out—by oversight, most probably—as to the giving up of the old flags, or what was to be done with them.

It may have been that Napoleon desired that the standards of the Consulate and the Eagles of the Empire should be displayed together on that day. None knew better than he the deep attachment of the older men in the ranks for their former battle-flags. Some of the old soldiers, indeed, even there on the Field of Mars, as we are told, were unable to restrain their feelings at the idea of having to part that day from their old colours. "More than one tear was shed," relates an officer, "amidst all the cheering and shouts of '*Vive l'Empereur!*'"

Enthusiastically as most of the soldiers might welcome the new Eagles in the presence of the Emperor, all did not desire to part with colours which had led through the battle-smoke on many a victorious field of the past, even in exchange for the glittering "*Cou-cous*," as barrack-room slang had already dubbed Napoleon's Eagles, giving them in advance a soldier's nickname that stuck to them as long as the Army of the Empire lasted.

Both sets of standards were carried in the march past, which proceeded without incident to a certain point.

It was an effective display of the lusty manhood of France, of the pick of the Grand Army in its prime; not yet made *chair au canon* to gratify the ambition of one man. A curious commingling, too, of fighting costumes did the review present for the general spectators; those of yesterday side by side with those of the coming time. Three-fourths of the soldiers went by wearing the stiff Republican garb of the expiring *régime*, as adopted hastily at the outset of the Revolution: the long-skirted coat, cut after the old Royal Army fashion, but blue in colour instead of white, and with white lapels and turn-backs; long-flapped white waistcoats, white breeches, and high black-cloth gaiters above the knee, such as their ancestors had worn in the days of Marshal Saxe; the old-style big cocked hat, worn cross-wise, or "*en bataille*," as the soldiers called it, with a flaunting tricolour cockade in front.

The new Napoleonic style was represented by the Imperial Guard and Oudinot's Grenadier Division from Arras and the Light Infantry battalions, whose turn out in smartly cut *coatees* faced with red and green, with the tall broad-topped *shakos* pictures of the time make us familiar with as the normal presentment of the soldiers of the Empire, attracted special attention. [1]

During the March Past, *Frimaire* suddenly reasserted itself, and brought about the regrettable incident that was to wind up the day.

The parade was three parts through, when, all of a sudden, a tremendous downpour of cold rain set in, discomfiting and scattering all who were looking on. With the drenching effect of a shower-bath the rain commenced to pour down in torrents, causing an immediate stampede among the general public. The rearmost columns of the soldiers had to pass before empty benches, tramping along stolidly through the mud, "splashing ankle-deep through a sea of mud," as an officer put it.

The spectators one and all disappeared. The immense crowd of sightseers left the benches on the embankment round the Champ de Mars, and fled home *en masse*. The seat-holders on the open stands in front of the *Ecole Militaire* scurried off in like manner. The occupants of the pavilions and galleries, half drowned by the water that streamed down on them through the awnings, quitted their places in haste to seek shelter within the building. The downpour saturated the canopy of the Imperial Pavilion and dripped through. It compelled Josephine to get up from her throne and hurry indoors. The Princesses promptly followed the Empress's example, all except one—Napoleon's youngest sister, Caroline Murat. Caroline sat the March Past out to the end, together, of course, with Napoleon himself and the marshals, and those court officials who had to stay where they were. Soaked through, she smilingly remarked that she was "accustoming herself to endure the

---

1. Pigtails, too, were missing; for the first time at a military display of the kind in Paris. Even the soldiers of the Revolution, the rank and file, had kept up the old style of clubbed-hair. The new *régime*, however, had altered all that. "*Le petit tondu*" ("The little shorn one"), a camp-fire nickname for Napoleon, from his close-cropped head, had made every soldier cut his hair short; by a general order of six months before. The order, it may be mentioned incidentally, at first nearly raised a riot in the Imperial Guard, and led to a number of duels between "*les canichons*," the "lap-dogs" or "poodles," as the men who obeyed the order at the outset were sneeringly dubbed by comrades who refused to do so, and the others,.

inconveniences inseparable from a throne!"

Then, at the close of the review, came the *contretemps*.

After the last Eagle had gone past the throne, when Napoleon had left on his way back to the Tuileries, as the troops were moving off the ground to return to their quarters, unanticipated trouble suddenly arose in connection with the old flags. What happened may best, perhaps, be described in the words of an eyewitness, a general present on the Field of Mars, Baron Thiébault:

> Immediately after the Emperor had gone and the seats all round were empty, finding it tiresome to be loaded with the double set of standards, all the more so, no doubt, as it was raining, the standard-bearers apparently could think of nothing better than to rid themselves of the superseded flags. They began everywhere to throw them down, that is, to drop them where they stood in the mud. There they were trampled under foot by the soldiers as they passed along on their way back to quarters.

The outrage scandalised the older soldiers, and very nearly brought about a mutiny among some of them. To continue in General Thiébault's words:

> Indignant, at such an outrage to national emblems which the Army had been honouring and defending for thirteen years past, many of the men in the regiments began to grumble and make angry protestations. Presently oaths and violent imprecations burst out on all sides; and then some of the grenadiers became mutinous and defiant. They declared that they would go back, regardless of the consequences, and forcibly recover possession of the old colours.

The situation speedily became so threatening that General Thiébault hastened off to warn Murat of what was happening. As he went he came across one of the adjutants of the commandant of the Military School. On the spur of the moment he gave him orders to get together what men he could of the party who had been keeping the parade ground. Of these Thiébault took personal charge and sent them round at once to collect the thrown-down colours and carry them inside the *Ecole Militaire*.

Apparently that satisfied the soldiers—anxious, most of them, to get out of the wet as soon as possible.

General Thiébault tried after that to find Murat, intending to report to him; but Murat had by then left the Field of Mars. In the end the general decided, as perhaps the wisest course, to refrain from saying anything; not to take official notice of what had happened. After all he was not on duty at the parade; he was only in Paris as an invited guest at the Coronation festivities. Nobody, as a fact, said a word of the affair. By the authorities all reference to it seems purposely to have been hushed up. Not a hint of anything of the sort appeared in the *Moniteur*, which published a fairly full report of the day's proceedings; not a word in any of the other Parisian papers.

For the soldiers a dinner of double rations at the Emperor's expense wound up the Day of the Eagles; for the great personages there was:

> A banquet at the Tuileries, at which the Pope and the Emperor sat side by side at the same table, arrayed in their Pontifical and Imperial insignia and waited upon by the Grand Officers of the Crown.

Afterwards, without delaying in the capital, the deputations set off on their return to rejoin their regiments. Their arrival at their various destinations was celebrated everywhere, by Imperial order, by a full-dress parade and State reception of the Eagle by each corps; the occasion being further treated as a *fête*-day and opportunity for a general carousal in camp or garrison. At Boulogne the regiments of the "Army of England" took over their Eagles at a grand review on December 23, Marshal Soult presiding over the ceremony.

The old standards of the Consulate, some bearing on them the battle-scars of Marengo and Hohenlinden, remained where General Thiébault's assistants had left them stacked, leaning up against the wall in one of the corridors of the Military School, until they were carted off in artillery tumbrils to the central *dépôt* at Vincennes. There, on New Year's Day of 1805, they were officially made away with; burned to ashes in the presence of an ordnance department official told off to certify to their complete destruction. That was the authorised method in France of disposing of the standards of a discredited regime; but all the same it was a hard fate for national emblems that had waved victoriously over so many a hard-fought field.

Such were the principal scenes and incidents of the Day of the Field of Mars when Napoleon presented the Eagles of the Empire to the Soldiers of the Grand Army.

CHAPTER 3 - IN THE FIRST CAMPAIGN:
Under Fire With Marshal Ney

The Eagles made their *début* on the battlefield amid a blaze of glory. Within a twelvemonth of the Field of Mars they had swooped irresistibly across half the Continent, leading forward victoriously through the cannon-smoke in combat after combat, to achieve the crowning triumphs of Ulm and Austerlitz. Within the twelvemonth they witnessed the overwhelming defeat of more than 200,000 foes, the capture of 500 cannon, while 120 standards had been paraded before them as spoils of victory.

In the first fortnight of September 1805, Austria and Russia, as the protagonists in Pitt's great European Coalition against Napoleon, declared war on France, and an army of 80,000 Austrians traversed Bavaria in hot haste, to take post at Ulm by the Danube, on the frontiers of Württemberg. There they proposed to hold Napoleon in check, until their Russian allies, whose advance by forced marches through Poland had already begun, could join hands with them. After that they would press forward in resistless force to cross the Rhine and invade France.

But Napoleon was beforehand with them from the outset. Within twenty-four hours of the ultimatum reaching his hands he had made the opening move in the campaign: the lion, whose skin had been sold, had crouched for the fatal spring.

General Mack, the Austrian commander-in-chief, entered Bavaria on September 8. On September 1 Napoleon's "Army of the Ocean" had struck its tents in Boulogne camp and started on its way, with plans laid that ensured Mack's overthrow. A hundred and eighty thousand soldiers were hastening along every highroad through Hanover, Holland, and Flanders, and in eastern France, towards the great plain of Central Bavaria, to deal the Austrians the heaviest and most resounding blow ever yet dealt to a modern army.

Napoleon, screening his movement by means of Murat's cavalry, sent ahead on a wide front to occupy the attention of the Austrian out-posts, made a bold sweep right round Mack's right flank. Before the Austrian general had any suspicion that there was a single Frenchman on that side of him, the entire French army had passed the Danube in his rear, and had blocked the great highway from Vienna. Napoleon at the first move had cut the Austrian line of communication with their base. He had barred the only route by which the Russians could approach to Mack's assistance.

That done, swiftly and successfully, while Mack, startled and utterly staggered at the sudden appearance of the enemy in his rear, was hurriedly facing about in confusion, to try to hold his ground, Napoleon struck at him hard. He hurled attack after attack in force on the Austrian flanking divisions, on both wings of Mack's army, and broke them up. Taking thousands of prisoners and many guns, he drove the wreck, a disorganised mass of scared and helpless battalions, in rout to the walls of Ulm itself. Penned in there, ringed round by 100,000 French bayonets, with the French artillery pouring shot and shell into the doomed fortress from commanding heights within short range, General Mack, left now with barely 30,000 men, after a despairing interview with Napoleon, was terrorised into immediate surrender at discretion.

Amid such scenes did the Eagles of the Field of Mars undergo their baptism of fire. Ever in the forefront under fire, brilliantly, time and again, did those who bore them do their duty.

It was round the Eagles of Marshal Ney's corps, "the Fighting Sixth," that the fiercest contests of the campaign centred; and on every occasion they gained honour.

In the sharp brush at the bridge across the Danube at Reisenburg, near the small town of Günsburg, on October 8, one of the opening encounters of the campaign, the Eagle of the 59th of the Line showed the way to victory. The Austrians, whom Ney surprised on the south side or right bank, retreating as the French approached, had partially broken down the bridge before Ney's men could reach the place.

The Danube flows wide and deep at Reisenburg, and there was no other means of getting over.

Ney had explicit orders from Napoleon to cross over and occupy Günsburg, and to hold the river passage. As the 59th, who led the attack, got to the bridge, a long and narrow wooden structure, the

Austrian sappers were hard at work destroying it; covered by a rearguard brigade of infantry and artillery. The planking had been ripped away, but most of the bridge framework and supporting beams still stood. The 59th came up and opened fire, compelling the sappers to withdraw. Then a hasty effort was made by the pioneers of the regiment under fire to repair part of the bridge. They made a way across with planks wide enough for a few men to scramble over together. "In places only one man could get across at a time."

At once the 59th rushed forward cheering, but the concentrated Austrian fire from the other side was too hot to face. They were beaten back three times, the dead and wounded falling into the rushing stream below. But were they not the 59th? No other of the regiments following them in rear should have the honour of being the first to make the passage! The Eagle-bearer of the 59th, waving the Eagle aloft, headed a fourth attack; with Colonel Gérard Lacuèe, the colonel of the regiment, a distinguished officer and an Honorary A.D.C. to the Emperor, beside him. The two led out in front, regardless of the storm of bullets round them.

Colonel Lacuèe fell mortally wounded. An officer ran forward and carried the Colonel back to die on the river-bank, but the Eagle-bearer went on. "Soldiers," the brave fellow stopped for an instant to turn round and shout back to his comrades, "your Eagle goes forward! I shall carry it across alone!" The men of the 59th, thrown into a frenzy at the sight of their Eagle's peril, rallied instantly to follow. The four leading companies held on bravely and got across. Then they charged the Austrians at the point of the bayonet and drove them back into the village. That, though, was not all. Fresh Austrians had turned back to help their rearguard troops. Firing from the riverbank on either side of the village, for a time they stopped the other French regiments from crossing the bridge after the 59th.

Austrian dragoons and infantry at the same time charged the gallant regiment, entirely isolated now on that side of the river. But they could not break the 59th. Forming square, the two battalions, with their Eagles held on high as rallying-centres, kept a host of foes at bay. Three fierce Austrian charges did they beat off—and then help arrived. A second regiment, the 50th, had by then managed to get across the bridge. The two regiments maintained themselves there all the afternoon until nightfall and then bivouacked on the ground they had won until morning, "passing an anxious time, under arms, unable to light a fire. Fortunately, in the dark the Austrians did not realise our small numbers.

They were more anxious to cover their own retreat." Before daylight the Austrians fell back and the passage of the Danube was won.

There was another morning's work on October 11.

At Haslach, on the north bank of the Danube, not far from Ulm, a brigade of Dupont's Division of Ney's corps, advancing on that side on its own account, was suddenly set on by five times its number of Austrians. The brigade was made up of three regiments: the 9me Légère (or 9th Light Infantry), the 32nd, and the 69th. They stumbled, as it were, suddenly on the Austrians, whereupon General Dupont, who was riding with the brigade, on the opposite side of the river from the rest of his troops, "judging that if he fell back it would betray his weakness," made a dash at the enemy. His daring deceived the Austrians, who believed that he was the advanced guard of a large force close behind. They held back at first and awaited attack.

Throwing the 32nd into Haslach to hold the village, Dupont boldly charged with the two other regiments, and at the first onset made 1,500 prisoners, numbers equal to a quarter of his total force. The Austrians, however, rallied and returned to the fight. They brought up reinforcements and entrenched themselves in the village of Jüningen, nearby, where again Dupont attacked them. Five times did the 9th Light Infantry take and retake Jüningen at the point of the bayonet, their two battalion Eagles heading the attack each time. No fewer than six officers, bearing the Eagles in turn, fell in the fight. "*Ces corps ne devaient étonner de rien*," commented Napoleon in praising Dupont and his men.

At Elchingen, a village in the immediate neighbourhood of Ulm, the scene of the brilliant victory by which Marshal Ney won his title of Duc d'Elchingen, the Eagles of two regiments won distinction, through the individual heroism of the, officers who, holding them on high, "*En haut l'Aigle!*" was the charging cry led the onset that stormed the place. [1]

Ney headed the 6th Light Infantry personally, "in full uniform

---

1. Ney rode up to head the 6th Light Infantry at the outset, immediately after a chaffing challenge to Murat. The two, who had been operating together during the previous days, had had some difference over their methods of attack. Said Murat arrogantly on one occasion, after Ney had been laboriously trying to get into his brother-marshal's head an elaborate scheme of his proposed tactics: "I don't follow your plans. It is my way not to make mine till I am facing the enemy!" Ney, on the morning of Elchingen, got his chance to pay Murat back. They were together, riding close to Napoleon, with all the staff nearby, and not far from the Danube bank. As the guns began to open, Ney suddenly turned (continued next page).

and ablaze with decorations, offering a splendid target to the enemy." Ney led the 6th with the Eagle of the First Battalion carried close at his side. Fifteen thousand Austrians with forty guns held Elchingen, and the post is described as being "one of the strongest positions that could be imagined." The village itself, a large place, consisted of "successive piles of stone houses, intersected at right angles by streets, rising in the form of an amphitheatre from the banks of the Danube to a large convent which crowns the summit of the ascent. All the exposed points on heights were lined with artillery; all the windows filled with musketeers." The village was on the north bank, and the river had to be crossed to get to it.

First the gallant 6th Light Infantry stormed the bridge. It had been partly destroyed by the Austrians on the day before, and its tottering arches were now swept by cannon-balls, plunging down from batteries on the heights in rear, and a tornado of bullets from sharpshooters in the houses near the riverside. Fighting their way forward step by step, the 6me Légère went on. Their Eagle headed the advance. Its bearer was wounded, but he proudly brandished on high the standard; its silken flag torn to tatters by bullets, and with one wing of the Eagle broken by a shot. With the 6th fought the 69th of the Line.

The two regiments forced their way along the steep crooked main street up hill, fired down on furiously meanwhile from the windows. Parties of men at times entered the houses at the sides and fought the enemy inside bayonet to bayonet, from floor to floor. The 6th and the 69th pressed forward, broke down the enemy's resistance, and carried Elchingen. The Austrians finally, after a gallant attempt to hold out in the convent on the hilltop, abandoned it as fresh French troops came up from across the river.

On the battlefield, when the fight was over, Napoleon, with the Imperial staff round him, publicly congratulated Marshal Ney (he named him later "Duc D'Elchingen") in the presence of the 6th Light Infantry and the 69th, specially paraded at the spot for the occasion.

The Eagles of Ney, again, were foremost at the winning of the

---

and laid hold of Murat's arm. Giving his colleague a rough shake, before the Emperor and everybody, Ney exclaimed: "Now, Prince, come on! Come along with me! and make your plans in the face of the enemy!" The astonished Murat drew himself back, whereupon Ney spurred up his horse and dashed forward; "galloping off to the riverbank, he plunged into the water up to his horse's belly amidst a shower of cannon-balls and grape, to direct the mending of the bridge." That done, he galloped on to head the leading column of attack across the bridge..

final fight at Ulm. They led the furious onrush that stormed the steep heights of Michelsberg and Les Tuileries, the key of the last Austrian position. Thence Napoleon looked down directly into the fortress; and within an hour of Ney's brilliant final feat the French shells, from batteries, quickly galloped up to the heights, were bursting in Ulm, carrying terror and death into every quarter of the city.

On that came the surrender of General Mack. The curtain next rises on the intensely dramatic Fifth Act of the tragedy, the march out of the Austrians to lay down their arms.

In that display the Eagles had their allotted place. Before them, brought forward and prominently paraded, each Eagle in advance of its own corps in line, with the whole Grand Army ranged in battle order as spectators of the scene, the standards of the vanquished foe defiled out of the gates of Ulm, and were laid down on the ground in formal token of surrender.

Napoleon proved himself at Ulm a born stage-manager.

Hardly ever before, never in modern war, had such a spectacle been witnessed as that presented on that chill and cheerless October Sunday forenoon, October 20, 1805, in the heart of central Germany, beside the banks of the rushing Danube, roaring past, a yellow foaming torrent after weeks of autumn rain, amid pine-clad summits extending far and wide on either hand.

Along the lower slopes of the high ground to the north and east of Ulm, drawn up in lines and columns over a wide semi-circle, stood the victorious army; massed round, as it were, in a vast amphitheatre. They formed up by army corps, and took post grim and silent, drawn up in battle array, with muskets loaded and bayonets fixed. The cavalry with sabres drawn were on one side; the infantry on the other, facing them and leaving a space between, along which the Austrians were to pass. Fifty loaded cannon, in line along one ridge, pointed down on the city. In front, towards the river, there rose a small knoll, an outlying spur of rock. On that Napoleon took his station beside a blazing watchfire which marked the spot from far. Accompanying him were most of the marshals and the assembled *Etat-Major* of the Grand Army, a numerous and brilliant gathering. Immediately in rear stood massed the 10,000 men of the Imperial Guard.

Two army corps, a little way from the rest, had a special post of honour. They were drawn up at the end of the wide semi-circle of the main army nearest the Augsburg gate of Ulm; immediately where the defilading column of captives would present themselves before passing

Napoleon to lay down their arms and standards. The two corps were: that on the right, Ney's, the Sixth Army Corps, the heroes of the day *par excellence*; on the left, the Second Corps, Marmont's, who had been doing notable work elsewhere in the neighbourhood of Ulm. Ney, with his personal staff beside him, was on horseback in front of the centre of his corps; Marmont had his post in like manner in front of his men. As his personal reward for the leading part Ney and the Sixth Corps had had in bringing about the triumph, that marshal had the special honour of being designated to superintend the surrender.

A few minutes before ten o'clock the French drums began to beat, and the regimental bands to play. Immediately after that the long-drawn-out procession of sullen and woebegone-looking Austrian captives began silently to trail its way out of the Stuttgart gate of the fortress.

> Suddenly we saw an endless column file out of the town and march up in front of the Emperor, on the plain at the foot of a mountain.

General Mack himself headed it, wan-faced and pale as the white uniform coat he wore, his eyes filled with tears, his head bowed, a pitiful and abject figure to behold. After him followed eighteen Austrian generals—a surprising number—most of them as wretched and downcast-looking as their chief. "Behold, Sire, the unfortunate Mack!" was the ill fated leader's address to Napoleon, as he formally presented his sword. Napoleon, in a mood—as well he might be—in that hour of unparalleled triumph, to show courtesy to the fallen foe, desired Mack to keep his sword and remain at his side. He said the same to the eighteen other generals as, one by one, they came up in turn to tender him their swords. He returned each his sword and bade them all place themselves near their chief. When all the swords had been presented and returned, Napoleon made the Austrian generals collectively a short harangue:

> "Gentlemen, war has its chances! Often victorious, you must expect sometimes to be vanquished!

He did not really know, Napoleon went on, why they were fighting. Their master had begun against him an unjust war. "I want nothing on the Continent," said Napoleon in conclusion, "only ships, colonies, and commerce!"

It was on the day before Trafalgar that these memorable words were spoken. The Austrian generals stared at Napoleon blankly, but not one uttered a word.

They were all very dull; it was the Emperor alone who kept up the conversation.

Then they took their stand beside their conqueror and looked on at the bitterly humiliating scene of the defilade of their fellow soldiers.

In an almost incessant throng the columns of the Austrian Army streamed by: white-clad *cuirassiers*; hussars in red and blue and grey; battery after battery of cocked-hatted, brown-garbed artillerymen, riding with or on their rumbling dull-yellow wheeled guns; battalion after battalion of white-coated linesmen; dark-green coated *jägers*; Hungarian grenadiers, and so on. Twenty-seven thousand officers and men and sixty field-guns in all defiled past the Eagles, proudly arrayed there above them, in front of the serried lines of glittering French bayonets along the hillsides. For five hours on end the host of captives plodded on before the rocky brow from which Napoleon surveyed the spectacle; tramping by, their muskets without bayonets and unloaded, their cartridge-boxes emptied.

In several regiments the men maintained a fair semblance of discipline and military order; but the ranks of all were sadly bedraggled-looking, the white uniforms torn and soiled and besmirched with powder-smoke, with many of the men hatless, or limping from wounds, or with bound-up heads, and their arms in blood-stained slings. As had been ordered by Napoleon, they carried with them their standards; no fewer than forty silken battle-flags—for the most part cased, but here and there was to be seen one not furled, displaying, as though in futile defiance, its flaunting yellow folds with the double-headed Black Eagle.

As the Austrian linesmen came abreast of where Napoleon stood, the pace of the men slackened. Every eye was turned to look at "him"; at the small grey-coated figure on foot beside the watchfire, standing near the crestfallen group of their own generals, a few paces from the bright and brilliant-hued cavalcade of French marshals and the staff. All stared at Napoleon, gazing as if under a spell. Then, in the midst of it all, this happened. Suddenly, as they passed Napoleon, a shout rose from among the ranks of the defeated army: "*Es lebe der Kaiser!*" ("Long live the Emperor!") The cry burst forth with startling effect. It was repeated, and then several men took it up. But what did it mean? "*Es lebe der Kaiser!*" was the national German greeting in salute to their own Austrian sovereign as Head of the Empire, to the *Kaiser* at Vienna, the Emperor of Germany.

Did the soldiers who first raised the cry intend it for that, or to hail Napoleon, as his own men did, with a *"Vive l'Empereur!"*? The words bore the same meaning. Or did the men fling the words at Napoleon in a sort of bravado, as a show of defiance? Some of the Austrians assuredly did mean them so; to relieve the breaking strain, the terrible tension of the ordeal. At least some of the French officers near Napoleon took that view of it. One describes:

> As they passed by the prisoners, seized with wonder, with admiration, slowed down in their march to gaze at their conqueror, and some cried out 'Long live the Emperor!' but no doubt under very different emotions; some with evident mortification.

From the presence of Napoleon the captive army passed to the scene of the act of final humiliation: to the place where, midway between the lines of bayonets of the troops of Ney and Marmont, they were to lay down their colours and ground their arms.

The colours were first surrendered, a French general, Andréossi, formerly Napoleon's ambassador in London, receiving them, with half a dozen staff officers and orderlies, who deposited the flags one by one in two commissariat wagons drawn up close by.

It was a moment of the deepest and keenest anguish for proud and gallant soldiers. All round them on the hillsides most of the French, overcome by excitement over the unprecedented and amazing spectacle, were by that time almost beside themselves, rending the air with exulting shouts and cheers. Under the cruel stress of the ordeal, as the supreme moment came on, the self-possession of some of the Austrians, tried beyond endurance, gave way.

The men of the cavalry and artillery bore themselves throughout with well-disciplined steadiness. As they came to the appointed place where groups of French cavalry troopers and gunners, told off to take over their horses and guns, were standing near the roadside awaiting them, they dismounted at the word of command from their own commanders and stood back. With hardly a murmur from the ranks the Austrian troopers unbuckled their swords and carbines and pistols, and dropped them in heaps at the places pointed out to them. With quiet dignity the officers relinquished their gold-embroidered banners into the enemy's hands. In grim silence they saw the victors—who there at any rate behaved with courtesy and soldierly consideration for the feeling of the vanquished—step forward to take possession of their horses and their cannon. Many of the Austrians had tears running down their cheeks; some stood trembling with suppressed passion;- but all preserved order and behaved with complete decorum as became disciplined soldiers.

With others unfortunately, with some of the infantry corps, it was otherwise. At the very last, before arriving at the place where they were to give up their weapons, a number of the men in some of the marching regiments broke down under the fearful strain of the moment and lost their heads. In many regiments, no doubt, the soldiers obeyed mechanically, acting like men half stunned after a violent shock; they did as they were told, and passively grounded their arms to order.

But in others the final scene was attended by acts of wild frenzy, pitiful to behold. In, as it were, a paroxysm of exasperation at the disgrace that had befallen them, the rank and file of these broke out recklessly, and got at once beyond all efforts of their officers to control. With one accord they began smashing the locks and butts of their muskets on the ground with savage curses, flinging away their arms all round, and stripping off their accoutrements and stamping on them, trampling them down in the mud. These, though, as has been said, were only some of the men; and in certain regiments. The majority of the Austrians bore themselves with fortitude and calmness.

At the end of the afternoon the Imperial Guard, headed by their Eagle and band, marched into Ulm and through the city, as we are told, "amid the shouts of the whole populace."

So terminated the tragedy of Ulm, in the presence of the Eagles on their first triumphant battlefield.

The spoils of the Eagles at all points, as announced by Napoleon in the Ulm Bulletin of the Grand Army, were 60,000 prisoners, 200 pieces of cannon, and, in all, 90 flags. The 40 standards surrendered at Ulm itself Napoleon sent to Paris forthwith—after a grand parade of the trophies at Augsburg, in which ninety sergeants of the Imperial Guard bore in procession the Austrian flags. The Ulm trophies were made an Imperial gift for the Senate. Wrote Napoleon:

It is a homage, which I and my army pay to the Sages of the Empire.

They were the flags, it may be added, which were displayed at the head of Napoleon's coffin on the occasion of his State funeral in 1840: they form four-fifths of the trophies now grouped round Napoleon's tomb. Alone of the trophies of the Ulm campaign, and also of the Austerlitz campaign which followed it, they escaped destruction in the holocaust of Napoleon's trophies that took place at the Invalides in March 1814, on the night of the surrender of Paris to the Allies. How that came to pass will be told later.

There was a very interesting sequel to the Ulm campaign for one of Ney's regiments. A brief but brilliant campaign in the Tyrol on their own account followed for Ney's men immediately after Ulm.

Entering the Tyrol with two of his divisions, Ney attacked and by brilliant tactics overthrew the Tyrolese forces and Austrian regulars who barred his way in a position among the mountains deemed impregnable. The battalion Eagles of the 69th gave the signal for the frontal attack which stormed the enemy's position. Guided by chamois-hunters the soldiers with the Eagles scaled the face of a precipitous line of crags which overhung in rear the Austrian centre, by inserting their bayonets into fissures in the rocks and clinging to shrubs and creepers, their *havresacs* tied round their heads as protection from the stones that the Tyrolese above showered down on them. At the top, driving in the defenders, they held up the gleaming Eagles in the sunlight on the brink of the precipice to the marshal below, firing down on the Austrians at the same time to demoralise their resistance and clear the way for Ney's main effort:

Les Aigles du 69me plantées sur la cime des rochers servirent de signal a l'attacque de front que le Maréchal Ney avait preparé.

Innsbruck, the capital of the Tyrol, and the headquarters of the Austrian army corps garrisoning the country, was the immediate prize of the victory. It was there that this incident took place.

One of Ney's regiments, the 76th, had fought in the Tyrol six years before; in Masséna's campaign of 1799, in one of the battles of which-at Senft in the Grisons, on August 22—two of its battalions lost their colours. An officer of the regiment, while visiting the arsenal at Innsbruck after Ney's capture of the city, came across the two flags there, in tatters from bullet-holes, hung up as trophies. He made known his discovery, and the place was quickly filled with the soldiers of the regiment, eager to see the old flags. "They crowded round them and kissed the fragments of their old colours, with tears in their eyes."

Ney had the flags removed at once. He restored them to the custody of the regiment with his own hand at a grand parade in the presence of the rest of his army, which the marshal attended with his staff, all in full uniform. The old colours were received with an elaborate display of military ceremonial. They were borne along the lines while the regimental band played a stately march, and the Eagles of both battalions were formally dipped in salute to them.

On receiving Ney's report, Napoleon thought fit to give the recovery of the flags a bulletin to itself. Relating how they had been lost in battle, and the "*affliction profonde*" of the regiment in consequence, he set forth how they had been found and handed back by Marshal Ney to the regiment:

> With an affecting solemnity that drew tears from the eyes of both the old soldiers and the young conscripts, proud of having had their share in regaining them!

The bulletin concluded:

> *Le soldat Français, a pour ses drapeaux un sentiment qui tient de la tendresse; ils sont l'objet de son culte, comme un présent reçu des mains d'une mère.*

A medal was specially struck to commemorate the event; and Napoleon, in addition, specially commissioned an artist, Meynier, to paint a picture for him of Marshal Ney presenting the recovered colours to the regiment. The painting is now in one of the galleries of Versailles.

THE MIDNIGHT BATTLE BY THE DANUBE

A startling and dramatic episode of the first campaign of the Eagles comes next. It took place during the second stage of the war; in the midst of Napoleon's impetuous advance on Vienna down the Danube valley after Ulm. Intent on dealing a shattering blow at the advanced army corps of the Russians, which had reached Lower Austria and was making an effort to cover the capital, Napoleon made a false move, and left one of the headmost French divisions in an exposed position, temporarily isolated. It got trapped by the Russians at Dürrenstein, or Dirnstein, on the north side of the Danube, to the west of and about seventy miles up the river from Vienna; and was all but annihilated. There was nearly twenty hours of continuous fighting, including a night battle of the fiercest and most desperate character in which three Eagles were temporarily lost; fortunately to be recovered later among the dead on the battlefield. (*See note following.*)

Note:—Napoleon himself, it so chanced at the outset, heard the fierce cannonading from afar, and, becoming suddenly alarmed at what might be happening, was thrown into a fever of anxiety over it; into a state of violent agitation. It was on the evening of November 11. Napoleon just then was on his way to take up his quarters at the Abbey of St. Polten, whence only a few miles intervened between him and Vienna. As he was nearing St. Polten he was suddenly alarmed by "the smothered, distant echo of heavy firing, which was not even interrupted by night."

So one of the *aides de camp* on the Emperor's staff, De Ségur, describes. "What unforeseen danger could suddenly have overtaken Mortier? It was almost certainly he who, going forward with an advanced guard of five thousand men, had unexpectedly come across Kutusoff with forty thousand. It was impossible, though, at first, to imagine the destruction of the marshal and his unhappy division."

At St. Polten they listened, and in the end feared for the worst. "One could only offer up prayers and await the decision of fate! The wide and deep Danube separated us from the marshal. This stream had just delivered over to the enemy one of Mortier's generals, who in despair had tried to make his escape in a boat. Everything announced a catastrophe: the Emperor no longer doubted it. In his anxiety, as he drew nearer to the sound of the combat, while advancing from Moelkt to St. Polten, the fear of a reverse usurped the place of Napoleon's former confidence of victory. Now, his agitation increasing with the noise of the firing, he despatched everybody for news: officers, *aides de camp*; every officer who happened to be near him. With his mind full of Mortier's peril he suspended the progress of the invasion. He stopped Bernadotte and the flotilla behind at Moelkt. He recalled Murat, dashing on for the gates of Vienna; and Soult, following Murat. Not indeed until three on the next afternoon, the 12th of November, was Napoleon's anxiety allayed by the arrival of an *aide de camp* from Mortier."

It was on an extemporised corps, specially placed under the command of Marshal Mortier, that the blow fell.

While Napoleon and the Grand Army in force advanced along the south, or right, bank of the Danube, Mortier had been detached across the river to hold in check any attempt to interfere with the main operations from the Bohemian side. A body of Austrian cavalry, under the Archduke Ferdinand, had managed to cut their way through from Ulm at one point just before the closing of the net round General Mack. With the aid of the local militia levies these might prove troublesome on the line of communications. To deal with them, three divisions, drawn from as many corps, were amalgamated as Mortier's special corps, which numbered in all between twenty and twenty-five thousand men: Gazan's division, lent by Marshal Lannes; Dupont's, lent by Ney; Dumonceau's, lent by Marmont.

To keep Mortier in touch with the main body of the army, and that he might be reinforced in emergency, a flotilla of Danube craft was at the same time improvised, and placed in charge of the Seamen of the Guard, a battalion of whom had accompanied Napoleon for the campaign. The flotilla was to keep pace with Mortier and link him with Napoleon. Mortier crossed at Linz and moved forward; his three divisions each a day's march apart, for convenience of provisioning. He marched so fast, however, that he outstripped the connecting boats.

At the moment the fighting opened, the flotilla was miles in rear. It had been stopped and its progress blocked near Moelkt, unable in the swollen state of the Danube to pass the dangerous Strudel, or whirlpool, there, raging just then, after the heavy autumn rains, with the force of a swirling maelstrom. The flooded river had made it extremely difficult work all the way, even for the picked Seamen of the Guard, to navigate with safety the assortment of boats and timber rafts, clumsy structures of logs and spars lashed together, 160 feet long each, and planked over, with cabins on the planks, which composed the flotilla. On them, together with a quantity of spare stores and ammunition for the army, convalescents and footsore men of various regiments were being carried, who, it was intended, would thus be on the spot to reinforce Mortier first of all in case of danger.

Immediately after passing Dürrenstein, the leading division, General Gazan's, numbering some 6,000 men, unexpectedly stumbled across part of the Russian rearguard. All unknown to Mortier, the Russian army corps which had been entrenched in front of Vienna had abandoned its position and had hastily withdrawn north of the river, crossing a short distance from Dürrenstein.

Mortier, after clearing a narrow and difficult pass on the eastern side of Dürrenstein, with steep and rocky hills on one hand and the Danube on the other, first learned of the presence of the enemy by catching sight of the smoke of the burning bridge of Krems, which the Russians had set fire to after passing over. Then he suddenly found his further advance barred by troops with guns, who rapidly formed up across his path. The Russians took up a formidable-looking position, but the marshal decided to attack without waiting for Dupont to come up with the Second Division, or for the flotilla; both miles in rear.

The sight of the burning bridge and the apparent haste of the enemy to get across the river, it would seem, misled Mortier into thinking that the Russians had been in action with Napoleon, and were in flight, trying to escape. He went at them without pausing to reconnoitre. He assumed that they were only making a show of defence. The troops before him he would sweep aside easily. Then he would press on and complete the rout of the rest of the Russians, whom he took to be retreating in confusion, screened by the force he saw, across his front. Confident of easy success, Mortier entered into the fight then and there.

The sudden rencontre, as has been said, was a surprise for the marshal. Half an hour previously a battle had been almost the last thing in Mortier's thoughts. His guns were on board a number of river boats which were being drifted downstream abreast of the troops, the artillery horses being led with the marching columns along the bank. The boats had been requisitioned a few miles back, so as to enable the troops to get on faster over the rough stretch of road through the Pass of Dürrenstein. The guns were hastily disembarked and raced forward into the firing line in order to stop a forward movement that the Russians, who promptly took advantage of the opportunity offered by Mortier being apparently without artillery, began by making.

The Russians came on and quickly increased in numbers, to Marshal Mortier's further surprise. Were those beaten troops in full flight? They began to swarm down to meet the French; heading for the guns as these were being brought forward. The fight rapidly became general, and charge after charge was made by the Russians to carry Mortier's guns. They captured them, but were then beaten back and the guns recaptured. Twice were the guns taken and retaken. The two French regiments nearest the guns, the 100th and 103rd, defended them with brilliant courage, their four battalion Eagles conspicuous in the forefront and repeatedly the centre of desperate fighting, as the Russians essayed again and again at the point of the bayonet to make prize of the gleaming emblems.

But more and more Russians kept joining in, and after four hours of very severe fighting the marshal began to get anxious. He had gained ground towards Krems, and had made some 1,500 prisoners; but every foot of the way had been stubbornly contested, and his losses had been serious.

Mortier after that left the troops, and with an *aide de camp* galloped back through the pass in order to hasten up Dupont. But the Second Division was still at a distance. Dupont's men were still a long way beyond Dürrenstein and could not arrive for some time yet. Mortier could only tell them not to lose a moment, and then retrace his own steps. On his way back, to his amazement, he came upon a second Russian column in great strength in the act of debouching from a side pass and entering Dürrenstein. It had come round by a track among the hills on the north to take Gazan's division in rear, and interpose between it and Dupont's reinforcing troops. At considerable personal risk the marshal managed to evade discovery by the Russians. By following a devious by-path he at length got back to where Gazan's division was; as before, in hot action and slowly forcing the Russians back.

Mortier stopped the advance at once. He faced his troops about, and, while keeping off his original enemy, retreated; closing his columns and rushing all back as fast as possible to repass the defile of Dürrenstein and confront the new enemy on the further side, in a position he might hold until Dupont could reinforce him. But it was already too late. The French reached the entrance of the pass on the near side to find it already occupied by the Russians, who were pouring through in dense masses. There were nearly 20,000 of them on that side of him and 15,000 on the other, his former foes now fast closing in from behind hard on his heels. Mortier's reduced ranks numbered barely 4,000 all told.

Owing to the high, steep rocks on one hand, and the river on the other, it was impossible to push past the Russians on either flank. All that could be done was to attack in front and try to cut a way through. That; or to surrender! With reckless impetuosity the French attacked, firing furiously and flinging themselves on the Russian bayonets; while their rearguard, facing round, kept their first foes back. For two long hours they fought like that; their ranks swept by the enemy's cannon on each side. At length they forced the entrance to the pass: but they could get no farther. They had by then lost all their guns but two: but they still had all their Eagles. With bullet-holes through some of them, and their silken flags shot away or torn to tatters, the Eagles did their part. Now they were rallying-centres; now they were leading charges. There was hardly a battalion in which the first standard-bearer had not gone down.

All were fighting almost without hope, holding out in sheer despair as long as they had cartridges left, when, as that dreadful November afternoon was drawing to its close, suddenly, from beyond the far end of the pass was heard the booming of a distant cannonade. The soldiers heard it and hope revived. It could only be Dupont! Help, then, was coming! The despairing rank and file took heart again—but the hour of rescue was not yet.

They had four long hours more to go through; every hour making their terrible situation worse. At nightfall "our cavalry gave way, our firing slackened, our bayonets, from incessant use, became bent and blunted. The confusion became terrible. Things, indeed, could hardly have got worse." So an officer describes. The enemy, in places, had got right in among them, but "our soldiers, being the handier and more agile, had an advantage over the great clumsy Russians." Here and there "the men were so close, that they seized each other by the throat." In the midst of the fiercest of the fighting the tall figure of the marshal was conspicuous. He was seen amid the flashes from the muskets "at the head of a party of grenadiers, sword in hand, laying about him like any trooper."

The Battalion-Eagles of the 100th, with their Porte-Aigles and a handful of soldiers, got cut off together, amid a surging *mêlée* of Russians. The major of the regiment, Henriot by name, the senior surviving officer—the colonel of the 100th, as also the colonel of the 103rd, had fallen earlier in the fight—saw what was happening and the extreme peril of the Eagles. Calling for volunteers, he got together some of his men, cut his way through to the Eagles, and rescued them. Major Henriot, after that, having saved the Eagles for the moment, determined as a last resource to attempt a forlorn-hope charge; to get beyond the enemy and reach Dupont with them. It might be possible to save them under the cover of darkness.

One of the *Porte-Aigles* of the 6th Light Infantry with his Eagle, nearby at the moment, joined the devoted band of men that the intrepid major now managed to rally round the Eagles of the 100th. With half a dozen stirring words Henriot called on them to follow him.

> Comrades, we must break through! They are more than we, but you are Frenchmen: you don't count numbers! Remember, your duty is to save the Eagles of France! (*Souvenez vous qu'il s'agit de sauver les Aigles Françaises!*)

There was a hoarse shout in reply: "We are all Grenadiers! *Pas de charge!*"

They dashed at the Russians, Henriot leading, and, after fighting their way through the pass and nearly to Dürrenstein, fell to a man. Yet the three Eagles did not fall into Russian hands, thanks to the darkness. They were found next morning by French search-parties under a heap of dead, where the last survivors, fighting back to back, had fallen while making their final stand.

So desperate, indeed, did things look for the French at one time, a little before midnight, that some of his staff appealed to Mortier to make his escape and get across to the other side of the Danube in a boat, "so that a marshal of France shall not fall into the hands of the enemy!"

But the gallant veteran flatly refused to listen to the proposal, his answer was:

No, certainly not! I will not desert my brave comrades! I will save them or die with them! Keep the boats for the wounded. We have still two guns and some case-shot—rally and make a last effort

Almost immediately afterwards an opportunity did offer for the marshal to save them.

Two of Dupont's regiments at that moment reached the battle. By persistent exertions, outstripping the rest of the Second Division, and continuing in the dark, guided by the flashes of the guns, they had made their way by a goat-path along the steep rocky slopes at the side of the defile and taken the Russians barring Mortier's retreat in rear. Instantly the new arrivals flung themselves hotly into the fight. They were the 9th Light Infantry and the 32nd of the Line, that old favourite of Napoleon's in the days of the Army of Italy, whose flag on the Eagle-staff bore, as has been said, the golden inscription which Napoleon had placed there—"*J'étais tranquille, le brave 32me était là.*"

The golden legend was of good omen for Mortier.

Their interposition put the Russian main force between two fires, weakening the attack on Mortier and compelling a portion of them to face about. Its effect was speedily felt, and at once; although a desperate effort by the two regiments to break through and join hands with Mortier, in which the Eagles of the 9th and 32nd were "taken and retaken," was beaten back under pressure of numbers.

The arrival of the two regiments so opportunely put heart into all: Dupont's whole division, declared the marshal, could not be far off. He himself would make an effort to meet him on the farther side of

Marshal Mortier

the pass, as is described by Napoleon's *aide de camp,* Count de Sègur:

> Then, rallying and closing up the remaining troops, he brought up the only two guns left him. One was to point towards Krems and against Kutusoff's troops; the other Mortier placed at the head of the column, in the direction of Dürrenstein. As all the drums had been broken he had the charge sounded on iron cooking-cans.
>
> At that moment the Austrian general, Schmidt, who had led the Russian corps from Dürrenstein, headed a final charge which was to strike a crushing blow and complete the destruction of our column. But Fabvier (the colonel in charge of Mortier's artillery) heard them advance. Concealed by the darkness, he let Schmidt approach quite near. Then he suddenly fired the gun on that side, at the shortest range, in among the headmost of the attacking troops. The discharge threw the enemy into confusion and killed their leader. Into this bloody opening Mortier and Gazan precipitated themselves, overthrowing everything before them. Dürrenstein itself was retaken in the impetuous dash.

It was indeed a *tour de force*; a sudden reversal of the fortunes of the fight. The feat in its complete accomplishment surprised even Mortier's expectations. "The marshal, in fact, could hardly believe his own success." So an officer puts it. But he had done more than burst through the toils. As daylight next morning showed, the Russians, driven headlong, had abandoned six of their guns, and left in the hands of the French no fewer than twelve standards. Two of them were taken by the two Dupont regiments which had so gallantly flung themselves on the Russian rear. .

That was as concerned honour and glory. As a set off, barely 2,000 remained of Mortier's corps of 6,000 men. Two-thirds of the total when the roll was called next day were found to have fallen on the field.

Mortier's men regained Dürrenstein, all in flames; set on fire by the Russians as they evacuated the village. But where was Dupont and his Division? They had heard Dupont's distant guns just before dark; but except the two regiments who had been rushed forward independently, ahead of the main body, starting immediately after Mortier's visit in the early afternoon, no help from Dupont had reached them. Gazan's wearied survivors of the midnight battle dared not even yet lay aside their arms. The fight was not all over. The enemy were still nearby; just beyond the outskirts of the village. Both the Russian divisions that they had been fighting with in front and rear had in the end united. Outnumbering Mortier's men as they did by ten to one, the Russians would certainly turn back and be on them before long with re-formed ranks, eager to take vengeance for their defeat and the rough handling they had undergone.

But the end was near.

Suddenly, from the farther side of Dürrenstein, from the direction in which the enemy had fallen back, there came a violent outburst of firing. Immediately on that followed sounds of shouting. Then there was the trampling rush of a great host of men all making for the village.

> With despair in our hearts we were preparing for another battle, when, in answer to our challenge of '*Qui vive?*' came back, with electrifying effect, the answer 'France!' It was Dupont. At last he had arrived to the rescue of his marshal.
>
> We recognised each other in the light of the blazing houses, and with transports of joy and gratitude and cries of 'Long live our rescuers!' our men threw themselves on the necks of their deliverers.

In that dramatic fashion the battle of Dürrenstein reached its close. The Russians fell back under cover of the night, retreating up the lateral valley-pass, by which way at the outset they had worked their way round, guided by the Austrian general, Schmidt, to surprise and cut off Gazan's division. Napoleon, in his great relief at learning that Mortier had come through without disaster, for once blamed nobody. He knew that he himself was most of all to blame, for exposing to sudden attack a comparatively weak detachment of his army in the face of an enemy still full of fight, on the farther side of a deep and rapid river. In Marbot's words:

> It seemed as if no explanation of this operation beyond the Danube satisfactory to military men being possible, there was a desire to hush up its consequences.

By way of covering up his own glaring blunder Napoleon heaped praises on the troops engaged. He expressed unbounded admiration at the stand they had made. In the 22nd "Bulletin of the Grand Army," issued from Schönbrunn, near Vienna, two days later, the Emperor declared that "*le combat de Dürrenstein sera à jamais mémorable dans les annales militaires.*" Gazan, he said, had shown "*beaucoup de valeur et de conduite.*" The 4me and 9me Légère and the 32nd and 100th of the Line, wrote Napoleon, "*se sont couverts de gloire.*"

CHAPTER 4

On the Field of Austerlitz

Austerlitz, the crowning triumph of the First War of the Grand Army, set its *cachet* to the fame of the Eagles.

Napoleon there lured the enemy on into attacking him at apparent disadvantage on ground of his own choosing. Then, availing himself to the fullest extent of the flagrant blundering of his assailants, he struck at them with a smashing, knock-down blow from the shoulder.

By making believe that his army was separated in detachments, out of touch, and beyond possibility of early concentration, and causing it to appear further that he had become alarmed for his own safety and was on the point of commencing a retreat, he decoyed them into a false move. He tempted the Czar Alexander, whose main force had arrived within a few miles of Vienna, and was confronting him, into making a rash manoeuvre designed to cut his line of communications and defeat him before the second Austrian army in the field, under the Archduke Charles, hastening from the Italian frontier to join hands with the Russians, could reach the scene.

In the confident belief that by themselves they outnumbered Napoleon at the critical point by two to one, with nearly 90,000 men to 40,000, the Russians made a risky flank march to interpose between Napoleon and his base, and drive him in rout into the wilds of Bohemia. They began their advance suddenly, on Thursday, November 2, but immediately afterwards wasted two days through faulty leadership. Before they could get within striking distance of Napoleon he had called in his detached corps and had massed 70,000 men at the point of danger. Foreseeing the possibility of the enemy's move, his apparent disposal of the various corps had been elaborately arranged so as to ensure concentration at short notice in case of emergency.

From hour to hour during Sunday, December 1, the Russian army in dense columns streamed past within six miles of the French position in full view of Napoleon, all marching forward in stolid silence, intent only on getting between Napoleon and Vienna. No countermove meanwhile was made from the French side. Strict orders were sent to the outposts that not a shot was to be fired. But by the early afternoon all was ready for action. Completely seeing through the enemy's plans, Napoleon exclaimed in a tone of absolute confidence: "Before tomorrow night that army is mine!"

On Napoleon's right flank, in a strong defensive position, stood Marshal Davout's corps, thrown back at an angle to the main front of the army, so as to induce the enemy to extend themselves widely on that side before opening their attack. Marshal Soult's corps, the most powerful in the Grand Army, formed the centre; supported by the Imperial Guard, Oudinot's Grenadier Division, and two divisions of Mortier's corps. Marshal Lannes' corps, with Bernadotte's, was on the left, as well as Murat's cavalry. Napoleon proposed to allow the Russian leading columns to circle round his right flank and get into action with Davout.

Then, as soon as they were committed to their attack in that quarter, Soult's immense force would hurl itself on the Russian centre and break through it by sheer weight of numbers. Thus the Allied Army would be cleft in two, after which Napoleon would only have to fling his weight to either side for the enemy to be destroyed in detail. During Soult's move, Lannes on the left flank was to hold in check by a brisk attack the Russian right wing and reserves, which would prevent assistance reaching the centre until too late to save the day. So the battle was planned; so it was fought and won.

The Allied columns were seen during Sunday afternoon to be steadily moving southward over a high ridge opposite the French camp, crowned near the centre by the lofty plateau of Pratzen, the key of the position on the Russian side. They streamed along from the direction of the village of Austerlitz, a short distance away to the north-east, from which the battle took its name. A tract of low marshy country, the valley of the little river Goldbach, four miles across, with two or three hamlets dotting it here and there, connected by narrow cart-roads, divided the two armies. The French position, facing eastwards, was on a range of tableland along the west side of the valley of the Goldbach.

Monday morning came, and the "Sun of Austerlitz"—so often apostrophised by Napoleon in after days—rose in a cloudless sky

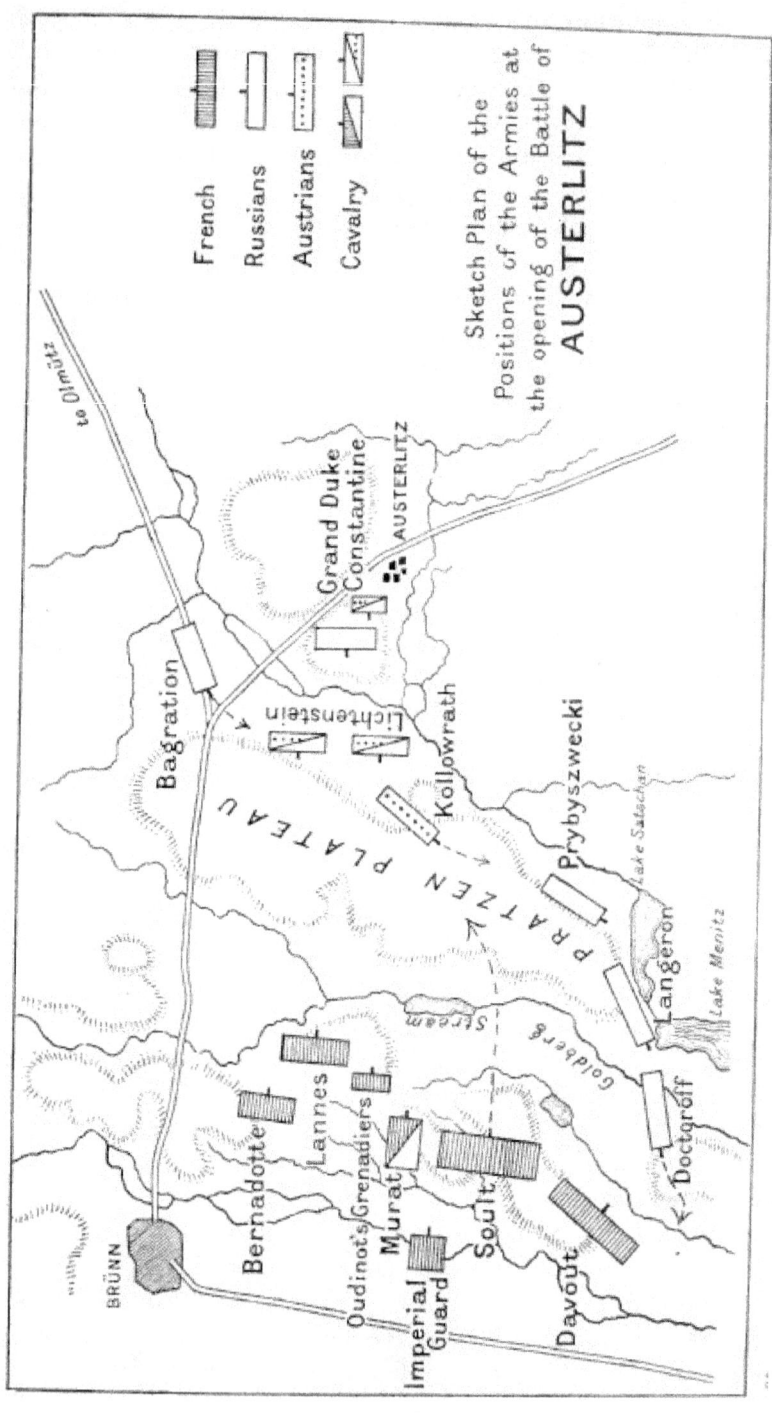

above the early mists lying dense over the marshy ground of the low-lying valley between the armies. The dominating crest of the Pratzen plateau showed above the mist almost bare of troops. On the evening before it had bristled with Russian bayonets, glistening in the rays of the setting sun. Pratzen, the master-key of the battlefield, had been left unoccupied. The enemy's corps had taken no measures to hold it in their haste to get forward to attack the French right wing, and cut Napoleon off.

Soult's corps—the entire French Army had been under arms since four o'clock—was ordered to descend into the valley before the morning mist dissipated as the sun rose. Under cover of the mist Soult was to get as close as possible to the foot of the Pratzen Hill, so as to be on the spot ready to seize the height immediately the battle opened on the right.

Napoleon waited, standing among the marshals on foot near the centre of the position, until between seven and eight o'clock. Then sharp firing suddenly broke out from the direction of Davout's corps, and a few minutes later an *aide de camp* came galloping up with the news that the enemy were attacking the right wing in great force. "Now," said Napoleon, "is the moment." The marshals sprang on their horses and spurred off to head their corps.

So Austerlitz opened.

Its first brunt, as Napoleon had foreseen, fell hard and heavily on the French right wing; but Davout's men there proved well able to maintain their ground. The sturdy linesmen on that side disputed every foot of the position at the point of the bayonet against four times their numbers.

Right gallantly, time and again, did the Eagles on that part of the field fulfil their *rôle* and take their part; now heading charges, now rallying round them the men who had sworn to die in their defence.

The 15th Light Infantry—a corps in the ranks of which were many young soldiers, now under fire for the first time in their lives-stormed the village of Tellnitz, which the Russians had carried in their first rush on the French outposts. The leading battalion of the 15th drove the Russians out; and, dashing on beyond the village, met a reinforcing Russian column hastening to the spot. They charged it without hesitation, but could not break through, and then they began to recoil before superior numbers. The Eagle-bearer was shot down, and fell badly wounded. He had to leave hold of his Eagle, and amid the surging throng of soldiers in disorder it was in great danger of being trampled underfoot and lost.

Fortunately the officer in command, *Chef de Bataillon* Dulong, saw what had happened, and sprang from his horse and seized the Eagle. Holding it on high with one hand, he shouted to his men to stand fast. "Soldiers, I stay here!" he called. "Let me see if you will abandon your Eagle and your commander." The act and words checked the disorder. The battalion rallied at once, re-formed ranks, and made head against the enemy until help arrived, when the Russians were driven back.

The Eagle of another battalion in the same division of Davout's army corps, General Friant's, the 111th of the Line, a little time later had its part. The 111th had suffered heavily in the earlier fighting, but towards eleven o'clock were called on to lead a counter-attack beyond the line of fortified hedgerow that the regiment was holding, against a fresh Russian column which was advancing with loud shouts and bayonets at the charge to storm their position. Immediately in front was a wide, open stretch of ground, across which a Russian battery, to cover the attack, was pouring a tremendous fire of shell, the bursting projectiles tearing up the ground as if it were being ploughed. Just as the order to advance was given, the *Porte-Aigle* fell dead.

An old sergeant, Courbet by name, took his place. He seized the Eagle and looked round, for several of the men were wavering. They were unwilling to leave cover for certain death, as it looked, on the shell-swept space of open ground before them. Courbet climbed over the hedge, and, waving the Eagle and flag with both hands, stood by himself amid the bursting shells, some twenty yards in front. "Come on, comrades!" he shouted "come on!" Then with the words, "*A moi, soldats du 111me!*" brandishing the Eagle, he ran straight at the fast-nearing Russians.

"The effect," says one who saw the brave deed done, "was electric." The men streamed over the hedge instantly, re-formed line in spite of the cannon-balls, and, led by the grenadiers of the battalion, charged the approaching enemy, broke them, drove them before them, and seized the village in front, whence the Russians had made their advance.

The Eagle of the 48th, another of Friant's regiments, in like manner was rallied in the moment of supreme crisis by the daring of its Eagle-bearer.

The Eagle of the 108th, which regiment was fighting nearby, all but fell into the enemy's hands through a blunder. It was early in the morning, at the very beginning of the fight, in crossing a marshy strip under cover of the mist, to take in flank the Russian attack. In the uncertain light another French regiment, the 26th Light Infantry, one of Soult's regiments, moving about a hundred yards on the left of Davout's men, mistook the 108th for the enemy, and fired heavily into it. The Eagle-bearer was among those shot down, and fell with the Eagle. This sudden blow from an unexpected quarter staggered the 108th. They fell back hastily to re-form in rear, leaving their Eagle, whose fall had been unobserved in the mist, lying beside its dead bearer on the ground. The loss was discovered just as another force of Russians, who came up in front, reached the place; but before they could carry off the trophy a charge forward by some hastily rallied men of the 108th recovered the Eagle and bore it back to safety.

So far then with Davout's corps.

Soult, meanwhile, in the centre, was striking hard. His attack, in its effect on the Allied Army, was a complete surprise. Soult's advance began the instant that the marshal, riding at full gallop from the presence of Napoleon, could reach his men. At that moment the third of the Russian columns in the order of march, pressing ahead to overtake the first and second, and join in the attack on Davout, had not long descended the southern slope at the foot of the Pratzen heights; while the fourth Russian column, a mile or more in rear, was just about to ascend the northern slope to cross the Pratzen Hill and follow.

Up the steep western hillside face of the Pratzen clambered Soult's regiments. Unseen by the enemy at any point, without a shot being fired at them, or by them, until just as they were nearing the crest-line of the ridge, they emerged from the mists of the valley and seized the high ground.

They moved on a front of three divisions. Legrand's was on the right, *echeloned* in the direction of Davout's left flank so as to keep touch with that marshal. St. Hilaire's was in the centre, advancing in a long line of battalions in attack formation. Vandamme's division was on the left.

The Allied fourth column caught a glimpse of Vandamme's men as they were climbing the last ascent, and raced forward to form up and bar their way. There were 14,000 troops in the column, half Austrians, half Russians; and the Czar Alexander with the Emperor of Austria rode with them.

Attacking at once, the French broke through the Allied front line, and, after a hard fight for the Austro-Russian regiments, fighting under the two Sovereigns' eyes, resisted with desperate valour—forced it

Marshal Soult In the uniform of colonel-in-chief of the Chasseurs of the Guard.

back on the second line with the loss of several guns.

Again there the Eagles took their part. On the right of St. Hilaire's attack, the brigade of General Thiébault became separated in the fighting with the Russian foremost line. Its three regiments—the 10th Light Infantry, the 14th, and the 36th—became separated, and one of them, the 36th, was for a time in danger of being overpowered by part of the Russian third column, which had faced about on hearing the firing in rear and was hastening back up the hill. Two Russian regiments raced up towards them on that side. Some Austrian infantry of the fourth column, extending in their direction, were at the same time coming at them on the left. In front the 36th was faced by two Russian batteries, which dashed up, unlimbered, and blazed away, firing grape and case shot at barely thirty paces; as well as by some Russian dragoons, who made as if about to charge.

To keep the dragoons off, the leading battalion attempted to form square; but the men, breathless after their rush uphill, were in some disorder and for the moment out of hand. The square, while yet half formed, was then nearly torn to pieces by a staggering discharge of grape, and several of the men began to get unsteady. It looked bad for the 36th, when, of a sudden, Adjutant Labadie, of the First Battalion, snatched the Eagle from its bearer and ran out in front. He stopped short and held the Eagle-staff with both hands planted firmly on the ground. Then he called to the men, in a momentary pause while the Russian gunners were reloading: "Soldiers of the 36th, rally to the front! Here is your line of battle!"

The men saw him, and obeyed. The disorder ceased. Quickly deploying to right and left, they dashed at the Russian guns. At the same moment the other two regiments of the brigade, led by St. Hilaire and the brigadier, sword in hand, came up at the *pas de charge*, bayonets levelled. The 10th Light Infantry brilliantly repulsed the Austrians on one side: the 14th on the other side drove Kamenskoi's Russians back down the hill.

Supporting the 10th Light Infantry was the 59th of the Line, one of Mortier's corps, of Dupont's division, which had been sent forward to help in holding the Pratzen heights. Some of the Russian dragoons dashed in among them as they deployed to follow the 10th. A Russian officer cut down the Eagle-bearer and seized the Eagle. Sergeant-Major Gamier, the *"Porte-Aigle,"* struggled to his feet in spite of his wounds, wrested the Eagle back, and with his free hand fought with his sword and killed the Russian, saving the Eagle.

On St. Hilaire's left, during this time, Vandamme's division had had to fight its way forward against the Russians and Austrians of the fourth column, several battalions of which, with artillery, had rapidly taken post along a range of knolls towards the northern edge of the Pratzen plateau. Driving back at the outset six Russian battalions, which charged forward to meet them, springing up from the shelter of a dip in the ground, Vandamme's men, "without firing a shot, with the bayonet only, advanced on the main enemy with shouldered arms, not replying to the Russian musketry." When within forty yards, they halted, fired a volley, and dashed in with bayonets lowered. The attack was successful beyond expectation. The enemy before them were routed, and all their guns taken, with many prisoners. Then Vandamme received orders to wheel his division to the right and take in flank the enemy, at that moment in hot fight with St. Hilaire.

Vandamme was in the middle of the move when one of his brigades met with a sudden and unexpected disaster. Two battalions belonging to the 24th Light Infantry and the 4th of the Line, who fought side by side on the extreme left of Vandamme's command, were all but annihilated. As they were wheeling round, the Russian Imperial Guard came up, hurrying forward from the Reserve, and set on them fiercely. It was just to the left of the village of Pratzen, as approached from the French side, on the farther side of the plateau. The Russian Foot Guards forced the 4th and the 24th Light Infantry back into some vineyards adjoining the village in disorder.

The last to retire was the First Battalion of the 4th. They had hardly gained the edge of the tract of vine-yards, when, without the least warning of their approach, coming up on their flank and unseen in the smoke and turmoil of the contest, a more formidable enemy still assailed them. The Russian *Cuirassiers* of the Guard, 2,000 horsemen, troopers of the finest cavalry in the world, came down on them, and charged them at a gallop on the flank. The Grand Duke Constantine, brother of the *Czar*, in person led the *cuirassiers*. Disaster, hideous, overwhelming, crushing, for the two hapless battalions—that of the 24th Light Infantry was, in like manner, caught just beyond cover exposed in the open—was the instant result. They tried to form square at the last moment, but the *cuirassiers* were on them before they could begin the evolution. Both battalions were practically hurled out of existence within three minutes.

They were ridden down, trampled on by the huge Russian horses, and slashed to pieces mercilessly by the giant Russian troopers with their long straight swords. Both battalions lost their Eagles. That of the 24th Light Infantry was picked up later on the field and restored to what was left of the ill-fated corps.

The Eagle of the 4th was carried off by the Russians, and is now in the Kazan Cathedral at St. Petersburg. Yet it was lost with honour; bravely defended to the last. The Eagle-bearer was cut down. A lieutenant tried to get hold of the Eagle and save it; he, too, was cut down. A private then snatched it from the dead officer's hands, and was in the act of waving it on high when he in turn was sabred and fell. The Russians made prize of the trophy at once, and it was carried direct to the Czar Alexander on the battlefield.

Napoleon, who had moved up near the fighting in the centre, witnessed the disaster with his own eyes.

The corps, as it happened, too, was one he had taken an interest in. The 4th of the Line had been in favour with him, and he had appointed his brother Joseph as its colonel when the 4th was at the camp of Boulogne as part of the "Army of England." He had, indeed, specially chosen that particular corps for its steadiness. He announced Joseph's appointment to it in a message to the Senate on April 18, 1804:

> In order that he should be allowed to contribute to the vengeance which the French people propose to take for the violation of the Treaty (of Amiens) and be afforded an opportunity of acquiring a fresh title to the esteem of the nation.

In wild panic the survivors of the disaster fled to the rear, tearing by close past where Napoleon and the Staff were.

> They almost rushed over us and the Emperor himself, (*describes De Ségur, who as an aide de camp was close to the Emperor at the moment.*) Our effort to arrest the rout was in vain. The unfortunate fellows were quite distracted with fear and would listen to nothing. In reply to our reproaches for so deserting the field of battle and their Emperor, they shouted mechanically '*Vive l'Empereur!*' and they fled away faster than ever.

Napoleon smiled pitifully. With a scornful gesture, he said to us: 'Let them go!' Retaining all his calmness in the midst of the confusion he despatched Rapp to bring up the Cavalry of the Guard.

Rapp,[1] another of the Imperial *aides de camp*, was also colonel of the Mamelukes of the Guard. He was at the moment riding close be-

---

1. *Rapp: The Last Victor* by Jean Rapp is also published by Leonaur.

hind the Emperor. Rapp darted off, and, after taking Napoleon's order to charge the Russian *cuirassiers* to Marshal Bessières, in command of the Cavalry of the Guard, he himself led their headmost squadrons forward; his own swarthy Mamelukes with two squadrons of *chasseurs* and one of Horse Grenadiers. Waving his sabre and calling at the top of his voice, "*Vengeons les! Vengeons nos drapeaux!*" "Avenge them! Avenge our standards!" he led them forward at full gallop.

"We dashed at full speed on the artillery and took them," described Rapp in a letter. The guns were those of a Russian battery which had just come into action close by where the Guard *Cuirassiers* had charged.

> The enemy's horse awaited our attack at the halt. They were overthrown by the charge and fled in confusion, galloping like us over the wrecks of our squares.

But the Russians rallied quickly. Reinforced by the superb regiment of the Chevalier Guards, a corps in which all the troopers were men of birth, they came on to meet the French again. Just at that moment Bessières, with at his back the magnificent cavalry of Napoleon's Guard, came up at full speed. Rapp's squadrons rejoined, and both Imperial Guards met in full career. Rapp says:

> Again we charged, and this charge was terrible. It was one of the most desperate cavalry combats ever fought, and lasted several minutes. The brave Morland, colonel of the mounted *Chasseurs* of the Guard, fell by my side. We fought man to man, and so mingled together that the infantry on neither side dared fire, lest they should kill their own men.

They fought it out until the Russians gave back and broke and fled—in full sight of the *Czar* and the Austrian Emperor, who from some rising ground nearby had been spectators of the desperate affray.

The survivors of the hapless First Battalion of the 4th of the Line had meanwhile recovered themselves. Rallied by their officers, they had been brought back into the battle. They returned with their nerve restored, now only anxious to make amends for the disgrace they had brought on the Grand Army. They were in time to join in the final advance beyond the Pratzen heights and cross bayonets with an Austrian regiment, from which they took its two standards. That feat, as will be seen, was to serve them in good stead later on.

The charge of the Cavalry of the Guard practically decided the fate of the day at Austerlitz. Napoleon at once brought up Oudinot's grenadiers, Bernadotte's battalions, and the regiments of the Old Guard to further reinforce Soult's divisions. The Allied centre was shattered and driven in at all points, and forced back for a mile-and-a-half beyond the field of battle. It resisted desperately to the last, and several fierce counter-attacks were made; but in vain.

In one of these the Eagle of the *Chasseurs à Pied* of the Imperial Guard had a narrow escape. According to the story it was saved by a dog—"Moustache," a mongrel poodle that had attached himself to the corps and become a regimental pet. The Eagle-bearer of the First Battalion, to whom the dog was much attached, and whom he was following, was shot, and the Eagle dropped to the ground beneath the man's body. An Austrian regiment was making a counter-attack at that point, and before the Eagle could be picked up, three Austrian soldiers ran forward to seize it. Two of them attacked the two men of the Eagle escort. The third was faced by "Moustache," who kept him off, growling savagely and snapping at the Austrian from behind the dead body of the Eagle-bearer.

The man dropped his musket, drew his hanger, and cut at "Moustache," slicing off a paw. But in spite of that the dog managed to keep him off until assistance came. Then the three Austrians were bayoneted and the Eagle was saved. Marshal Lannes, on hearing the story, had a silver collar made for "Moustache," with a medal to hang from it, inscribed on one side, "*Il perdit une jambe à la bataille d'Austerlitz, et sauva le Drapeau de son regiment*"; and on the other, "*Moustache, chien Français; qu'il soit partout respecté et cheri comme un Brave.*" "Moustache," in the end, it may be said, died a soldier's death. He was killed by an English cannon-ball at Badajoz, and was buried on the ramparts there, with a stone over him, inscribed: "*Cy git le brave Moustache.*"

The Allied centre broken through, the end came on swiftly all over the field of battle.

On Napoleon's left wing, Lannes and Murat had engaged the Russian rear column (or right wing as they fronted to fight) immediately after Soult opened the main attack. They had done their part by holding in play the enemy in front, thus preventing the Allied troops on that side from moving up to reinforce the centre. There, too, as elsewhere, the Eagles of Napoleon's battalions fulfilled their *rôle*; one Eagle in particular, that of the 13me Légère, achieving special distinction. When the Allied centre gave way, Lannes and Murat pressed forward impetuously, forcing their antagonists back, and driving them off the field to the north-east, past the village of Austerlitz.

Davout, on Napoleon's right, finished his task at the same time; in no less workmanship fashion. As Soult swung round his victorious divisions to the right to take the Russian left wing in rear, Davout's moment came and he gave the order to advance. Surging forward with exultant shouts the stout-hearted defenders of that fiercely contested side of the field swept down on the assailants they had kept at bay for five long hours. The Russians did their best to make a brave resistance, but the day was lost. Formed in close-packed columns they fell back, losing guns and colours, and hundreds of prisoners. [2]

As darkness closed in, the last shots were fired at Austerlitz. Crushing and complete had been the overthrow. The Allied army fled in wild panic. It left on the field 30,000 men, dead, wounded, or prisoners, 100 guns, and 400 ammunition caissons. Forty-five standards were in the hands of the victors. Twelve thousand men in killed and wounded was the price Napoleon paid. It was a big price; but the victory to him was worth the sacrifice. At five next morning an *aide de camp* from the Austrian Emperor presented himself before Napoleon to beg for an immediate suspension of hostilities. The Emperor Francis himself had an interview with Napoleon during that afternoon, and, as the result, terms of peace—to include the Austrian Emperor's Russian allies—were mutually agreed on; to be formally settled between the diplomatists as soon as possible, Pressburg in Hungary being named for the meeting-place.

We come now to the dramatic sequel to Austerlitz which awaited the ill-fated First Battalion of the 4th of the Line. They had to face

---

2. It was to one of these retreating columns that the historic "Ice Disaster" happened. Everyone knows the story, as related in Napoleon's Austerlitz Bulletin, and mentioned also by Ségur, Marbot, and Lejeune in their memoirs, how a column from the Russian left wing tried to escape over the frozen surface of the lake of Satschan, how Napoleon turned a battery on them while in the act of crossing the ice and broke it, and how "thousands of Russians, with their horses, guns, and waggons, were seen slowly settling down into the depths." The actual facts are recorded in the recently discovered report of the "*fischmeister*" (or overseer) of the Carp Fishery of Satschan Lake, setting forth the results of draining off the water in the spring of 1806. There were found at the bottom, recorded the *fischmeister*, twenty-eight cannon, one hundred and fifty dead horses, but only three human corpses. The column, it would appear, had been composed of five batteries of artillery, and when the ice was broken, the guns, all but the two nearest the shore, sank through and dragged the horses with them to the bottom; but the gunners, it would seem, were all able to scramble out, except the three unfortunates who had been either hit by French round-shot, or were entangled in the harness of their teams. The loss of human life was therefore, presumably, only three men out of the five hundred or so who must have been riding on, or with, the guns.

Napoleon and render account to him personally for the loss of their Eagle. The dreaded interview came some three weeks later; at a grand parade of Soult's corps before the Emperor at Schönbrunn—as it befell, on Christmas Day.

Napoleon, attended by the Imperial Staff, most of the marshals, half a hundred other officers of rank, and nearly as many *aides de camp*, passed down the long line of troops, congratulating most of the regiments on the parts they had individually taken on the different battlefields. In due course the Emperor came to the regiments of Vandamme's division, ranged in their allotted place, the 4th of the Line among them. Its First Battalion, reduced by the disaster to a quarter of the normal strength, stood at the head of the regiment, looking gloomy and disconsolate, the only corps on parade without its Eagle.

Napoleon approached the place with a frown on his face and a look as black as thunder. He reined up opposite the battalion and addressed it in a loud angry tone.

"Soldiers," he began hoarsely. "What have you done with the Eagle which I entrusted to you?"

The colonel of the regiment replied that the Eagle-bearer had been killed at Austerlitz in the *mêlée* when the Russian *cuirassiers* charged the regiment, and the Eagle had been lost in the tumult and confusion of the moment. There was no survivor of those who had seen the Eagle-bearer fall. The battalion, indeed, did not know of its loss until sometime later. One and all deeply deplored what had happened, but they desired to inform His Majesty most respectfully that they, single-handed, had captured two Austrian standards, and implored his consideration on that account, begging that he would allow them to receive a new Eagle in exchange.

The whole regiment supported the colonel's request with loud shouts, "*reclama à grands cris.*" But Napoleon's countenance remained unchanged.

He replied coldly and contemptuously: "These two foreign flags do not return me my Eagle!" Then, after a pause, he launched out into words of the severest censure and rebuke, telling the men that he had seen them with his own eyes in flight at Austerlitz. He poured bitter scorn on their conduct, "in phrases, stinging, burning, corrosive, which those present remembered long afterwards—to the end of their lives."

Again the unhappy colonel pleaded his hardest for his men. He entreated the Emperor's clemency, once more beseeching Napoleon to allow that they had wiped out the slur on their good name, and to grant the battalion a new Eagle.

Napoleon said nothing for a moment. Then he again addressed them in an abrupt tone:

Officers, sub-officers, and soldiers, swear to me here that not one of you saw your Eagle fall. Assure me that if you had done so you would have flung yourselves into the midst of the enemy to recover it, or have died in the attempt. The soldier who loses his Eagle on the field of battle loses his honour and his all.

"We swear it!" came the reply at once.

At that there seemed to come a change in the Emperor's mood. He paused once more for a few moments, during which there was dead silence. Then he raised his voice:

I will grant that you have not been cowards; but you have been imprudent! Again I tell you that these Austrian standards—even, indeed, were they six—would not compensate me for my Eagle.

He stopped short. He seemed to be musing for a moment, looking straight into the eyes of the men. After that, with a curt "Well, I will restore you yet another Eagle!" Napoleon turned his horse and rode on down the line of troops.

It was quite true, as the colonel told Napoleon, that the regiment was unaware at the time that their Eagle had been lost. As a fact, search-parties—practically all the survivors of the First Battalion—were out on the day after Austerlitz hunting over the battlefield among the dead for their lost Eagle. By the irony of fate it was they who picked up and restored the Eagle of the 24th Light Infantry to their fellows in adversity; the Russians, it would seem, had not marked its fall in the confusion of the fighting. At any rate it was left where it fell and where it was found.

There was, as it curiously happened, no reference in the Austerlitz Bulletin published in France—the 30th "Bulletin of the Grand Army"—to the loss of its Eagle by the 4th of the Line, although the disaster to the battalion is reported. "*Un bataillon du 4me de Ligne fut chargé par la Garde Impériale Russe à Cheval et culbuté.*" That was all that was said on the subject. Yet, on other occasions later, when Eagles were lost, mention was made of the misfortune in one or other of the Bulletins, with, generally also, some remark by way of explaining away the unpleasant fact, and now and then a caustic comment by Napoleon. A picture connected with the incident was, however, painted—at whose request is unknown. It is now in the national collection of military pictures of the campaigns of Napoleon at Versailles. It shows the First Battalion of the 4th of the Line at the Schönbrunn review:

> Presenting Napoleon with two Austrian standards taken by them from the enemy, and claiming in exchange a new Eagle for themselves.[3]

This closing word may be said of the spoils of the Eagles at Austerlitz.

The forty-five flags captured in the battle, with five others selected from those taken at Ulm, making fifty in all, were presented by Napoleon to the Cathedral of Notre Dame. With the trophies he sent this message:

> Our intention is that every year on the 2nd of December a Solemn Office shall be sung in the Cathedral in memory of the brave men who fell on the great day.

The flags were borne in triumph, together with the trophies of the Ulm campaign,—120 captured standards and colours in all—through the streets of Paris on January 15, 1806, amid a tremendous demon-

---

3. Incidentally, that Christmas Day morning of the Schönbrunn review has an interest for us in this country. Napoleon left the palace for the review in a vile temper, which no doubt was one reason why he vented his spleen so savagely on the unfortunate soldiers of the 4th in his speech of censure. This was probably the prime cause. Late on the night before, on Christmas Eve, a courier from Paris had arrived at the Imperial headquarters, bringing the defeated Admiral Villeneuve's Trafalgar despatch, his *Compte Rendu*, written while Villeneuve was a prisoner on his way to England, and dated from "*A bord de la frégate Anglaise Euryalus—le 15me Novembre 1805.*" It had been sent to France under a flag of truce, as an act of inter-national courtesy, and the Minister of Marine forwarded it to Napoleon. The news of the disaster had reached the Emperor some five weeks before, at Znaim in Moravia, a fortnight before Austerlitz; first, from some Austrian officers taken prisoners by Augereau in the Tyrol, then from the English papers. It had been enough then to give him a bad night, and make him morose for a week. Now that he learned the story from his own admiral, it made him more furious than ever. The original despatch received by Napoleon at Schönbrunn that Christmas Eve exists, with its pathetic closing appeal, the pitiless response to which sent Admiral Villeneuve to a suicide's grave." "*Profondément pénétré,*" it ran, as written by Villeneuve's own hand, "*de toute l'etendue de mon malheur et de toute la responsibilité que comporte un aussi grand désastre, je ne désire rien tant que d'être bientôt à même d'aller mettre aux pieds de S.M. ou la justification de ma conduite ou la victime qui doit être immolée, non a 1'honneur du pavilion, qui, j'ose le dire, est demeuré intact, mais aux manes de ceaux qui auroient péri par mon imprudence, mon inconsidération ou l'oubli de quelqu'un de mes devoirs.*"

stration of popular enthusiasm. "The behaviour of the people," wrote Cambacérès, "resembled intoxication." Four days later the Austerlitz flags were received at Notre Dame by the assembled cathedral clergy, Cardinal du Belloy at their head, with elaborate religious ceremonial.

Said the Cardinal-Archbishop of Paris in his address from the altar-steps:

> These banners, suspended from the roof of our Cathedral, will attest to posterity the efforts of Europe in arms against us; the great achievements of our soldiers; the protection of Heaven over France; the prodigious successes of our invincible Emperor; and the homage which he pays to God for his victories.

Not one of the flags exists now. They disappeared mysteriously, in circumstances to be described later, in the early hours of March 31, 1814, the day on which the victorious Allies entered Paris, and Napoleon withdrew to Fontainebleau.

Fifty-four of the other trophies paraded through Paris, flags taken in the Ulm campaign, were presented by Napoleon, as has been said, to the Senate. In return a picture of the scene at the reception of the trophy-flags was ordered to be painted for presentation to the Emperor. It is now at Versailles.

The remaining sixteen trophies were divided by order of the Emperor. Eight were sent to the Assembly Hall of the Tribunate; eight to the Hotel de Ville as a gift to the city of Paris.

Thus did France receive the first spoils of the Eagles.

Napoleon said to the Grand Army, in his Austerlitz Proclamation;

> Soldiers, I am satisfied with you. You have justified my fullest expectations of your intrepidity. You have decorated your Eagles with immortal glory!

CHAPTER 5: IN THE SECOND CAMPAIGN
Jena and the Triumph of Berlin

The curtain rises this time on an act in the War Drama of the Eagles unique in the startling incidents of its historic *dénoûment*.

Prussia, in September 1806, threw down the gage to Napoleon and drew the sword for a trial of strength, with the full assurance of victory. There was no doubt in Germany as to the issue; not the least anxiety was felt. No troops in the world, declared one and all, could stand up to the Prussian Army. It was easy, they said at Potsdam and Berlin, to account for what had happened last year on the Danube. Any sort of army could have won in that war. Timidity and want of skill in the Austrian generals, deficient training in the men, had been, beyond dispute, the reason of the disasters.

It would be otherwise now. Napoleon would have to meet this time the Army of Prussia; the best drilled and smartest soldiers in the world, organised and trained under the system that the Great Frederick had originated and himself brought to perfection. "His Majesty the King," said one of the Prussian generals, addressing a parade at Potsdam, "has many generals better than Napoleon!" In the Prussian Army, from veteran field-marshal to drummer-boy, there were no two opinions as to what must be the outcome of a clash of arms with France. The wings of Napoleon's Eagles would be clipped once for all.

But to hurl defiant words was not enough. Yet further to display contempt for their French foes, the young officers of the Prussian Guard marched one night in procession through the streets of Berlin to demonstrate in front of the French Embassy. Shouting out insults and jeers, they brandished their swords before the windows of the mansion and made a show of sharpening the blades on the Ambassador's doorsteps. The Prussian king's ultimatum went forth, couched in language there was no mistaking, and the Royal Guard Corps set out from the capital for the frontier with flags displayed and their bands playing triumphal airs, chanting songs of the victories of the Great Frederick, and shouting themselves hoarse with cries of "*Nach Paris!*" All over Prussia it was the same. The marching regiments tramped through the towns and villages, their colours decked with flowers, their bands playing, and with the swaggering gait of victors returning from conquest.

The Prussian ultimatum, delivered on September 1, haughtily demanded a reply from France within a week. It was accepted with alacrity. Napoleon had foreseen all and laid his plans. "Marshal," he said to Berthier, with a grim smile, as he read the ultimatum, "they have given us a rendezvous for the 8th; never did Frenchman refuse such an appeal."

The Eagles never swooped to more deadly purpose, with results more amazing and more dramatic, than in that campaign.

Within three days of the firing of the first shot, a Prussian division of 9,000 men had been routed with heavy loss at Schleitz in Thuringia; and Murat's cavalry had captured elsewhere great part of the Prussian reserve baggage-trains and pontoon equipment. On the fourth day of the war, at Saalfeld in Thuringia, 1,200 Prussian prisoners were taken and 30 guns. In the battles of Jena and Auerstadt, both fought on the same day, October 14, 20,000 Prussian prisoners, 200 guns, and 25 standards were spoils to the Eagles. At Erfurth, on the next day, a Prussian field-marshal with 14,000 men, 120 guns and the whole of the grand park of the reserve artillery of the army were taken. At Halle 4,000 Prussian prisoners were taken, with 30 guns; at Lübeck 8,000 prisoners and 40 guns.

Magdeburg, one of the strongest fortresses in Europe, with immense magazines and 600 guns on the ramparts garrisoned by 16,000 troops, surrendered after a few hours' partial bombardment. Stettin, a first-class fortress mounting 150 guns, with a garrison of 6,000 men, surrendered without firing a shot. The strong fortress of Cüstrin on the Oder, with 4,000 men in garrison and 90 cannon on the ramparts, surrendered, also without firing a shot, to a solitary French infantry regiment with four guns. The fortress of Spandau, garrisoned by 6,000 men, hauled down its flag and opened its gates to a squadron of French hussars, no other French troops being within many miles, bluffed into surrender.

Within twelve days of Jena, Napoleon had made his entry as a conqueror into Berlin, and the Prussian Army had ceased to exist.

"We have arrived in Potsdam and Berlin," announced Napoleon in a Bulletin to the Grand Army, "sooner than the renown of our victories! We have made 60,000 prisoners, taken 65 standards, including those of the Royal Guard, 600 pieces of cannon, 3 fortresses, 20 generals, half of our army having to regret that they have not had an opportunity of firing a shot. All the Prussian provinces from the Elbe to the Oder are in our hands." Before the end of the year, in little more than three months from the firing of the first shot, a total of 100,000 prisoners, 4,000 cannon, 6 first-class fortresses, and many smaller ones, were in the hands of the victors.

Never had the world witnessed such an over-throw in war, so complete and appalling a catastrophe. Two battles sufficed to prostrate Prussia and annihilate the model army of Frederick the Great: the twin battles of Jena and Auerstadt, both fought, as has been said, on the same day, October 14, and within ten miles of one another. Jena was fought under Napoleon's own eye; Auerstadt by Marshal Davout, practically single-handed, with his one army corps confronting the King and Blucher with the main Prussian army. The Prussian generals indeed gave themselves into Napoleon's hands at the outset. They separated their main army into two bodies out of touch with each other, in the immediate presence of the enemy. Ruin, swift and irreparable, was the penalty.

At Jena, Prince Hohenlohe's army was flung roughly back and dashed to pieces, its scattered remnants flying in wild disorder. At Auerstadt, Davout defeated numbers nearly double his own, through the confused tactics of the Prussian generals. Immediately after that came on the *débâcle*. The Prussian Auerstadt army was falling back, disheartened and demoralised, but still in fair military formation to a large extent, when, all of a sudden, not having had up to then the least inkling of what had happened at Jena, the retreating troops came upon the shattered fragments of Hohenlohe's battalions, streaming in wild confusion across their path; masses of fugitives running for their lives in frantic panic before the sabres of Murat's pursuing cavalry.

That ended everything for the Prussian army in five minutes. The sight of their fugitive comrades struck confusion and sheer fright into the retreating columns from Auerstadt. All order was instantly lost: the soldiers threw away their arms and spread over the country in headlong rout. And there was no means of stopping it. In their blind self-confidence the Prussian generals had made no arrangements in the event of a reverse. No line of retreat had been arranged for, no rallying-point had been thought of.

The disaster of a single day made an end of the Prussian Army as a force capable of meeting the enemy in the field.

For the Eagles it was a day of adventures on both battlefields. Swiftly alternating rushes forward, the Eagles showing the way at the head of their regiments at one moment; hasty halts to form in rallying squares, the Eagles in the midst, the next moment, to check the incessant Prussian cavalry counter-charges—that was what the fighting on the French side was like, all through the day, at both Jena and Auerstadt. At one time the Eagles were leading forward charging lines of exultantly cheering men, firing fast and racing forward at the *pas de charge*; immediately afterwards they were standing fast, each the centre of a mass of breathless and excited soldiers, surging round and closing up to form square, with bristling bayonets levelled on every side, to hold the ground they had won against the charging squadrons of Prussian horsemen that came at them, thundering down impetuously at the gallop.

"I want to see the Eagles well to the front today!" said Napoleon to several regiments in turn, as he rode at early dawn along the lines of Marshal Soult's two foremost divisions who were to open the attack at Jena. To them the task had been appointed to push forward in advance, and hold the exits from the narrow defiles through which the French troops had to pass, before reaching the Prussians on the high ground beyond, in order to give time to the main army, following close in rear, to deploy and form in battle order. "Lead out your Eagle, Sixty-fourth!"

Napoleon said to one of the regiments told off to go forward in the forefront of all. "I wish today to see the Eagle of the Sixty-fourth lead the battle on the field of honour!" How that Eagle led its regiment, how those who fought under it did their duty, the prized honour of special mention in the Jena Bulletin of the Grand Army, and a shower of crosses of the Legion of Honour, distributed among all ranks, bore testimony. Five times did the Eagle of the 34th, the regiment fighting next to the 64th, lead a charge, each charge crossing bayonets with the enemy, twice in hand-to-hand fight with the picked corps of the Prussian Grenadiers.

It was on the battlefield of Jena that Marshal Ney won his historic *sobriquet* of "The Bravest of the Brave." He personally led forward his attack, with, at either side of him, the Eagles of the 18th of the Line, the 32nd, and the 96th. Carried away by his impetuous valour, soon after the opening of the battle, Ney made his attack with only at hand the three regiments of his First Division. The other two divisions of Ney's corps had not yet reached the field. A regiment of *cuirassiers* headed the column, and at their first charge captured 13 Prussian guns; but the Prussian cavalry, charging back at once to recover the guns, overpowered the *cuirassiers*.

The Prussian cavalry broke the French horse, and enveloped the infantry in such numbers as would inevitably have proved fatal to less resolute troops; but the brave marshal instantly formed his men into squares, threw himself into one of them, and there maintained the combat by a rolling fire on all sides, till Napoleon, who saw his danger, sent several regiments of horse, under Bertrand, who disengaged him from his perilous situation.

Ney's other troops then joined the marshal, coming up with their Eagles gleaming through the battle-smoke: the Eagles of the 39th and the 69th, of the 76th, the 27th, and the 59th. Ney, extricated from his difficulties, went on again at once.

With intrepid step he ascended the hill, and, after a sharp conflict, stormed the important village of Vierzehn-Heiligen, in the centre of the Prussian position. In vain Hohenlohe formed the flower of his troops to regain the post; in vain these brave men advanced in parade order, and with unshrinking firmness, through a storm of musketry and grape; the troops of Lannes came up to Ney's support, and the French established themselves in such strength in the village as to render all subsequent attempts for its recapture abortive.

This was the spirit in which, at Jena, Ney's men fought under the Eagles. One instance will suffice. The 76th of the Line, after the village of Vierzehn-Heiligen had been taken, were in the act of advancing across the open to a fresh attack, when a charge of Prussian cavalry swept fiercely down on them. The regiment formed in square, each battalion rallying round its Eagle, held up aloft for all to gather round. The Prussians had come up suddenly. They were within 150 yards before the 76th were ready. Then the 76th were ordered to "present" and fire. Instead of doing that, the men, as if moved by one common impulse, took off their *shakos*, stuck them on their bayonets, and waved them in the air, with defiant cheers of "*Vive l'Empereur!*" "*Donnez feu, mes enfants! Donnez feu!*" ("Fire, men, fire!") shouted out their colonel, Lannier, anxious lest the enemy should get too near.

"We have time: at fifteen paces, Colonel; wait and see!" came back in answer from the ranks. They did wait, and, at just fifteen paces, fired a crashing volley which so staggered the Prussians that, leaving half their men on the ground, they turned and galloped back. The regiments of Lannes' corps, with the fiery marshal cantering at their head and waving them on, cocked hat in hand, entered the battle with drums beating and the Eagles proudly displayed in the centre of the leading lines.

One regiment lost 28 officers and 400 men. It had made good its first attack and was advancing to a second, when it was charged in the open by the Prussian cavalry, while in the act of forming square. It all but lost its Eagle. The Eagle-bearer was cut down, and the Eagle was broken from its staff in the trampling tumult of horsemen intermingled with infantry, savagely fighting with their bayonets. A soldier saved the Eagle, and in the hurry of the moment stuffed it into the pocket of his long overcoat. Then he went on fighting. Apparently the man had no time or opportunity to think of the Eagle again.

The regiment was re-forming towards the close of the battle, when Napoleon himself, riding across the ground near them, with his quick glance, missed the Eagle. He cantered up to the spot, and, on being told by an officer that he did not know where it was, angrily accused the men of having lost their Eagle on the field. He began upbraiding them indignantly: "What is this? Where is your Eagle? You have brought disgrace on the army by losing your Eagle!" Those were his opening words.

He was rating the men angrily, when he was abruptly interrupted by a voice from the ranks. "No, your Majesty, no! they did not get it: they only got a piece of the *bâton*! Here is the *Cou-cou*! I put it in my pocket!" The soldier drew out the Eagle as he spoke and held it up. There was a loud outburst of laughter from the soldiers at the unexpected turn of events, amid which Napoleon, without a word more, turned and rode off elsewhere.

At Auerstadt, where 30,000 French faced and defeated 60,000 Prussians, the fighting was even fiercer than at Jena. Recklessly the Prussian horsemen, led in person by the dauntless Blucher, repeatedly charged down on the French, who formed in square everywhere to beat them back. They did so at all points, and the Prussians only wrecked themselves beyond recovery by their efforts. In vain did the Prussian cavalry, as at Jena, gallop up to the French bayonets again and again.

In vain these gallant cavaliers, with headlong fury, drove their steeds up to the very muzzles of the French muskets. In vain they rode round and enveloped their squares: ceaseless was the rolling fire which issued from those flaming walls: impenetrable the hedge of bayonets which, the front rank kneeling, presented to their advances.

Erect in the centre of each French battalion square glittered its Eagle, raised on high defiantly above the smoke as the volleys flashed out all round.

Marshal Davout was seen at every point wherever the regiments were hardest pressed. From square to square the marshal galloped, as opportunity offered in the intervals of the Prussian attacks, "his face begrimed with sweat and powder-smoke, his spectacles gone,[1] his bald head bleeding from a wound, his uniform torn, a piece of his cocked hat shot away," to exhort the men to stand fast and hold their ground. To one regiment he called out, as he reined up beside its square: "Their Great Frederick said that God gave the victory to the big battalions. He lied! It's the stubborn soldiers who win battles; that's you and your general today!"

Davout personally brought up support at one point to rescue a sorely pressed division of four regiments, General Gudin's,[2] holding the village of Herrenhausen, on the right of the battlefield; a post of vital importance to the fate of the day. Taken by a brilliant dash forward early in the battle, the village was held to the last, in spite of the utmost endeavours of the Prussians to regain it.

The French kept the post at the cost of half their numbers. One regiment, the 85th, on the side of the village fronting the Prussians, lost two-thirds of its men and was forced back and compelled to abandon the outskirts. It kept the Prussians at bay, however, within the village, behind a barricade of overturned carts, farm implements, and cottage furniture heaped together. Close behind the firing line across the village street the Eagle-bearer took his stand, amidst a hail of bullets, mounted on a wheel-barrow and brandishing the Eagle and calling on the men to stand firm and fire low.

Marshal Davout brought up his First Division of five regiments to rescue Gudin, heading them sword in hand as he galloped forward. In doing so he received his wound and had a narrow escape of his life.

---

1. The spectacles which Marshal Davout wore at Auerstadt—an extremely primitive-looking pair of goggles in thick-rimmed frames—were picked up on the field, and are treasured to this day by the family of the present Duc d'Auerstadt.
2. Gudin's division was officially returned as having lost 124 officers and 3,500 men.

Marshal Davout.

"One bullet went through the marshal's hat just above the cockade."³

The 111th of the Line, of Davout's Third Division, had three Eagle-bearers shot down in succession, a fresh officer coming forward to carry the Eagle as his predecessor fell. All the drummer-lads of the regiment were killed, whereupon Drum-Major Mauser, dropping his staff, picked up a drum and beat it as the regiment advanced in its final charge. He ran forward close beside the Eagle until he in turn fell shot dead. This was in storming the village of Spielberg, nearly at the close of the battle. Napoleon in the Fourth Bulletin of the campaign, commending with warmth wrote:

> The corps of Marshal Davout performed prodigies, the rare intrepidity of the brave corps.

He ordered 500 crosses of the Legion of Honour to be distributed in Davout's corps, directing that when the army reached Berlin, Davout and the Third Corps should take precedence, and their Eagles lead the triumphal entry through the streets of the Prussian capital. At a special review of Davout's corps, calling the marshal and his generals round him, he declared his unbounded admiration of the feat of arms they had achieved. "Sire," replied Davout, deeply moved at Napoleon's words, "the soldiers of the Third Corps will always be to you what the Tenth Legion was to Caesar."

At the attack on Halle, three days after Jena, the 32nd of the Line, near the Eagle of which regiment Ney had ridden at Jena, distinguished themselves brilliantly. The Prussian Reserve Army Corps was holding Halle and making a gallant effort in a rearguard fight to safeguard the passage there over the River Saale. Led by the commander of Ney's First Division, General Dupont, in person, they stormed the bridge in the face of a tremendous fire of grape and case shot. Then, backed up by their comrades in Ney's First Division, the 18th and 96th and 9th Light Infantry, they fought their way through the city and, breaking open the gates, stormed the heights beyond, foremost throughout in the attack.

Four times the Eagle-bearer of the 32nd was shot down: each time a fresh officer sprang forward to lead the regiment on. The 97th of the Line, while fighting their way through the streets of Halle at another point, found the Prussian cannon mounted at a barricade too deadly to face in the open, and the regiment recoiled in confusion. Taking

---

3. Davout's cocked hat, with one end shot away and a bullet-hole through the crown, is now one of the battle relics of Napoleon's wars kept at the Invalides,

the Eagle from the Eagle-bearer, Colonel Barrois called forward the grenadier company. Leading them on himself on horseback, holding up the Eagle with his right hand, he went straight at the barricade, which was stormed without touching a trigger. Thenceforward there was only left for the Eagles to choose the slain; to parade in triumph across a conquered land. "*Veni, Vidi, Vici,*" sums up the story of the after-events of the war for the Eagles of Napoleon.

The army of the great Frederick committed suicide after Jena. Its resistance collapsed: the army that had gone forth in September to cross the Rhine and dictate peace at the gates of Paris had ceased to exist within six weeks. How completely indeed the *moral* of the Prussians had been shattered, this story, from a report from Marshal Lannes to Napoleon, serves to show.

> Three hussars, having lost their way towards Grätz, found themselves in the midst of an enemy's squadron. They boldly drew their carbines and, levelling them at the enemy, called out that the Prussians were surrounded; and must surrender at discretion. The Prussians obeyed. The commander of the squadron, without apparently a thought of resistance, ordered his men to dismount, and they surrendered their arms to those three hussars, who brought them all in prisoners of war.

General Lassalle, with a handful of hussars, as has been said, captured the fortress of Stettin, with 150 guns on its walls and a garrison of 6,000 men, by sheer effrontery. He rode up to the main gate and demanded the surrender within five minutes; and the governor capitulated on the spot. Napoleon wrote to Murat, on hearing the news:

> If your hussars take strong fortresses like that, I have nothing to do but break up my artillery and discharge my engineers.

Prince Hohenlohe with 14,000 men and 50 guns, his troops including the Royal Prussian Guard and six regiments of Guard cavalry, laid down their arms at Prentzlau. A few miles away, 8,000 more Prussians surrendered on the same day to a French brigade of dragoons. The unfortunates were remnants of the troops beaten at Jena, and had been relentlessly pursued for ten days.

The 7th Hussars forwarded to Napoleon as their spoils from a three days' chase, 7 Prussian cavalry standards; those of the Anspach and Bayreuth Dragoons; the Queen of Prussia's regiment; and 4 standards of the Light Cavalry of the Guard. Marshal Lannes sent Napoleon 40 Prussian standards taken between Jena and Berlin. Bernadotte and

Soult presented 82 more trophies, the spoils of Blücher's army, forced to surrender at Lübeck after a forlorn-hope fight in the course of which the city was stormed.

Marshal Ney took the fortress of Magdeburg without having a single siege-gun, and with only 11,000 men at hand to deal with 24,000 in the garrison and 700 guns on the ramparts, some of these being the heaviest artillery of the time. It was perhaps the most surprising event of the war. The taking of Magdeburg, wrote Junot, "is the finest feat of arms that has illustrated this campaign." Ney had been ordered to blockade Magdeburg until a sufficient army was available for the siege of the fortress, which Napoleon expected would be a long and difficult affair. But so tedious a task as a blockade was not at all to Ney's taste. To hasten matters he sent for half a dozen mortars, taken at Erfurt, and began throwing shells into the suburbs on the side nearest him.

The bombardment caused a scare among the townsfolk. Panic-stricken at seeing their houses set on fire and destroyed by the bursting shells, they hastened to General Kleist, the governor of Magdeburg, an elderly, and nervous old gentleman of between seventy and eighty years of age, and implored him to ask terms of the French marshal. Dismayed himself at the prospect of a siege, with disorder rampant among the military—nearly half the garrison was made up of fragments of fugitive regiments from Jena who had fled to Magdeburg for shelter from the pursuing French—Kleist, losing his nerve in the face of the alarming situation, agreed to negotiate for terms. Ney's reply was a demand for instant surrender, whereupon the wretched governor, although he had more than enough good troops at disposal, without counting the Jena fugitives, to have made a stubborn defence, tamely hoisted the white flag.

The march out of the garrison of Magdeburg was a repetition of the Austrian humiliation of Ulm on a lesser scale. The standards of the Black Eagle in their turn had at Magdeburg publicly to acknowledge defeat before the Eagles of Napoleon.

Ney drew up his 11,000 men in a great hollow square outside the Ulrich gate of the fortress. His troops were drawn up along three sides of the square; the fourth side, that nearest the city, being left open. In front of the regiments stood their Eagles, all paraded as at Ulm, the Eagle-guards beside them, and the regimental officers standing in line with their swords at the carry. The Prussians marched out and, to the music of the French bands, passed in procession along the three inner sides of the square, and in front of Marshal Ney and his staff. The miserable Kleist led them, and then took his stand beside Ney, to answer the marshal's questions as to who and what the various regiments were, as each set of downcast Prussians trailed past. They tramped by, with their muskets on their shoulders unloaded and without bayonets, and with their colours furled.

The hapless prisoners, after they had defiled past, were at once marched away under escort on the road to Mayence. Twenty generals, 800 other officers, 22,000 infantry, and 2,000 artillerymen, with 59 standards, underwent the humiliation of the defilade.[4] There were several painful scenes at the laying down of the arms. One of the French lookers-on describes:

> Their soldiers openly insulted their officers. Most of them looked terribly ashamed of themselves; the faces of not a few were streaming with tears.

At Magdeburg, as in the other surrenders elsewhere, it was not the personal courage of the officers and soldiers that was wanting—there were men by thousands in the various garrisons ready to give their lives for the honour of their country; it was the generals in command whose nerve lacked. The generals were men past their prime, and mostly physically incapable of enduring hardships. They had been appointed to their posts, in accordance with the system in vogue in Prussia, for the sake of the emoluments. To use the words of a modern writer:

> The overthrow of Jena, had been caused by faults of generalship, and cast no stain upon the courage of the officers; the surrender of the Prussian fortresses, which began on the day when the French entered Berlin, attached the utmost personal disgrace to their commanders. Even after the destruction of the army in the field, Prussia's situation would not have been hopeless if the commanders of the fortresses had acted on the ordinary rules of military duty. Magdeburg and the strongholds upon the Oder were sufficiently armed and provisioned to detain the entire French army, and to give time to the King to collect upon the Vistula a force as numerous as that which he

---

4. In his instructions to Ney in regard to the trophies taken, Napoleon wrote this, specially with reference to a number of flags belonging to Prussian regiments elsewhere which had been temporarily stored at Magdeburg: "*Les drapeaux prussiens pris dans l'arsenal de Magdeburg ne signifient rien: donnez l'ordre qu'ils soient brûlés, mais vous ferez porter en triomphe par votre premier division les drapeaux pris à la garnison, pour être remis par vous à Berlin a l'Empereur. On ne doit porter en triomphe que les drapeaux pris les armes à la main, et brûler ceux pris dans les arsenaux.*"

had lost. But whatever is weakest in human nature—old age, fear, and credulity—seemed to have been placed at the head of the Prussian defences.

Küstrin on the Oder:

> In full order for a long siege, was surrendered by the older officers, amidst the curses of the subalterns and the common soldiers: the artillerymen had to be dragged from their guns by force.

At Magdeburg, indeed, before the march out, the younger officers of the garrison mobbed General Kleist, hooting at him and cursing him to his face; some of them, further, being with difficulty stopped from acts of personal violence.

There yet remained one day more for the Eagles. The triumphal parade of the victorious Eagles through Berlin was the crowning humiliation that Napoleon imposed on vanquished Prussia.

Davout's corps, as Napoleon had promised, marched through the Prussian capital first of all. The marshal was waited on as he entered by the *Burgomeister* and civic authorities, humbly bowing before him, and offering in token of submission the keys of Berlin. The offer, however, was declined. "You must present them later," was the reply; "they belong to a greater than I!" After marching through Berlin, Davout camped a mile beyond the city, posting his artillery "in position as for war, pointed towards the place as in readiness to bombard it." The soldiers were then allowed to go about Berlin in parties. They behaved very quietly, and made eager sightseers, we are told. The shops, which had been closed during the march through, reopened later, and the people went about the streets as usual, "mortified and subdued in demeanour, but apparently very curious to see what they could of the French officers."

Augereau's corps, and then those of Soult, Bernadotte, and Ney made their triumphal entry and march through Berlin in turn, on different days later on, bands playing and Eagles displayed at the head of the regiments—the people turning out on each occasion in crowds to line the streets and gaze at the show, "expressing great surprise at the small size of our men and the youth of most of the officers." Marshal Ney's corps brought with them their fifty-nine trophies from Magdeburg, and, after parading them through the streets of Berlin, ceremoniously presented them to Napoleon in public, in front of the statue of Frederick the Great.

Napoleon himself made his triumphal entry into Berlin on October

28, three days after Davout's march through. He rode from Charlottenburg through the Brandenburg Gate and along Unter-den-Linden to the Royal Palace, at the head of the Old Guard and six thousand *cuirassiers* in gleaming mail. Squadrons of *Gendarmerie d'Elite* and Chasseurs of the Guard and the Horse Grenadiers, in their huge bear-skins, led the long procession, all in *grande tenue*, with their bands playing and the Eagles glittering in the brilliant sunshine of a perfect autumn day.

Napoleon came next, "riding by himself, twenty paces in front of the staff, with impassive face and a stern expression," passing amid dense silent crowds, "the men all wearing black, as in mourning; the women mostly with handkerchiefs to their eyes." The people lined both sides of the roadway, and filled the windows of all the houses overlooking the route. All Berlin, young and old, was in the streets that day, staring at the spectacle in mute silence, looking on dumbly, pale-faced and miserable of aspect. Not a mutter of abuse was heard, not the least sign was apparent of the deadly hatred to their conqueror that one and all felt. With rage and despair in their hearts, with compressed lips and clenched fists at their sides, the men watched the splendid array sweep proudly past them in all the insolent pomp of victorious war.

For once, on that historic occasion, Napoleon discarded his customary wear of the green undress uniform of his pet corps, the Chasseurs of the Guard. He entered Berlin as the head of a conquering army, wearing the full-dress uniform of a French general, crimson plumed cocked hat with blue and white *aigrette*, blue coat heavily embroidered with gold, and with glittering bullion epaulettes, and the blue and gold sash of a general round his waist. Four marshals, Berthier, Lannes, Davout, and Augereau, riding abreast, followed Napoleon, immediately in front of the Imperial Staff, a cavalcade of a hundred and more brilliantly decorated officers, all in their most gorgeous parade uniforms, in celebration of the day.

The keys of the city were presented to the conqueror, and accepted by him, as Napoleon passed through the Brandenburg Gate. Ten thousand infantry of the Old Guard, in a vast solid column of glistening bayonets, marched, twenty abreast, in rear of the staff. Their famous band playing triumphantly, with the Eagle of the Grenadiers of the Old Guard above its flag of crimson silk and gold, heading the veterans. They also were all in the full-dress uniform they wore on gala-day parades before the Tuileries. By Napoleon's special order, the Old Guard on all campaigns carried in their knapsacks their full-dress uniform, specially for donning on occasions such as that at Berlin.

But the cup of humiliation for the miserable citizens of the Prussian capital was not yet full. They had yet another military spectacle with a significance of its own to witness; one the deep humiliation of which they felt more bitterly even than Napoleon's triumphant ride in person through their streets. The citizens of Berlin had to look on their own officers of the Royal Prussian Guard being led in procession through their midst under the armed escort of Napoleon's grenadiers. That was Napoleon's way of settling accounts for that August night of wanton insult to France, for the sharpening of the sword-blades on the steps of the French Embassy.

Nor, too, did Napoleon spare the Prussian prisoners of the rank and file. Writing from Berlin to the Minister of the Interior in Paris, he gave directions that the Prussian captives should be made use of as hewers of wood and drawers of water for their conquerors. They were to be farmed out to municipalities and district councils in the departments.

> Their services should be turned to account at a trifling expense in the way of wages for the benefit of our manufacturers and cultivators and replace our conscripts called to serve in the ranks of the Grand Army.

Napoleon stayed in Berlin for four weeks, while the marshals were leading the Eagles through Eastern Prussia towards the Polish frontier. Russia had taken up the cause of her defeated neighbour, and the armies of the *Czar* were on the move to rescue what was left of the Prussian army. Less than 15,000 men were all that remained in the field to show fight, of 200,000 soldiers who, not two months before, had been on the march against France in full anticipation of victory.

In the Royal Palace of Berlin Napoleon received with elaborate ceremony the deputation of the French Senate sent from Paris specially to congratulate the victor of Jena in the enemy's capital. He took advantage of the unique occasion for the formal presentation and handing over to their charge, for conveyance to Paris, of the trophies of the war 340 Prussian battle-flags and standards.[5] Forty of the tro-

---

5. The *Moniteur* made this notification in addition: "The Emperor has ordered a series of eight pictures, sixteen feet by ten, each, with life-size figures, from MM. Gérard, Lethière, Gautherot, Guérin, Hennequin, Girodet, Meynier, and Gros. The pictures are intended for the galleries of the Tuileries, and will depict the most memorable events of the campaign in Germany." They are now in the Louvre, badly "skied," and only paid heed to by the batches of recruits who from time to time are conducted round to see them under the guidance of under-officer instructors as lecturers.

phies presented to the Senate on that day at Berlin are now among the array of trophies grouped round Napoleon's tomb in the Invalides.

Napoleon handed over to the charge of the deputation at the same time, for transfer to the Invalides, his own personal spoil—the sword of Frederick the Great. It was removed all the world knows the story of the unpardonable outrage—by Napoleon's own hand from its resting-place on the royal tomb at Potsdam. He said to the officers beside him in the royal vault as he took possession of the sword:

> I would rather have this than twenty millions. I shall send it to my old soldiers who fought against Frederick in the campaign in Hanover. I will present it to the Governor of the Invalides, who will guard it as a testimonial of the victories of the Grand Army and the vengeance that it has wreaked for the disaster of Rosbach. My veterans will be pleased to see the sword of the man who defeated them at Rosbach!

The trophies started for France forthwith under military escort, and Paris went mad with exultation at the sight of them. On the day of the State Procession which escorted the trophies from the Tuileries to the Invalides it proved almost impossible to keep back the enormous crowds that thronged the streets along the route, in spite of cordons of *gendarmerie* and regiments of dragoons. Deputations of veterans and National Guards, with the Eagles of the Departmental Legions, led the way. Then came Imperial carriages with exalted official personages.

The trophies had their place next, displayed in clusters of flags all round a gigantic triumphal car. Marshal Moncey, the acting Governor of Paris, rode a few paces behind the car of Prussian standards, holding up the trophy of trophies before the eyes of the wildly cheering onlookers—Frederick the Great's sword. A gaily attired train of generals and staff officers attended the marshal. The rear of the procession was brought up by the battalions of the Guard of Paris, their Eagles being borne amid rows of gleaming bayonets. Salvos of artillery from the Triumphal Battery greeted the arrival of the trophies at the Invalides, where the veterans awaited them, drawn up on parade before the Gate of Honour.

As Napoleon had specially directed, the Hanoverian War veterans of the Invalides met and escorted Marshal Moncey to the chapel at the head of other specially nominated veterans, who bore, marching in procession, the Prussian trophy-standards. The trophies were deposited with an elaborate display of ceremonial in front of the High Altar, after which Fontanes, the Public Orator of the Empire, delivered an address full of glowingly eloquent passages on the glorious achievements of the Grand Army and the "resplendent magnificence of the leader who had led the Eagles to surpassing triumphs!"

THE TWELVE LOST EAGLES OF EYLAU

Napoleon passed from the victorious fields of Prussia to the rough experiences of the Eylau and Friedland campaigns, which followed as the sequel to Jena on the plains of the Polish frontier. The Eagles there had to undergo under fire vicissitudes of fortune that were a foretaste of the fate in store for some of them later on, at the hands of the same enemy, in the Moscow campaign. No fewer than fourteen of the Eagles borne in triumph through Berlin after Jena were on view within a twelvemonth as spoils of war in the Kazan Cathedral at St. Petersburg.

The Eagle of Marshal Ney's favourite regiment in the battle-days of the Ulm campaign, the 9th Light Infantry, was the first to meet adventures in the Polish War. It was on the occasion of the surprise of Bernadotte's army corps, at Mohringen near the Vistula, in the last week of January 1807. The Grand Army was lying in winter quarters to the north of Warsaw, awaiting the reopening of the campaign in the early spring, when the Russian army, breaking up unexpectedly from its cantonments beyond the Vistula in the depth of winter, made a dash at Bernadotte's outlying troops, posted by themselves at some distance from the main army and scattered in detachments over a wide tract of country for reasons of food-supply.

Bernadotte only got news of the enemy's approach just in time; practically at the eleventh hour. He was rapidly concentrating his corps at Mohringen, but barely half his troops had been able to reach the point of danger when the Russians struck their blow. He was able with the troops nearest at hand to avert destruction, but the escape was a narrow one and his losses were very heavy, all his baggage falling into the hands of the enemy. Fortunately for the French the Russian advanced guard attacked prematurely and was beaten back, after which Bernadotte made good his retreat to a safer neighbourhood.

The 9th Light Infantry were in the forefront of the fighting, which was at the closest quarters, the soldiers on both sides meeting man to man. Four Eagle-bearers of the 9th fell, one after the other. Four times the Eagle was taken by the Russians and recaptured at the point of the bayonet. A fifth time the Eagle-bearer went down, and on his fall this time the Eagle disappeared, while the 9th were driven back, broken and in disorder. They were quickly rallied again, however, and led once more to the charge, "going forward to the combat with the fury of despair."

This time their impetuous onset forced the Russians to give ground. Advancing with shouts of victory, they stormed the village of Psarrefelden, immediately in front of them, and there seized part of a Russian ammunition train. While searching for fresh cartridges in one of the enemy's ammunition wagons to replenish their empty *cartouche*-boxes an officer, to his surprise, came upon the lost Eagle. It had been broken from its staff in the last fight round it, and its Russian captor, probably having enough to do to look after himself without carrying it about, had apparently thrust it hastily into the ammunition wagon on top of the cartridges. At any rate there the Eagle of the 9th Light Infantry was found, and so it was regained.

The broken staff and flag were missing and were never seen again, but the all-important Eagle had been recovered. It was hurriedly mounted on a hop-pole, found leaning against a peasant's hut nearby, which was improvised for a staff, and on that the Eagle was carried to the close of the fighting that day, after which the 9th retreated with the rest of Bernadotte's corps.

Napoleon specially decorated the lieutenant who recovered the Eagle, and who also had led more than one of the charges to rescue it in the earlier fighting. He gave him the cross of the Legion of Honour with a money grant. He further recorded the recovery of the Eagle—though without mentioning how it was got back—in the 55th Bulletin of the Grand Army, dated Warsaw, January 29, 1807:

> The Eagle of the 9th Light Infantry was taken by the enemy, but, realising the deep disgrace with which their brave regiment would be covered for ever, and from which neither victory nor the glory acquired in a hundred combats could have removed the stigma, the soldiers, animated with an inconceivable ardour, precipitated themselves on the enemy and routed them and recovered their Eagle.

So Napoleon wrote history.

Two Eagles met their fate in the first day's fighting at Eylau—in the preliminary combat on February 7, which formed the opening phase of the terrific encounter next day. At Eylau—a small township some twenty-two miles to the south of Königsburg—Napoleon in person commanded with 80,000 men in the field, and met with his first serious check in a European war. In following up the Russian rearguard on the afternoon of the 7th, as it fell slowly back to rejoin its main body, drawn up in position on the farther side of Eylau, on ground chosen before-hand by the Russian leader for making a stand, two of Napoleon's battalions, while pressing hotly forward after the enemy over the open plain, some two miles from Eylau, were overpowered and cut to pieces. They had charged and were driving in the nearest Russians to them, when a Russian cavalry regiment, the St, Petersburg Dragoons, unexpectedly came on the scene.

Sweeping round amidst the tumult of the fighting, the dragoons rode into them on the flank. The two battalions were slaughtered almost to a man within five minutes, before help could get to them, and their Eagles were snatched up and borne away. It was an act of expiation for the St. Petersburg Dragoons. On the previous day Murat's pursuing hussars had charged and broken them, putting them to flight, and in a wild panic they had ridden over one of their own regiments, trampling their comrades down, with loss of life. To retrieve their character the St. Petersburg Dragoons now went savagely at the two French battalions, riding them down with reckless daring and relentless fury, giving no quarter. Their capture of two of Napoleon's Eagles in one charge, the taking of two Eagles by a single regiment, stands on its own account as a unique achievement.

Eylau—the historic battle of February 8, 1807—was fought in the depth of winter; in the midst of a flat expanse of a desolate snow-plain and ice-bound marshes; under dreary lowering skies of leaden grey; amid howling gusts of piercing wind, with driving snow-storms sweeping intermittently across the field of battle. A hundred and fifty thousand men on both sides faced each other at the break of day, after passing the night with their outposts within shot of one another, the soldiers, all lying in an open bivouac on the snow, round their watch-fires, wrapped up in their cloaks, the only shelter from the bitter cold. They fronted each other in the grey dawn "within half-cannon shot, their immense masses distributed in dense columns over a space in breadth less than four miles. Between them lay the field of battle, a wide stretch of unen-closed ground, rising on the Russian side to a range of small hills. All over the plain, ponds and marshes intersected the ground, but far and wide all was now covered over with ice and deep snow."

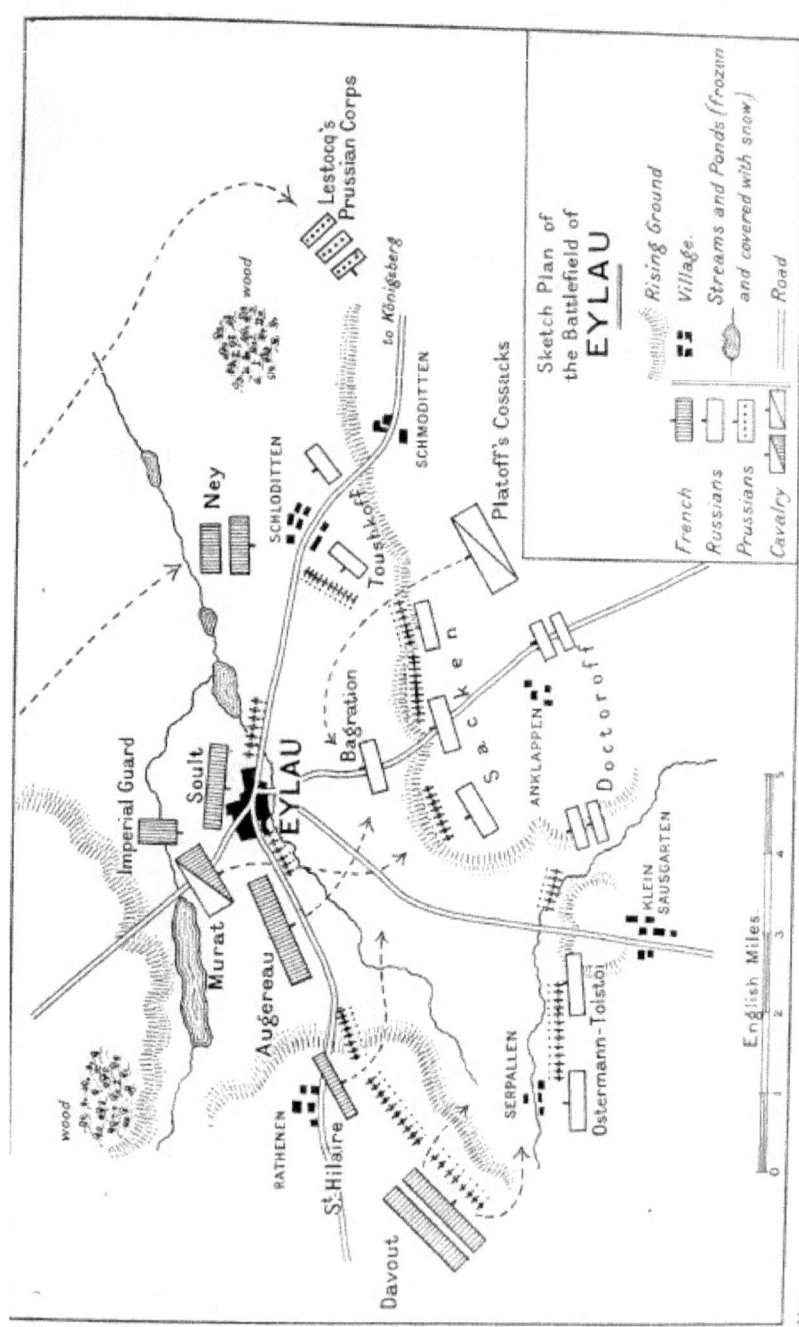

Napoleon began the battle with a fierce cannonade, opening a terrific fire all along the line with no fewer than 350 guns. The Russians replied at once, firing back even more furiously and with yet more guns. For almost an hour nearly 800 cannon belched forth shot and shell on either side; an artillery duel perhaps unparalleled in war. Then, in the midst of the cannonade, Napoleon launched his first attack. Fifteen thousand men of Augereau's corps moved out from the centre of the French line to storm the Russian position. They went forward, massed in two immense columns, with, in support, a third column of one of Soult's divisions.

They went forward to their doom: to meet disaster, swift, terrible, overwhelming, and to leave two of their Eagles in the hands of the enemy as mementos of their fate. Yet they were not given up; neither of those Eagles was surrendered. They remained on the field amid the dead; left behind because there was not a man living of their regiments to defend them. They lay where they fell, surrounded by the soldiers who had died in their defence; lying on the snow for the *Cossacks* to pick up and carry away. They were the Eagles of the 14th and the 24th of the Line.

The Russians turned their guns on Augereau's corps directly it commenced its advance; it was sheer massacre for the French, as the fierce tornado of cannon-balls crashed into the thick of the densely massed columns. Whole companies were swept away, mowed down, on every side. "Within a quarter of an hour, half of the corps were struck down." The rest, though, with stolid endurance, held firmly on their way. The soldiers went doggedly on; only halting for a moment now and again to close up their shattered ranks. At that moment, as they were nearing the Russian position, a furious snow-storm burst over the battlefield, the snow blowing right in the faces of the French. "It was impossible," one of the survivors told, "to see anything at all in front; we could at times barely see a foot before us." All, in spite of that, however, laboured bravely to get forward; without wavering, and regardless of the merciless fire of the Russian guns, which never ceased for one moment.

Then, as the snow-blinded soldiers struggled on, when the storm of whirling snow was at its worst, all in an instant the catastrophe happened. Without warning, coming from nowhere, as it seemed, an enormous mass of Russian horse, dragoons and *Cossacks*, charged suddenly, amid an infernal din of furious shouting, into them. "So thick was the snow-storm, and so unexpected the onset, that the assailants were only a few feet off, and the long lances of the *Cossacks* almost touching the French infantry when they were first discerned." The Russians swept down on all sides of the two divisions; charging them in front and flanks and rear at once, the dragoons sabring them right and left, the *Cossacks* stabbing at them with their long eighteen-foot lances.

> The combat was not of more than a few minutes' duration; the corps, charged at once by foot and horse with the utmost vigour, broke and fled in the wildest disorder back into Eylau, closely pursued by the Russian cavalry and Cossacks, who made such havoc, that the whole, above 15,000 strong, were, with the exception of 1,500 men, taken or destroyed; and Augereau himself, with his two generals of divisions, Desjardins and Heudelet, was desperately wounded.

Cut off in one part of the field and hemmed in, the 24th of the Line, "one of the finest regiments in the Grand Army, and itself almost equal to a brigade," as a French officer speaks of it, was destroyed to a man. It refused to turn its back to the enemy, and stood its ground to face its fate. The 24th were slaughtered as they stood in their ranks. Colonel Séméle and a devoted band of soldiers fought round the Eagle to the last, and fell dead beside it. A *cossack* picked the Eagle up and rode off with it.

The 14th had led the attack. It had lost heavily from the Russian cannonade, but was still pressing on when the cavalry came charging down. The regiments next following it, however, had suffered still more heavily from the artillery fire. They were swept away *en masse* by the *Cossack* rush. Thus the 14th were cut off and left by themselves, barely half a battalion of men in numbers, in the midst of the raging torrent of *cossacks* and dragoons. The survivors hastily threw themselves into a square on and round a low elevation or hillock of snow. There, with their Eagle in their midst, they stood at bay, refusing to retire without direct orders from their marshal.

Marbot, in his *Memoirs*, describes the fate of the 14th, to which he was sent with a message from Napoleon. He was one of Augereau's *aides de camp*. It was just after the wounded marshal had been carried back to the churchyard of the village of Eylau, the centre of the French position, whence Napoleon, on horseback, among his personal suite, had witnessed the disaster. All could see the 14th standing there, isolated and surrounded:

We could see that the intrepid regiment, surrounded by the enemy, was brandishing the Eagle in the air, to show that it still held its ground and wanted help.

Napoleon, touched by the grand devotion of these brave men, resolved to try to save them. He gave orders that an officer should be sent to tell them to try to make their way back towards the army. Cavalry would charge out to help them. It looked almost impossible to get through the thronging *Cossacks*; (but Napoleon's command had to be obeyed).

A brave captain of engineers named Froissart, who, though not an *aide de camp*, was on Augereau's staff, happened to be nearest him, and was told to carry the order to the 14th. Froissart galloped off: we lost sight of him in the midst of the *Cossacks*, and never saw him again or heard what became of him. The marshal, seeing that the 14th did not move, then sent an officer named David. He had the same fate as Froissart; we never heard of him again. Probably both were killed and stripped, and could not be recognised among the many corpses which covered the ground. For the third time the marshal called, 'The officer for duty!' It was my turn.

Marbot had seen his two predecessors go off with their swords drawn, as though they intended to defend themselves against attacks on the way. He had remarked that, and now proposed another method for himself.

To attempt defence was madness; it meant stopping to fight amidst a multitude of enemies. I went otherwise to work. Leaving my sword in its scabbard, I considered myself rather as a rider who is trying to win a steeple-chase and goes as quickly as possible by the shortest line towards the appointed goal without troubling about what is to right or left of his path. My goal was the hillock on which stood the 14th, and I resolved to get there without taking heed of the *Cossacks*. I tried to put them out of my mind entirely. The plan answered to perfection.

Lisette (Marbot's charger), flying rather than galloping, moving more lightly than a swallow, darted over the intervening space, leaping the heaps of dead men and horses, the ditches, the broken gun-carriages, the half-extinguished bivouac fires. Thousands of *Cossacks* swarmed over the plain. The first who caught sight of me behaved like sportsmen who, while beating, start a hare and tell of its whereabouts to each other with shouts of 'Your side!' None of the *Cossacks* tried to stop me. Perhaps it was because of the amazing speed of my mare; perhaps—probably—because there were so many of them swarming round that each thought I could not escape from his comrades farther on. At any rate I got through them all, and without scratch either to myself or to my mare, and managed to reach where the 14th stood.

I found them in square on top of their hillock, but the slope all round was very slight, and the Russian cavalry had been able to attack them with several charges. All, though, had been beaten off, and the regiment stood surrounded by a circle of dead horses and dragoons. The corpses indeed formed a kind of rampart round our men, and made by now their position almost inaccessible to mounted men. So I found, for in spite of the help of our men, I had much difficulty in getting across this horrible entrenchment. At last, however, I was in the square.

The major of the 14th was the senior officer left alive, and to him Marbot gave Napoleon's order. But it was absolutely impossible to carry it out; there were too few men left to make the attempt possible. They would be overpowered, said the major to Marbot, before they had gone half a dozen steps. They were past hope now, unless the cavalry could cut their way to them at once. Marbot must save himself and get back at once. He must take their Eagle back with him and deliver it into Napoleon's own hands. The major's words were:

I see no means left of saving the regiment. Return to the Emperor, and bid him farewell from the 14th of the Line. We have faithfully obeyed his orders in defence of the Eagle. Bear him back his Eagle which he entrusted to us, which now we have no hope of defending longer. It would add too much to the bitterness of death for us to see it fall into the hands of the enemy.

The major handed the Eagle to Marbot and then saluted it, amid shouts of "*Vive l'Empereur!*" from the men round. Marbot took the Eagle, and, as the only means of preserving it during his ride back, tried to break it off from its stout pole so as to conceal it under his cloak. He was in the act of leaning forward to get a purchase in order to break the oaken staff, when he was suddenly rendered powerless by the wind of a grape-shot It was a marvellous escape from death.

The shot actually went through his hat, within a quarter of an inch of his head. It deprived him, as he describes, of all power and sensation, although he still remained fixed in his saddle, his eyes witnessing the last scene, the fate of the 14th. The square was finally rushed by a swarm of Russian grenadiers, as Marbot says, who came charging up to the spot—

> ... big men with mitre-shaped caps bound in brass.

These men hurled themselves furiously on the feeble remains of the 14th. Our poor fellows had little strength left for resistance, weakened as they were by hardships and privations. They had for days been only existing on potatoes and melted snow, and on that morning had not had time to prepare even that wretched meal. Yet they made bravely what fight they could with their bayonets, and when, as too soon happened, the square was broken, they tried to hold together in groups, fighting back to back and keeping up the unequal fight to the last man.

Those nearest Marbot, so as not to be bayoneted from behind, stood all round him with their backs to the mare, hemmed in by a ring of Russians, some shooting down the hapless Frenchmen, others killing them with the bayonet.

Marbot, recovering his senses, got at the last moment an unexpected chance of escape. His mare, Lisette, he says, "of a notoriously savage temper," was pricked by a bayonet apparently, for she suddenly sprang forward, lashing out and kicking and biting. She crashed through the nearest Russians and galloped off with Marbot on her back towards Eylau. He was mistaken by the Cossacks, he thought, for a Russian officer, and rode on until suddenly Lisette collapsed beneath him, and Marbot rolled off into the snow, where he lay insensible for some hours. He lay there until a marauder on the field after the battle tried to strip him of his gold-laced uniform. That roused him, and he cried for help, which came; but the Eagle of the 14th had disappeared.

Two Eagles of St. Hilaire's division of Soult's corps were taken at about the same time that the 14th met its fate. One was that of the 10th Light Infantry, ridden down while hastening forward to support Augereau. The 10th missed its way in the snowstorm and, blundering close under the Russian guns, was "decimated by grape." Immediately after that, while reeling under the shock, and trying to reform its ranks, the Russian dragoons dashed into it. They burst into its midst at full gallop, "unseen until they were actually among us."

No help was near, and in less than three minutes the luckless 10th Light Infantry had ceased to exist. The second of Soult's Eagles that was lost at Eylau was that of a battalion of the 28th of the Line, which also perished, victims to the sabres of the Russian horsemen. It was a little later in the day, just after the 28th had made a successful bayonet charge on the Russian infantry. They were in the midst of their combat when the dragoons dashed into them, rode through them, and scattered them, bearing off the Eagle, snatched from the hands of the Eagle-bearer, who was cut down in the *mêlée*.

The Heart of the "First Grenadier of France" nearly went to St. Petersburg at the same time, The 46th and 28th together formed General Levasseur's division in Soult's corps, and both were overwhelmed at the same time by the Russian dragoons. The more fortunate 46th saved both their Eagle and the silver casket in which the heart of La Tour d'Auvergne was kept enshrined. The casket was worn, strapped on a velvet shield, on the chest of the senior grenadier sergeant of the First Battalion, whose station was next the Eagle-bearer.

It was with the 46th, then known as the 46th Demi-Brigade, that the heroic "*Premier Grenadier de France*" was serving as a captain when he met his death in the year of Hohenlinden, while in the act of capturing an Austrian standard. The 46th of the Line of the modern French Army keeps up today the traditional practice, first ordered by Moreau, the victor of Hohenlinden, of calling his name first of all at regimental parades. It was revived some thirty years ago, after being in desuetude since 1809. One of the officers of the regiment describes:

> Immediately the colonel has saluted the flag, the captain commanding the colour-company steps forward and, facing the men, calls in a loud voice 'La Tour d'Auvergne,' on which the senior sergeant of the company steps out two paces and replies, in a loud voice also, '*Mort au Champ d'Honneur!*'—'Dead on the Field of Honour!'

The heart of La Tour d'Auvergne in its silver casket was ceremoniously deposited by the regiment at the Invalides in 1904, eight years ago.

The 25th of the Line saved its Eagle, but lost on the field every single one of its officers. A plainly built obelisk with the brief inscription, "To the Memory of the Officers of the 25th," was erected by Napoleon to commemorate their fate at Eylau.

Two Eagles of Davout's corps were lost at Eylau. One was that of the 18th—the sole loss of an Eagle in the battle, as it so happens, that it suited Napoleon's purpose to admit publicly. This is what he said of it in his Eylau Bulletin—the 58th Bulletin of the Grand Army:

> The Eagle of one of the battalions of the 18th Regiment is missing. It has probably fallen into the hands of the enemy, but no reproach can attach to this regiment in the predicament in which it was placed. It is a mere accident of war. The Emperor will give the 18th another Eagle when it has taken a standard from the enemy.

Comments on this, by the way, a British officer, Colonel Sir Robert Wilson, who was attached to the Russian army as British military commissioner:

> Admirable! the accidental loss of *one* Eagle and only one! Colonel Beckendorff, then, did not carry *twelve* Eagles (*and, moreover, several colours from which the Eagles had been unscrewed*) to Petersburg, where they now are for the inspection of the world!

Napoleon made no other open reference to the loss of Eagles at Eylau; but, as he showed a little later, he felt what had happened. On the other hand, outside France, many people disbelieved the Russian official despatches. Wrote the editor of a London newspaper:

> The number of Eagles said to be taken is astounding, indeed incredible.

The 18th lost their Eagle in the fierce fighting on the extreme right of the battlefield, where, after storming the village of Serpallen, Morand's division captured a Russian battery, bayoneting the gunners. As they took the guns a Russian cavalry brigade came hastening to the spot to the rescue. Taking the 18th on the flank, the Russians rode them down, breaking the regiment up and scattering it. The Eagle disappeared in the midst of the fight.

The Eagle of the 51st of the Line was the other that was lost in Davout's corps. That was taken by the Prussian division which fought at Eylau; the last remnant of the Jena army still combating in the field. The Prussians, some 12,000 in number, had made good their escape to the Polish frontier and reached the battlefield of Eylau at the close of the fight, in time to strike in and take vengeance for their countrymen. They were, however, deprived in the end of their trophy. The captured Eagle of the 51st was claimed from them by the Russian general after the battle, and sent with the eleven others to St. Petersburg, where it now is.

Two others of Davout's Eagles which came through at Eylau had narrow escapes. They were those of the 17th and 30th of the Line. The

17th was one of the regiments ridden down by Towazysky's dragoons, the troopers who carried off the Eagle of the 18th. In their charge the dragoons broke up the 17th as well, and the Eagle was left with only a few men nearby to defend it. They were in the midst of the dragoons as the Russians galloped through, slashing with their sabres at all within reach. As the only means of saving the Eagle, Locqueneux, a *fourrier*, or quartermaster-sergeant:

> Thrust the Eagle under the snow and stood on it shouting for help. Colonel Mallet heard the cry and ran to the rescue. With a few men who rallied to the spot he succeeded in getting the Eagle away from among the *débris* of the 17th.

At roll-call next morning only one man in five answered to his name. Napoleon, on his ride over the field, happening to pass by while the muster was being held, the gallant *fourrier* was brought before him and presented with a lieutenant's commission and an annuity of 2,000 *francs*. The Eagle of the 30th of the Line, another of Morand's regiments, was saved from capture in like manner by the personal devotion of another *fourrier*, Morin by name. All round him men were falling, and he himself had been severely wounded, but the brave fellow had just strength enough to bury the Eagle under the snow. He fainted from loss of blood as he did it. Morin was found next morning just alive, outstretched over where the precious Eagle lay concealed. He was able to make signs and indicate that it was lying underneath the snow, and then he died.

Four cavalry Eagles, those of *cuirassier* regiments, made up the tale of twelve lost by Napoleon in the two days at Eylau. Platoff's *Cossacks* of the Don captured the four. They swooped down on Murat's cavalry, while out of hand and partially dispersed after breaking through the Russian centre, at the close of Murat's desperate charge at the head of seventy squadrons to save the survivors of the massacre of Augereau's ill-fated battalions. Of one *cuirassier* regiment only 18 men managed to regain their own lines, leaving 530 of their comrades on the field to be stripped of their shining armour by the *Cossacks*.

The Eagle of the Old Guard led a charge at Eylau at the head of the grenadiers. The Guard came into action to beat back a daring Russian counter-attack on the centre of Napoleon's position, which immediately followed the annihilation of Augereau's corps. Napoleon himself gave the order for the Guard to go forward. Caulaincourt, who was on Napoleon's staff, and near him throughout, describes:

The Emperor, standing erect in the stirrups, his glass at his eye, was the first to realise that the black shadow steadily drawing near through the veil of the snowstorm must be the columns of the Russian reserve.[6] He immediately sent against them two battalions of the Grenadiers of the Guard commanded by General Dorsenne.

It was just after Murat had been ordered to make his charge.

Dorsenne—"*Le Beau Dorsenne*," he was universally called; he had the reputation of being the handsomest man in the whole of the Grand Army—started off on the instant, rapidly deploying his men into lines as he moved forward, and with the Eagle of the Grenadiers of the Guard in advance of the centre of the front line. The Old Guard moved out in stately order, marching with clockwork precision, muskets at the support—held erect at the side and steadied and supported with one arm held stiffly across. One of the officers who rode beside Dorsenne suggested to the general as they were nearing the Russians to open fire. "*Non!*" was the haughty answer. "*Grenadiers l'arme à bras! La Vieille Garde ne se bât qu'à la baïonette!*" "No! Arms at the support! The Old Guard only fights at the point of the bayonet!")

They reached the Russians, who, on their side, seemed for the moment as if spellbound at the sight of them. The nearest Russians stopped short. They stood stock-still, rooted in the ground as it were, gazing at the sudden apparition of the solid wall of 2,000 veteran giants in their huge towering bear-skins. The next instant the battalion guns of the Guard, which accompanied the advance on either flank, opened with a burst of fire at short range into the thick of the Russians. At once, down came the gleaming rows of bayonets, and, like one man, the Old Guard sprang forward and charged into the enemy. A moment before the bayonets crossed a squadron of the *Chasseurs* of the Guard, the men on duty as Napoleon's own personal escort, sent forward by the Emperor himself to assist the Grenadiers, dashed into the rear of the Russian column, and "drove it forward on our Grenadiers, who received it with fixed bayonets."

Just before that it was that the Eagle of the Old Guard had its adventure. A shell dropped right in front of it and burst. The fragments

---

6. The hat that Napoleon wore at Eylau is kept in the little crypt beside Napoleon's tomb in the Invalides. It is the identical one represented in the colossal picture of the battle by Gros, to be seen at the Louvre, and was given to Gros for the picture. At the second funeral of Napoleon in 1840, it figured beside the coffin, with the Emperor's decorations and the sword Napoleon wore at Austerlitz.

smashed the Eagle pole in two places, just above and below the hands of the Eagle-bearer. The Eagle fell to the ground at the feet of the Russians. But they had not time to get hold of it. Instantly Lieutenant Morlay, the Eagle-bearer, sprang forward and recovered it. Picking the Eagle up, with the flag and fragment of pole that was left, Morlay snatched hold of a grenadier's musket and jammed the piece of the staff into the muzzle beside the bayonet. He carried the Eagle in that manner throughout the rest of the battle. (*See note following.*)

Note:—A gallant young officer of the Guard was the first man to break through the Russian line in front. With half a dozen grenadiers he made a dash forward, just as the *chasseurs* made their attack. Captain Ernest Auzoni—that was the young officer's name—caught sight of a Russian flag a few paces from him, and, calling on the men of his company, led straight at it, cutting his way through. "Courage!" he shouted. "Brave comrades! Follow me!" Auzoni, describes Caulaincourt, "rushed forward sword in hand, followed by his company, and penetrated the compact centre of the Russian column: his sudden assault broke their ranks, and our grenadiers burst in through the passage opened to them by the brave Auzoni."

Napoleon, from his post near at hand, was also an eyewitness of the captain's daring. On the Russians falling back after the routing of the column, as the Guard were re-forming for a fresh advance, he summoned Auzoni and the men of his company before him. "Captain Auzoni," began Napoleon as they stood in front of him, "you well deserve the honour of commanding my 'veteran' *vieux moustaches*; you have most nobly distinguished yourself. You have won an officer's cross and an annuity of two thousand *francs*. You were made captain at the beginning of the campaign, and I hope you will return to Paris with still higher rank. A man who earns his honours on the field of battle stands very high in my estimation!" Turning then to the soldiers, Napoleon added: "I award ten crosses to your company!" With an enthusiastic cheer the company marched off to rejoin their comrades, and as Caulaincourt puts it, "the same men advanced to meet the enemy's fire with a degree of courage and enthusiasm which is impossible to describe."

The brave young Guardsman captain, though, did not see Paris again. Auzoni met his fate at Eylau. He fell later in the day, in another charge, in which he took a second Russian flag. Napoleon himself discovered him, lying at the last gasp among the mortally wounded on the field. It was next day, as Napoleon, in accordance with his invariable practice, was riding over the scene of the battle.

"Near a battery which had been abandoned by the enemy," to use again the words of Caulaincourt, "about 150 or 200 French grenadiers were lying dead, surrounded by four times their number of Russians. They were lying weltering in a river of blood, amid broken gun-carriages, muskets, swords, and other *débris*. They had plainly fought with the most determined fury, for every corpse showed numerous and horrible wounds. A feeble cry of '*Vive l'Empereur!*' was heard as we rode up.

"It came from the middle of this mountain of dead, and all eyes were turned instantly to the spot whence the voice proceeded. Half concealed beneath a tattered flag lay a young officer whose breast was decorated with an order. He was still alive, and, though covered with many wounds, as we stopped by him he managed to raise himself so as to rest on his elbow. But his handsome face was overcast with the livid hue of death. He recognised the Emperor, and, in a feeble, faltering voice, exclaimed: 'God bless your Majesty! Farewell, farewell! Oh, my poor mother!' He turned a look of supplication towards the Emperor, and with that, with the words on his lips, 'To my country, to dear France—my last thoughts!' he fell back dead.

"Napoleon seemed riveted to the spot. 'Brave men!' he exclaimed. 'Brave Auzoni! Noble young fellow! Ah, this is a frightful scene! The annuity shall go to his mother: let the order be presented for my signature as soon as possible!' Then, turning to Surgeon Ivan, who accompanied him, he. said: 'Examine poor Auzoni's wounds and see what can be done for him!' Nothing however, could be done: the brave youth was beyond medical aid."

A hundred and fifty thousand combatants had faced one another at daybreak. An hour before midnight, when the last shots were fired, 50,000 men lay dead or wounded on the field. If we may recall the grim picture of the scene next day that Alison has drawn:

> Never was spectacle so dreadful as that field presented on the following morning. Above 50,000 men lay in the space of two leagues, weltering in blood. The wounds were, for the most

part, of the severest kind, from the extraordinary quantity of cannonballs which had been discharged during the action and the close proximity of the contending masses to the deadly batteries, which spread grape at half-musket shot through their ranks. Though stretched on the cold snow and exposed to the severity of an Arctic winter, the sufferers were burning with thirst, and piteous cries were heard on all sides for water, or assistance to extricate the wounded men from beneath the heaps of slain or load of horses by which they were crushed.

Six thousand of these noble animals encumbered the field, or, maddened with pain, were shrieking aloud amidst the stifled groans of the wounded. Broken gun-carriages, dismounted cannon, fragments of blown-up *caissons*, scattered balls, lay in wild confusion amidst *casques, cuirassiers*, and burning hamlets, casting a livid light over a field of snow. Subdued by loss of blood, tamed by cold, exhausted by hunger, the foemen lay side by side, amidst the general wreck. The *cossack* was to be seen beside the Italian; the gay vine-dresser from the banks of the Garonne lay athwart the stern peasant from the plains of the Ukraine.

When Napoleon took his ride over the field:

The men exhibited none of their wonted enthusiasm; no cries of '*Vive l'Empereur!*' were heard; the bloody surface echoed only with the cries of suffering or the groans of woe.

Sixteen Russian standards were sent to Paris after Eylau; Napoleon's set-off to the twelve Eagles taken to St. Petersburg. They were to be hung, he directed, temporarily at the Invalides, until such time as the conversion of the former Church of the Madeleine into Napoleon's *grandiose* "Temple of Victory" should be effected—a project that was fated never to be accomplished. There, designed Napoleon, all the trophies of the Grand Army would find their final resting-place, in a splendid edifice, designed externally after the Parthenon at Athens. Within, the trophies would be displayed, amidst colonnades of Corinthian pillars of marble and granite and a mass of decorative sculptures, statues of marshals and generals who had met their death in battle, and *bas-reliefs* of famous colonels, before a lofty marble *curule* chair, which Napoleon would occupy as a throne on great occasions. Writing from his camp in Poland, he laid down:

It is a Temple I desire, not a church; and everything must be made in a chaste, severe, and durable style, and be suitable for solemnities at all times and all hours.

Two more Eagles had yet to go to St. Petersburg before the war was over—the Eagle of the 15th of the Line and another. They were the spoils that the beaten Russian army carried off from the battle of Friedland, fought some six months after Eylau, on July 14. Napoleon won one of his most famous victories at Friedland, and one that he afterwards recorded on the colours of all the regiments that fought in the battle; but the defeated army carried back with them two more of his Eagles.

The Eagle of the 15th of the Line, a regiment of Marshal Ney's corps, was lost in a bayonet charge while fighting the Russian Imperial Guard. The second Eagle was left among the dead in the repulse of a column of Marshal Lannes' corps in the earlier part of the battle. "A column of 3,000 men advanced straight against Friedland. They were permitted to approach close to the Russian cannon without a single shot being fired, when suddenly the whole opened with grape, and with such effect that in a few minutes a thousand men were struck down, the column routed, and the Eagle taken."

One of the regiments of the column saved itself as it fell back by rallying round its Eagle. As at Eylau, so at Friedland the Russian dragoons dashed down among the broken battalions while trying to re-form under the murderous cannonade. The 50th of the Line had been near the head of the column, and more than half of its men had been shot down. The dragoons were cutting their way through to the Eagle, when Adjutant Labourie snatched it from its wounded bearer, and, holding it up, shouted to the men: "Rally round the Eagle. We must defend it to the death!" A small square hastily formed round him, and, stubbornly resisting, they kept the Russian dragoons off and fought their way back to safety with the Eagle.

The Peace of Tilsit closed the war within a month of Friedland.

The welcome-home of Paris to the Old Guard, and public decoration of the Eagles with crowns of gold, was the curtain-scene and grand *finale* of the Jena-Friedland drama. To all the regiments of the Grand Army under fire at Jena, Friedland, and Eylau, wreaths of gold, to be affixed round the necks of their Eagles, were voted by the Municipality of Paris. The wreaths were to be publicly presented to each regiment on its return to France. The Guard were the first to receive theirs, and their arrival in the capital was made the occasion of a series of civic fetes; announced officially as being "offered in tribute to the Glory of the Grand Army." Wednesday, November 25, 1807, was the day on which the Guard were due to reach Paris. All had been made ready to accord them a magnificent reception.

The Prefect of the Seine, at the head of the City magistrates and the Municipal Councillors of Paris, all in their robes and chains and glittering insignia of office, escorted by a mounted cohort of National Guards, met the returning veterans at the Barrier on the Strasburg road. Marshal Bessières led the Guard, who marched up with bands playing and resplendent in their full-dress uniforms, horse and foot and artillery—12,000 men in all.

A gigantic triumphal arch was set up beyond the Barrier, wide enough for twenty men to march through abreast. It was the approach to a wide arena on which the troops drew up, massed in front of a lofty platform, decked out with flags and wreaths of evergreens and bright-coloured hangings. There the prefect took his place with his *entourage* as the soldiers drew near. Grand-stands to accommodate a crowd of sightseers surrounded the arena.

The Old Guard marched in and drew up in close order, on which the proceedings opened with the civic address. The *prefect* began:

> Heroes of Jena, of Eylau, of Friedland, conquerors of a splendid peace, immortal thanks are your due from France! We salute you, Eagles of war, the symbols of the might of our noble-hearted Emperor! You have made known throughout the world, with his great name, the glory of victorious France!

So, in grandiloquent style, the address commenced. At its close the regiments of the Guards defiled past the platform in turn *Carabineers* and *Cuirassiers*, *Chasseurs*, Dragoons, and Hussars, and the battalions of veteran Grenadiers. Round the neck of each Eagle, as its corps came up, the *prefect* hung a wreath of laurel-leaves in gold.

Then came the triumphal march through the streets of Paris to the Tuileries, amid cheering crowds, nearly beside themselves with excitement and enthusiasm, and with difficulty kept back from breaking through the rows of National Guards who lined the pavement, to hug the grim bearskin-hatted warriors. The Eagles deposited with ceremony in the Imperial Guard-room of the Palace of the Tuileries, the horsemen dismounted in the square of the Carrousel, muskets were piled, and all marched off to the Champs Elysées. An immense banquet awaited them there, under vast marquees—shelter that the men appreciated, for it turned out a miserably wet afternoon.

The banquet in the Champs Elysées was the first in the round of festivities with which Paris welcomed home the "Victors over Europe." The *fêtes* lasted over three days, and terminated in a grand reception given by the Senate to all ranks of "Our Invincible Guard" in the Gardens of the Luxembourg.[7]

---

7. The Old Guard was recruited from the *élite* of the Line. After every battle soldiers who had been particularly prominent in the fighting were specially transferred to the Old Guard; a form of advancement much coveted among the rank and file. At all times there was great competition to enter the Guard, and every regimental colonel kept "waiting lists," in anticipation of vacancies, on which names were sometimes down for years. Service in the Old Guard meant, in addition to the prestige of enrolment in so favoured a corps, life amid the gaieties and pleasures of Paris, with increased pay and personal privileges; and the highly estimated honour of a special weekly inspection by the Emperor himself in the courtyard of the Carrousel, at which Napoleon invariably walked in and out among the ranks, talking to the men; and any Guardsman who had a grievance might then personally lay it before the Emperor. The private in the Guard drew seven *sous* a day as compared with the one *sou* pay of the private of the Line. Off duty, the private of the Guard ranked on an equality with a sergeant of the Line, and in army social circles was entitled to be addressed by the Linesmen he met as "*Monsieur*."

Only men of unblemished record were qualified for admission to the Old Guard. A colonel of a Line regiment on one occasion sent a man into the Guard who turned out a *mauvais sujet*. Napoleon ordered the unfortunate colonel to be publicly reprimanded on parade, and confined to his quarters for three days; and further had his name and offence put in General Army Orders, issued for universal circulation from the War Office, and posted up at the headquarters of every regiment throughout the service.

Chapter 6: Preparing For The Future
The "Eagle-Guard"

The loss of twelve Eagles in one battle made a deep and lasting impression upon Napoleon. That twelve of his cherished emblems, those mementoes of victorious Caesar, for whose prestige he had advanced such exacting claims, should have fallen *en bloc* into the hands of the enemy came as a galling blow to Napoleon's military pride. Twelve Eagles reft from amid the bayonets of the Grand Army on one battlefield: twelve Eagles paraded together as trophies through the capital of an exulting foe! It was a poignantly felt humiliation for the mighty Imperator of the Field of Mars. And yet no default could be charged against the soldiers to whom these Eagles had been entrusted. All that men might do for their defence they had done. Most of the luckless battalions, indeed, had fought and fallen directly under the eyes of the Emperor himself, looking on from his post of vantage by the wall of Eylau churchyard.

Napoleon, however, had already realised that his distribution of an emblem to whose preservation he attached such extreme importance had been made on too lavish a scale. He had been imprudent in distributing such hostages to fortune broadcast; there were too many Eagles on offer to the enemy. Napoleon, indeed, had already tacitly admitted that. Within two months of the opening of the first campaign of the Grand Army—during the Austerlitz campaign—immediately after Murat's daring gallop on Vienna, Napoleon had summarily directed all the light cavalry Eagles to be sent back from the front. Every Hussar and *Chasseur* regiment was ordered to return its three squadron Eagles to headquarters forthwith, for sending back to France.

In future, a new army regulation laid down, those corps would not take their Eagles into the field at all. The regulation after that was extended to Dragoons; and later to all Light Infantry battalions. No doubt it was a step dictated by prudence. In these corps particularly, from the nature of the duties they had normally to perform, the Eagles were peculiarly exposed to risk of isolation and capture.

What had happened at Eylau, and several narrow escapes in hand-to-hand combats at Friedland, together with certain other incidents in that battle which had come under Napoleon's personal notice, where, through a nervous anxiety for the safety of their Eagles, some battalion commanders had kept back round them men whose bayonets were badly wanted elsewhere, led to a further step. Napoleon took advantage of the general scheme for the reorganisation of the Grand Army, which he carried out in 1808, to recast entirely his original arrangement as to the Eagles. He reduced the numbers by two-thirds.

Battalion Eagles were to be withdrawn in favour of Regimental Eagles. In the infantry, under the reorganisation scheme, there were to be five battalions to each regiment instead of three as heretofore; but there would be only one Eagle in future for the entire regiment. The existing Second and Third battalions were ordered to give up the Eagles they had hitherto carried, which would find a resting-place at the Invalides. The Regimental Eagle would be borne by the First Battalion. The other battalions would carry only "*fanions*," small pennon-shaped flags. Each would have one "*fanion*," a plain serge flag, of a distinctive colour for each battalion, without any mark or device on it, beyond the number of the battalion.

The Imperial edict, issued early in 1808, laid down that for the special protection of the Regimental Eagle in battle a commissioned officer and two picked veterans were to be appointed as the "Eagle-Guard," replacing the sergeant-major and escort of the Battalion Eagles. The three were to be known as the First, Second, and Third Eagle-Bearers or "*Porte-Aigles*." The officer to whose special charge the Regimental Eagle itself was committed was to be a senior lieutenant, "a man of proved valour, with not less than ten years' Army service, including service on the battlefield in four campaigns," specified as those of Ulm, Austerlitz, Jena, and Friedland. He would receive captain's pay, and wear a gold-laced cocked hat and gold epaulettes. The two other *Porte-Aigles* were to be, in Napoleon's own words, "*deux braves*," of ten years' service in the ranks, and "*non-lettrés*." On the last qualification, indeed, Napoleon laid peculiar stress. The two were to be, as the Emperor himself put it:

> Men who could neither read nor write, so that their only hope of promotion should be through acts of special courage and

devotion.

They would receive lieutenants' pay, have special privileges, and wear four gold lace *chevrons* on their arms. Only the Emperor could nominate or degrade *Porte-Aigles*. The Second and Third *Porte-Aigles* were to carry no weapons except heavy pistols, "to blow out the brains of an enemy attempting to lay hands on an Eagle." These were Napoleon's own words as to that, in his order of February 18, 1808:

> *Pour éviter que l'ardeur dans la mêlée ne les détourne de leur unique objet, de la garde de l'Aigle, le sabre et l'épée leurs sont interdits. Ils n'auront d'autres armes que plusieurs paires de pistolets, d'emploi que de veiller froidement à brûler la cervelle de celui qui avancerait la main pour saisir l'Aigle.*

After the Wagram campaign of 1809 Napoleon substituted a helmet and defensive brass scale-epaulettes as the First *Porte-Aigle's* equipment. He gave the two soldiers of the Eagle-Guard a halberd each, with a pennon or banderol attached—Red for the Second *Porte-Aigle*, White for the Third—as well as a sword and a pair of large-bore pistols. The pennons were for use should mounted men attack the Eagle; "for fluttering in front of the horses in order to make them rear and plunge and upset their riders."[1]

Two more soldiers were added to the Eagle-Guard in 1813, as the Fourth and Fifth *Porte-Aigles*. They were armed with the same weapons as the others, and had respectively Yellow and Green pennons on their halberds.

Yet further to add to the prestige of the Eagles, Napoleon, after Wagram, decreed the institution of a Special Order of Military Merit, which he called the "Order of the *Trois Toisons d'Or*"—something

---

[1] Baron Lejeune, on the Imperial staff at Wagram, who was clever with his pencil, was specially desired by Napoleon to design the costume for the Eagle-Guard, as he himself relates. "Anxious to confer distinction on those brave fellows who had taken part in the actual defence of the flag, the Eagle of their regiment, Napoleon conceived the idea of giving them a costume and equipment which should mark them out as specially honoured, and at the same time be suitable to the duties they had to per-form. The Emperor therefore sent for me and asked me to make a sketch of a costume such as he wished to give to what he called his 'Eagle-Guard,' or those non-commissioned officers whose office it was to surround and defend the actual standard-bearers. The chief weapons of each were to be a pistol, a sword, and a lance, so that in the heat of the battle they would never have to trouble themselves about loading a gun. There was to be gold on their epaulettes, sword-belts, and helmets. I made a drawing and took it to the Emperor, and he sent it to the Minister of War with his own instructions on the subject."

on the lines of our own Victoria Cross—certain of the provisions of which had direct reference to the Eagles. The decoration was to be conferred on men, whatever their rank, "distinguished in the defence of the Eagle of their regiment." Also, according to the 6th Article of the Constitution of the Order, "*Les Aigles des régiments qui ont assisté avec distinction aux grandes batailles seront décorés de l'Ordre des Trois Toisons d'Or.*"[2]

The special distinction of having the badge of the Legion of Honour affixed to its Eagle as a decoration to the regimental standard was in 1812 granted to one corps, the celebrated 57th. It was as a reward for magnificent intrepidity displayed under the eyes of Napoleon at the battle of Borodino. The 57th had at the same time a further and unique mark of Imperial regard awarded to it. Napoleon ordered that a representation of the badge of the Legion of Honour should be stamped on the uniform buttons of the regiment. No corps of the Grand Army, perhaps, had a finer fighting tradition than this splendid regiment the same "*Terrible 57me qui rien n'arrête,*" of the Army of Italy; which, too, as has been said, Napoleon singled out for a special word of encouragement on the morning of Austerlitz; calling to them as he rode past, "You will remember today, Fifty-seventh, how I once named you '*Le Terrible'!*"

But, with regard to the Regimental Eagles of 1808, even for Napoleon it was one thing to decree the abolition of Battalion Eagles, and another to obtain compliance with the order that the surplus Eagles should be returned to the War Minister for laying up at the Invalides.

A number of second and third battalions of regiments stationed at places out of the way of direct Imperial inspection—in garrisons

---

2. Colonel Lejeune was again called in to design the decoration for the Order, and has recorded what Napoleon said to him. "'The Order of the Golden Fleece,' he said, 'is typical of victory; my Eagles have triumphed over the Golden Fleeces of the King of Spain and the Emperors of Germany, so I mean to create for the French Empire an Imperial Order of the Three Golden Fleeces. The sign of this order shall be my own Eagle with outspread wings, holding in each of its talons one of the ancient Golden Fleeces it has carried off; whilst hanging from its beak it will proudly display the Fleece I now institute.' He then took a pen and roughly marked out the size I was to make my drawing. . . . I made the drawings as desired, and he issued the order accordingly. The institution of the new Order was duly announced in the *Moniteur*; but the terms of the treaty of peace compelled him to suppress a distinction the chief aim of which had been to humiliate the conquered countries of Spain and Austria."

beyond the frontiers, in subjugated countries, or in the remaining overseas possessions of France—continued for some time to evade the order recalling their Eagles. No doubt, too, they were unwilling to part with standards some of which had led the corps under fire at Austerlitz and Jena.

Napoleon had to repeat his order of recall twice: once during 1809; the second time in 1811. That second order was the outcome of a discovery made by the Emperor himself. At an Imperial review of the troops of the Amsterdam and North Holland garrisons on October 12, 1810, three of the regiments had the temerity to parade before the Emperor's eyes with four Eagles apiece—one to each battalion. Such flagrant disobedience could not be overlooked; and then subsequent inquiries brought out the fact that elsewhere there were many Battalion Eagles which had similarly been retained against orders. An additional discovery was made at the same time, that the Fourth-Battalion Eagles had been supplied surreptitiously, through some official at the Ministry of War, entirely without Napoleon's knowledge.

It made Napoleon excessively angry. He complained bitterly to Marshal Berthier at the way in which the department which had to do with the standards of the Army had been mismanaged. "*La partie des drapeaux des régiments,*" he declared, "*est aujourd'hui dans un grand chaos.*" To the Minister of War, General Clarke, Duc de Feltre, Napoleon sent a stinging letter of rebuke.

With the letter went the draft of yet another decree, to be communicated to every corps in the service.

> I only give one Eagle per regiment of infantry, one per regiment of cavalry, one per regiment of artillery, one per regiment of special *gendarmerie*. None to the departmental companies or guards of honour.
>
> No corps may possess an Eagle which has not been bestowed by my own hand.
>
> All regiments, further, of whatever denomination, if they did not receive the Eagle they are authorised to possess from the hand of the Emperor in person, either directly on parade, or through a regimental deputation, must return it to the Ministry of War for the will of His Majesty to be declared as to that Eagle.
>
> All other corps are to carry '*fanions,*' ordinary flags. Infantry regiments reduced below 1,000 men in strength, and cavalry regiments of less than 500 men, cannot retain their Eagle, and

must return it to the *dépôt*. They will be accorded a standard (*drapeau*) without the Eagle.

All the infantry regiments now in possession of an Eagle per battalion, and cavalry with one per squadron, are to send the extra-regulation Eagles at once to Paris, to be kept (*déposées*) at the Invalides until they can be placed in the 'Temple of Glory' (*the Church of the Madeleine, then being rebuilt*).

"*Jusqu'à ce qu'elles puissent être misées dans le Temple de la Gloire,*" was what Napoleon wrote.

Three of the British trophy-Eagles now at Chelsea, it may be remarked in passing, bear the number "82." They came into our hands in February 1809, at the surrender of Martinique to a conjoint British military and naval expedition. The 82nd was one of the regiments referred to as out of the way of direct inspection; in garrison across the Atlantic. It had not obeyed the order of 1808 to return its Second and Third Battalion Eagles to Paris—with the result that three Eagles at Chelsea represent the misfortune of this one regiment.

> The First Battalion, (*ordered Napoleon in his decree of 1811,*) is to carry the Eagle: the other battalions will have each a *fanion*, quite plain, as follows: 2nd Battalion, White; 3rd, Red; 4th, Blue. Where certain regiments may possess additional battalions, these are to have, the 5th a Green *fanion*, the 6th a Yellow *fanion*.[3]

In 1813, in Napoleon's conscript army levied to replace the host destroyed in Russia, the newly raised Line regiments, and "Provisional-Regiments," made up of the amalgamated *dépôt* battalions of various corps, had to earn their Eagles on the battlefield. Napoleon, ordered:

> No newly raised regiment is to receive an Eagle until after His Majesty has been satisfied with its service before the enemy.

The flags issued in 1808, and after that, to go with the Regimental Eagles, were much more elaborate than those of the Champ de Mars. They had white diamond-shaped centre panels, similar to those in the flags presented on the Field of Mars, but with Imperial crowns embroidered in gold on the red and blue upper corners of the flag, and golden Eagles on the lower corners. Gold embroidered wreaths of laurel, encircling the Imperial monogram "N." divided off the crowns

---

3. They were to be merely identifying tokens. "If by misfortune," Napoleon went so far as to say, "*fanions* should fall into the enemy's hands, it will be apparent from their plain appearance that their capture is a matter of no account." "*Une affaire sans consequence*" were Napoleon's words.

above from the Eagles below. A border of gold fringe round the entire flag, embroidered with bees, was another new enrichment. In these flags the regimental battle-honour inscriptions on the reverse side of the white centre space in the former flags appeared in a revised from. Only victories of importance since the institution of the Empire, and at which Napoleon had commanded in person, were admitted. Ulm, Austerlitz, Jena, Eylau, Fried-land, Eckmühl, Essling, Wagram, constituted the full list from which selection was made.

One regiment alone was allowed to record an earlier victory:— the Imperial Guard. They preserved their "Marengo" honour. Inscriptions such as "*Le 75e arrive et bât l'ennemi,*" "*J'etais tranquille, le 32e etait là,*" and the others which had been allowed on the flags of the Field of Mars, recalling deeds of the Army of Italy, disappeared from the revised pattern of 1808. A new inscription was specially authorised for the flag of one regiment, in honour of a feat of great distinction during the Wagram campaign. The 84th of the Line was permitted to inscribe "*Un contre dix*—*Grätz, 1809*"—but that only lasted for three years; the inscription was ordered to be taken off in 1811.

The design of the flag introduced in 1808 held until 1814. A less elaborate design was adopted for the Eagle-standards of the "Hundred Days," two specimens of which are in this country—the Waterloo trophies at Chelsea.

Attractive and handsome as the new flag was, the Army, as before, looked on it as but an appendage, as merely "*l'ornement de l'Aigle.*" The Eagle at the head of the staff, by itself, was all that nine soldiers out of ten troubled about. Not a few regiments, indeed, when on service, removed the flags altogether from their Eagle-poles and displayed as their standard the Eagle only. Particularly was this the case in Spain, where many regiments were in the field continuously, in some instances, for over six years—from 1808 to 1814. Asked one day after the Peninsular War about the inscription and battle-honours on the flag of his regiment, an infantry *chef de bataillon* frankly confessed that he had "never set eyes on it!" The silken flag, he explained:

> Had been removed from the Eagle-pole before he first joined as a lieutenant, and had always, as he understood, been kept at the *dépôt* of the corps in France, rolled up and locked away in the regimental chest. The Eagle on its bare pole was all he had ever seen.

Said another officer:

We never spoke of the regiment's 'colours,' and never saw them. We spoke only of 'the Eagle.'

This may be added. Napoleon was scrupulously exact in showing respect to the Eagle of a regiment whenever he passed one; whether on the line of march, or in bivouac, under a sentry, with the Eagle-Guard near at hand, resting horizontally on a support of piled muskets with bayonets fixed. If on horseback, Napoleon always uncovered and bowed low; if on the line of march, he sometimes stopped his carriage in passing, and got out, saluted the Eagle, and said a few words about the regiment's battle record to the Eagle-Guard.

Between the review on the Field of Mars in 1804 and the overthrow on the plains of Leipsic in 1814 the number of regiments in the Grand Army increased continuously, requiring the presentation of many new Eagles. Forty-four were presented in the period to the infantry alone; to the regiments of the Line bearing numbers from the 113th to 156th; besides others to the regiments of the "Middle Guard "and "Young Guard," and to two additional regiments of *Cuirassiers*. In every case Napoleon, in accordance with the stipulation that he so insisted on, made the presentation in person, with his own hand.

In not a few instances, indeed, the ceremony took place on campaign; and for one of these exceptionally interesting occasions we have available the notes of an eyewitness. It was at the presentation of the Eagle of the 126th Regiment of the Line, in Germany, in 1813.

Napoleon made his appearance in his campaigning uniform, the dark green undress of the *Chasseurs* of the Guard, and mounted as usual on a grey charger. His staff, all brilliant in full dress, attended him. Approaching the scene at a canter, they all slowed down to a walk as they neared where the regiment stood, with its battalions parading every available man, and drawn up to form three sides of a hollow square. The new Eagle, enveloped in the leather casing in which it had been brought from France, lay on a pile of drums on one flank of the First Battalion, and a little in advance. The fourth, or open, side of the square was for the Imperial staff, who drew up there, while the Emperor by himself rode into the middle of the square. As Napoleon reined up, the regimental drums beat the *Appel*, and the officers of the regiment stepped to the front, with swords at the carry, and formed in line before the Emperor.

Marshal Berthier, chief of the Headquarter Staff, then rode across to where the Eagle lay. He dismounted to receive it at the hands of the First *Porte-Aigle*, the Eagle being uncased at the same time. Berthier saluted the Eagle; then, holding it erect with both hands, the marshal bore it ceremoniously along in front of the row of officers, who saluted with lowered swords as the Eagle passed, the drums of the regiment now beating a long roll. Halting close in front of Napoleon, Berthier inclined the Eagle forward in salute, and the Emperor, on his side, uncovered and bowed in return. Then, drawing his glove from his left hand, Napoleon raised his hand and extended it towards the Eagle. He held the reins, according to his custom, in his right hand. Napoleon began his address to the corps in a deep, impressive tone:

> Soldiers of the 126th Regiment of the Line, I entrust to you the Eagle of France! It is to serve to you ever as your rallying-point. You swear to me never to abandon it, but with life! You swear never to suffer an affront to it for the honour of France! You swear ever to prefer death for it to dishonour! You swear!

The last words were pronounced with a peculiar stress, in a very solemn tone, with intense energy.

Instantly the officers of the regiment replied. Holding their swords on high, with one voice they shouted: "We swear!"

The next moment the words were taken up and repeated enthusiastically by the men: "We swear!"

Berthier, on that, formally handed the Eagle over to the colonel of the regiment, and the Emperor, raising his hand to his hat in salute to the Eagle, turned to rejoin the Staff and ride off elsewhere.

On the afternoon before the three days' Battle of Leipsic opened, on October 15, 1813, Napoleon, on the Marchfeldt, in the very presence of the enemy, presented with these formalities new Eagles to three newly raised regiments.

CHAPTER 7

Before the Enemy at Aspern and Wagram

Napoleon's regimental Eagles made their debut on the battlefield in the Wagram campaign of 1809, when Austria challenged Napoleon to a second trial of strength in her premature attempt to achieve the liberation of Germany. The gallant deeds of the regiments that fought round the Eagles in that war are commemorated on the standards of the French Army today by the legend "Wagram, 1809," a name and date that stand as the comprehensive memento of a conflict that lasted four months, and included no fewer than ten fiercely fought battles. They are superabundant as a fact; it would almost need a book by itself to tell the full story. It must suffice therefore to take here only these, picked out at random, as typical of the rest.

This is the achievement that "Wagram, 1809," inscribed in golden letters on the silken tricolour standard of the present-day 65th of the Line, serves to recall.

Napoleon's 65th was one of the regiments of Marshal Davout's corps at Ratisbon, where Davout had been stationed on the eve of the outbreak of the war. He was hastily recalled on the Austrians opening hostilities and advancing in greatly superior force. Davout fell back at once, leaving behind him the 65th to hold the very important bridge over the Danube at Ratisbon for forty-eight hours, until the bulk of his corps had gained a sufficient start on their way.

The 65th had not long to wait for the enemy. Within twelve hours of the marshal's retirement the Austrians swooped down on Ratisbon to seize the bridge. Two of their army corps led the advance. One took possession of the city, sending troops forward to secure the bridge. Part of the other crossed the Danube in the neighbourhood of the city in boats, in order to cut off and capture the French troops left behind. It was expected that in the presence of so over-powering an enemy the single French regiment holding the bridge would not venture to make a serious defence. The Austrians did not know the 65th.

To oppose the first comers three battalions of the 65th barricaded and loopholed the houses nearest the bridge on that side. The remaining battalion held a fortified outwork, or bridge-head, across the river.

For a whole day the battalions in the city held the Austrians at bay, resisting desperately in the streets and from house to house. Four hundred Austrian prisoners, together with an Austrian regimental standard and three other flags, testified to the way they did their duty. The battalion holding the bridge-head on the farther side of the river made meanwhile a no less stubborn resistance and kept the enemy off until nightfall. Then, however, it was found that their ammunition was exhausted. The three battalions fighting the city were by that time in a no less desperate plight. They on their side had been forced back to their last defences among the houses immediately surrounding the approach to the bridge. Still, though, they kept up a fierce resistance, at the last using cartridges taken from the *cartouche*-boxes of the Austrian prisoners and their own dead and wounded comrades. They held out until further defence of the bridge was impossible, until indeed further resistance at all was hopeless.

But the regimental Eagle? What was to become of that? The Eagle of the 65th must at all cost be kept from being surrendered into an enemy's hands. What was to be done? At first it was suggested that an officer, known to be a good swimmer, should try to swim down the river with it in the dark until he could land safely on the farther bank, after which he should do his best to make his way to wherever Napoleon might be, there to render personally into his hands the sacred Eagle. But the other surviving officers were loath to part with their treasured standard in that way. The risk of a man getting through the Austrians who were swarming on the other side of the Danube was considered too great. It was then suggested to sink it in the Danube, noting the spot, so as to be able to fish it up again on some future day.

Colonel Coutard, in command of the 65th, however, was against that. They might never be able, or have time, to find it at the bottom of a deep and swiftly flowing river like the Danube. He proposed to conceal the Eagle in the ground, burying it in some secret place. There it might without difficulty be recovered later on and brought back to France. The colonel's proposal was assented to, and then a further suggestion was made. Their Eagle should be given a fitting shroud by wrapping round it the captured Austrian flags they had taken that afternoon. That would preserve the trophies also for future days when the fortune of war again favoured the regiment. The idea was eagerly taken up, and the Eagle was buried in a cellar, wrapped up in the Austrian flags.

After that, at the very last, just as the Austrians were about to launch another attack it was impossible to withstand, Colonel Coutard had the *chamade* beaten, and the 65th surrendered. They were granted, as they well deserved, the honours of war, and were for the time being confined under guard in the city. Their captivity, however, was not for long. Their release came about in a very few days on the Austrian troops hurriedly evacuating Ratisbon before Napoleon's triumphant advance.[1] The Eagle was now dug up, and Colonel Coutard, with a deputation from the regiment, waited on Napoleon on his arrival, to present the Eagle before him, still wrapped up in the three captured Austrian flags.

In recognition of the endurance that the 65th had shown, the colonel was created a Baron of the Empire; crosses of the Legion of Honour were distributed broadcast among all ranks; forty soldiers who had shown exceptional gallantry in the fighting were, as a reward, specially transferred to the Old Guard.

Such is the fine story that the battle-honour "Wagram, 1809," lettered in gold on the regimental tricolour of the present-day 65th of the Line in the French Army commemorates, and care is taken that every young soldier on joining is made acquainted with it.

---

1. It was during the battle at Ratisbon that Napoleon, according to the story, was wounded for the only time in his life, and had to dismount, and, in the sight of the dismayed soldiers, have his wound dressed by a surgeon, the news causing consternation through the ranks of the whole army far and wide. Indeed, only this year there was placed in the Army Museum at the Invalides, as an historic relic of the highest interest, "the fragment of a shell that struck Napoleon at Ratisbon on the 23rd of April, 1809, and gave him the only wound he ever received in battle." The truth is revealed in M. Combes' journal, which, after telling how Napoleon carefully concealed everything which might detract from his reputation among his soldiers for invulnerability, enumerates his wounds in detail. After his death half a dozen scars were found on his body. There was the mark of a wound on his head, a hole above his left knee, either from a bayonet or a lance, the mark of the injury received at Ratisbon, another on one hand, and on the body the scars of sword cuts and slashes.

Equally fine as an exploit, and yet more renowned for the exceptional honour that Napoleon paid to the Eagle of the regiment, was the splendid heroism that the 84th of the Line displayed at Grätz in Styria. That episode of the campaign, indeed, is commemorated by a double battle-honour on the flag of the 84th of the modern French Army. Both "Wagram, 1809," and "*Un contre dix—Grätz, 1809*" are inscribed in golden letters on its tricolour. Napoleon himself, as has been said, bestowed the honour of the unique inscription on the regimental flag. He had also the words "*Un contre dix*" incised on the square tablet supporting the Eagle itself. Here is the story of the exploit as related by one of Napoleon's staff officers in the campaign, Colonel Lejeune:

> Amongst all these battles and victories there was one action so remarkable and so brilliant that I feel impelled to describe it here from the accounts of eye-witnesses. During the taking of Grätz by General Broussier, and when the struggle was at its fiercest, Colonel Gambin of the 84th Regiment was ordered, with two of his battalions, to attack the suburb of St. Leonard, where he made from four to five hundred prisoners. This vigorous assault led General Guilay on the enemy's side to imagine he had to deal with a whole army, and he hurried to the aid of the suburb with considerable forces. Gambin did not hesitate to attack them, and he took from them the cemetery of the Graben suburb, but was in his turn invested by the Austrian battalions, and found it impossible to rejoin the main body of the French.
>
> He accepted the situation, spent the whole of the night in fortifying the cemetery and the adjoining houses, and, his ammunition being exhausted, he actually kept at bay some 10,000 assailants with the bayonet alone, even making several sorties to carry off the *cartouches* on the dead bodies with which his attacks had strewn the ground near the cemetery. General Guilay now directed the fire of all his guns and five fresh battalions on this handful of brave men, who had already for nineteen hours withstood a whole army. General Broussier was at last able to send Colonel Nagle of the 92nd, with two battalions, to the aid of the 84th. The enemy vainly endeavoured to prevent the two regiments from meeting.
>
> Colonel Nagle overthrew every obstacle, got into the cemetery, and after embracing each other the two officers, with

their united forces, flung themselves upon the Austrians, took 500 of them prisoners, with two flags, and carried the suburb of Graben by assault, finding no less than 1,200 Austrian corpses in the streets. When the Emperor heard of this feat of arms, he was anxious to confer the greatest distinction he could on the 84th Regiment, and ordered that its banner should henceforth bear in letters of gold the proud inscription, 'One against ten.'

Seldom indeed did the soldiers of Napoleon encounter a more determined enemy than the Austrians proved themselves in the war of 1809. At Aspern, the battle on the Danube near Vienna, where Napoleon experienced his first defeat on the Continent, more than one Eagle came within an ace of being taken. The Eagle of the 9th of the Line, for instance, to save it from what appeared to be imminent capture, was actually buried on the battlefield in the middle of the fighting. One of the men of the 9th, wrote:

> Our colonel took the Eagle of the regiment, pulled it from its staff, and, after digging a hole in the ground with a pioneer's tool, buried and concealed there our rallying signal to prevent it from falling into the enemy's hands.

It was, though, after all, an unnecessary precaution. The hard-pressed 9th were rescued at the last moment, whereupon the Eagle made its reappearance.

Three other Eagles, less fortunate, are now in the Austrian Army Museum at Vienna; those of the 35th of the Line and of the 95th and 106th. The Eagle of the 35th was taken on the Italian frontier near Lake Garda, in a surprise attack at daybreak on the camp of the Viceroy, Eugène Beauharnais, by the troops of the Archduke John. The other two fell into Austrian hands on the night of the opening attack at Wagram, victims of a panic that suddenly seized one of the French columns. It had led the attack on the centre of the Austrian position with brilliant success.

Two thousand prisoners and five standards had been taken, and the French were advancing exultantly, when the Austrians counter-attacked with fresh troops, headed by the Archduke Charles in person. The French resisted stubbornly, and at first successfully. They held their own until, in the midst of furious hand-to-hand fighting, they were suddenly charged by cavalry. It was late evening, and in the gathering dusk a sudden panic seized a regiment on the flank. The panic spread instantly to the whole of the attacking column. All order was lost forthwith. The soldiers gave way in confusion, broke up, and went racing back headlong, a mob of fugitives, down the steep ascent that a few minutes before they had so gallantly won.

As they went back in a tumultuous rush, fresh French troops, coming up to their support, "in the darkness mistook the retreating host for enemies and fired upon it; they, in their turn, were overthrown by the torrent of fugitives." The Austrian prisoners taken in the advance escaped, the captured Austrian standards were recaptured, and two Eagles disappeared in the dark amid the turmoil. Those are the two now at Vienna.

Fortunately for Napoleon the Austrian leaders did not realise the smashing nature of the blow they had dealt. The fate of Napoleon's Empire otherwise might have been decided on that night. Unaware that the panic had "spread an indescribable alarm through the French centre as far as the tent of the Emperor, they stopped the advance, sounded the recall, and fell back to their original positions."

Of the Eagle-bearers of four regiments at Aspern, the 2nd, 16th, 37th, and 67th of the Line, not one came through the day alive, but the Eagles were saved. They were the four regiments that took the village of Aspern and held it all day and till after dark—12,000 men against 80,000 enemies. The village was the all-important key of the battlefield. Its defence was of supreme moment, for only part of Napoleon's army had been able to get across the Danube as yet, the main bridge of boats having been broken down and swept away.

They had seized Aspern at the outset, but had been forced to fall back before an Austrian counter-attack, returning after that to recapture it, and hold it until the end.

Marshal Masséna led the onset that retook the village. A French officer describes:

> The Austrians had entered Aspern, and it was absolutely necessary to dislodge them. Masséna therefore, who had had all his horses killed, marched on foot with drawn sword at the head of the Grenadiers of the Molitor division, forced his way into the village, crowded as it was with Austrians, drove them out, and pursued them for some twelve or fourteen yards beyond the houses. But here the French troops found themselves face to face with the strong force under Hiller, Bellegarde, and Hohenzollern, advancing rapidly in their direction. It was hopeless for the division to attempt to engage such superior numbers in the open plain, so Masséna recalled the pursuers, and ordered them to hold Aspern. The enemy, ashamed apparently of this

first defeat, returned to the charge with 80,000 men and more than a hundred pieces of cannon, which were soon pointed on the village.

It was impossible to stop the onrush of the Austrians. In spite of every effort of Masséna, who with his artillery "opened fire upon the densely packed masses of men, every shot working terrible havoc amongst them," they swarmed forward to the outskirts of the village. A life-and-death struggle in defence began.

In a very few minutes the village was completely surrounded by troops; and hidden from view in the dense clouds of smoke from the cannon, the musketry, and the fires which at once broke out, the combatants, almost suffocated by the smoke, crossed bayonets without being able to see each other; but neither side gave way a step, and for more than an hour the terrible attack and desperate defence went on amongst the ruins of the burning houses.

It was during the Austrian opening attack on the outskirts of Aspern that at one point a French regiment—the number of the regiment is not given in any account—was forced apart from the rest, and driven back in disorder beyond the village. Its colonel was killed, and, though the Eagle was kept from falling into the enemy's hands, the regiment fell back in confusion. Napoleon witnessed the check and galloped to intercept the troops as they were retreating. Riding into the midst of the fugitives, he personally rallied them, and then called angrily for the colonel. There was no answer from any one, and in high anger Napoleon again called for the colonel. Then somebody made the reply that the colonel was dead.

"I know that!" answered Napoleon sharply. "I asked where he was!"

"We left him in the village."

"What! you left your colonel's body in the hands of the enemy? Go back instantly, find it, and remember that a good regiment should always be able to produce both its colonel and its Eagle!"

Napoleon's stinging rebuke did its work. The men at once re-formed and turned back. Charging forward with a rush, they forced their way through to where the colonel had fallen and recovered the body. Then they joined in with the other defenders at the village, and did their duty to the end. The colonel's body was brought back and laid before Napoleon next morning.

The fearful contest in Aspern went on until four in the afternoon, by which time the Austrians had succeeded in taking half the village. They could not, however, get beyond that.

> Masséna still held the church and cemetery, and was struggling to regain what he had lost. Five times in less than three hours he took and retook the cemetery, the church, and the village, without being able to call to his aid the Legrand division, which he was obliged to hold in reserve to cover Aspern on the right and keep the enemy from getting in on that side. Throughout this awful struggle Masséna stood beneath the great elms on the green opposite the church, calmly indifferent to the fall of the branches brought down upon his head by the showers of grape-shot and bullets, keenly alive to all that was going on, his look and voice, stern as the *quos ego* of Virgil's angry Neptune, inspiring all who surrounded him with irresistible strength.

Even when the sun went down:

> The struggle was far from being over, and the awful battle was still raging in the streets and behind the walls of the village of Aspern. The enemy, irritated at the stubborn resistance of so small a body of troops, redoubled their efforts to dislodge them before nightfall, and went on fighting by the light of the conflagrations alone. The history of our wars relates no more thrilling incident than this long and obstinate struggle, in which our troops, disheartened by the ever-fresh difficulties with which they had to contend, worn out by fatigue, and horrified by the carnage round them, were kept at their posts by the example and exhortations of Masséna and his officers alone. General Molitor had lost some half of his men, and the enemy were hurrying up from every side. The struggle was maintained under these terrible conditions until eleven o'clock, when we remained masters of Aspern and of the whole line between it and Essling.

Five regiments of the French Army of today commemorate a splendid Eagle-incident in the name "Wagram, 1809," on their colours; the final charge of Macdonald's column which saved and decided the battle for Napoleon, besides gaming a marshal's baton for the Scottish officer who achieved the feat. That was on the final battlefield of Wagram itself, the outcome of which tremendous encounter settled the fate of the war.

It was the culminating event of the battle. The crisis was at hand for both armies when the order was given to Macdonald to go forward. On the Austrian side the powerful and fresh corps of the Archduke John was rapidly nearing the scene, and the fortune of the day yet wavered in the balance. Napoleon, as his last hope and final effort to break the stubborn Austrian array of the Archduke Charles' host which still confronted him, defiant still after ten hours of charges and counter-charges, holding out tenaciously in a strong position, massed his reserves and sent them at the centre of the Austrians, to press forward in a vast column of closely formed battalions. They went at the enemy with all the daring of a forlorn hope.

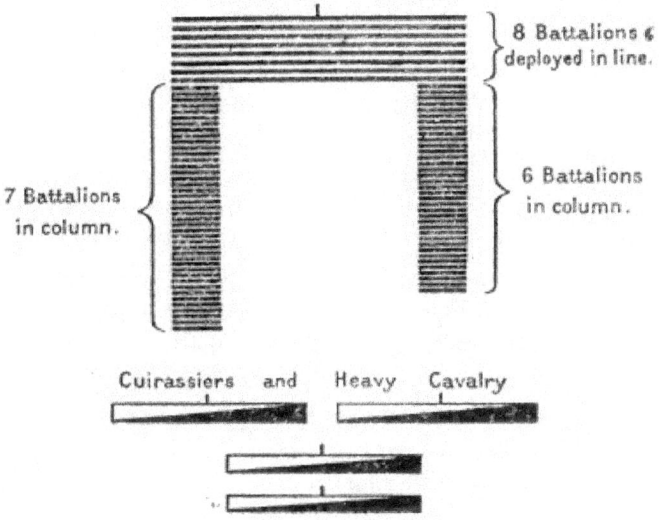

Moving steadily forward through the wreck of guns, the dead, and the dying, this undaunted column, preceded by its terrific battery incessantly firing, pushed on half a league beyond the front at other points of the enemy's line. In proportion as it advanced, however, it became enveloped in fire; the guns were gradually dismounted or silenced, and the infantry emerged through their wreck to the front. The Austrians drew off their front line upon their second, and both, falling back, formed a sort of wall on each side of the French column, from whence issued a dreadful fire of grape and musketry on either flank of the assailants. Still Macdonald pushed on with unconquerable resolution: in the midst of a frightful storm of bullets his ranks were unshaken; the destiny of Europe was in his hands, and he was worthy of the mission.

The loss he experienced, however, was enormous; at every step huge chasms were made in his ranks, whole files were struck down by cannon-shot, and at length his eight dense battalions were reduced to 1,500 men. Isolated in the midst of enemies, this band of heroes was compelled to halt. The Empire rocked to its foundations: it was the rout of a similar body of the Guard at Waterloo that hurled Napoleon to the rock of St. Helena.

The five regiments which formed the spear-point of the attack had paraded that morning 6,000 strong. They numbered now, the survivors, less than 300. They were at the extreme point of the advance, but were held fast and unable to go farther. The enemy were on every side of them, for in the last moments they had pressed on beyond touch of the troops that were following next, The Austrians saw their chance to charge them and annihilate them before the approach of French supports to the main column could get near. But General Broussier, the brigadier in command of the leading troops, knew his work and his men. As they halted he rapidly rallied the fragments of the nearest regiments and formed them in a single square. They drew up under the *feu d'enfer* of cannon and musketry, three deep in front, with, in the centre, held up on high, the five Eagles of the regiments; so as not to weaken the front, the firing line, "the Eagles were held up only by men who had been wounded."

Broussier marked the massing of the Eagles in the midst; and, as the firing round them for one moment seemed to lull, raising his voice, he called out for all to hear: "Soldiers, swear to die here to the last man round your Eagles!" "*Jurez moi, soldats, de mourir tous, jusqu'au dernier, autour de vos Aigles!*" were the brigadier's words. But there was fortunately no need for all to die. At that moment reinforcing troops came up, with the Young Guard at their head. The column, on that, moved forward again with a steady front:

> And the archduke, despairing now of maintaining his position, when assailed at the crisis of the day by such a formidable accession of force in the now broken part of his line, gave directions for a general retreat.

The Eagles had done their part and the Battle of Wagram was won.

CHAPTER 8

"The Eagle With the Golden Wreath" in London

There are thirteen of Napoleon's Eagles in England, among the trophies of the British Army at Chelsea Royal Hospital; or, to speak strictly, twelve Eagles and a "dummy "Eagle, the later reproduction of a very famous trophy, gone now, unfortunately, to the melting-pot of a thieves' kitchen. It is with the dummy Eagle, as it may be called for short, without disrespect to its gallant custodians, and five of the twelve Eagles at Chelsea, that we are for the immediate moment concerned. That represents the first of Napoleon's trophies won by British soldiers in hand-to-hand fight—the once celebrated "Eagle with the Golden Wreath."

The story opens on Saturday morning, May 18, 1811, a day that was a great occasion for Londoners. For the first time, on that Saturday, trophies taken from Napoleon were publicly displayed in the British Capital, and no pains were spared to make the most of the event. An elaborate and dramatic ceremonial was ordained for the occasion by the authorities at the instance of the Prince Regent. It was like nothing else of the kind ever witnessed or heard of in England before.

On many another day in bygone times London had been the scene of stately martial pageants in which the victor's spoils from many battle-fields were borne in triumph, amid blare of trumpets and clash of drums, to be deposited with due ceremony in their allotted resting-places. So had it been when the Marlborough trophies from Blenheim and Ramillies, the captured flags from Dettingen, Louisburg, and Minden, were borne along the crowded streets, preceded by bands playing triumphant music and accompanied by armed escorts of Foot and Horse.

Another Saturday, seventeen years before, May 17, 1794, had been the last occasion of trophy-flags being displayed in London, when the captured French Republican standards of the garrison of Martinique were publicly carried through the streets by Life Guards and Grenadiers, with the band of the First Guards leading the way and the Tower guns booming out an artillery *feu de joie*, from St. James's Palace to St. Paul's, to be received at the great west doors of the cathedral by the dean and chapter, and laid up "as a lasting memorial of the success of his Majesty's Arms." Some of the flags then displayed hang in the Hall of Chelsea Hospital today.

So, too, had it been in London in yet earlier times, in the far off, unhappy days of Civil War in England, when the citizens of those periods, in turn, saw the spoils of Bosworth, and of Mars-ton Moor and Naseby, of Worcester, Preston, and Dunbar, paraded through their midst, escorted by mail-clad men-at-arms, on the way to be hung up exultingly in St. Paul's Cathedral or in Westminster Hall. With his own Royal banners from Marston Moor and Naseby drooping down overhead from the roof of Westminster Hall, Charles the First faced his judges and heard his fate. But never before in London had so elaborately designed a ceremony attended the display of trophies taken from any enemy, as that planned for the *Royal Depositum*, as it was officially styled, of the first of the captured Eagles of Napoleon to be received in England.

There was to be a special display of trophies the London newspapers announced some days beforehand. The newspapers had not spared themselves in working up public interest. At the outset they had told how, on the night of March 24, Captain Hope, First A.D.C. to General Graham, had arrived in London with the *Barrosa* despatches and a "French Eagle with a wreath of gold," which, it was stated, "the general trusted his *aide de camp* might be permitted to lay at His Majesty's feet." Then Londoners were informed that the Barrosa Eagle was a trophy of unusual importance, and was being kept at the War Office, to be presented to the Prince Regent at the next *levée*. It was announced a week later that His Royal Highness had been so desirous of seeing it at once, that the War Minister, the Earl of Liverpool, instead of waiting five weeks for the *levée*, had already presented it to the Prince at Carlton House.

On that came the official notification that "the Eagle with the Golden Wreath," as the trophy was everywhere styled, together with a number of other French trophies, which had been previously received and had been some time stored away at the War Office pending instructions as to their disposal, would be deposited in the Chapel Royal, Whitehall, (now the Museum of the Royal United Service Institution). "The *Royal Depositum* ceremony will be very grand, and the martial music appropriate to the occasion, and as the orders have been issued by direction of his Royal Highness the Prince Regent, the chapel will be thronged with nobility." So one journal notified; another remarking that "in addition to the great religious and military ceremony, an anthem is to be performed after the manner of the *Te Deum*."

Thus popular interest was aroused and kept alive in advance, and the selected Saturday morning proving fine and pleasant, with the prospect of a genial and sunny forenoon, Londoners turned out in large numbers to see the show.

To the Brigade of Guards it fell to carry out the ceremony of the military reception of the Eagles.

The "Parade in St. James's Park," which we know now as the Horse Guards Parade, was the appointed place for the display, and as the clock struck nine the preliminaries opened with the arrival of a large body of Guards' recruits who were to keep the ground. From quite an early hour a crowd had been gathering there and along the side of the Park. Soon afterwards the first of the troops designated to attend the ceremony began to arrive. These were several companies of the First Guards and Coldstreamers "in undress, with side arms." They formed line along either side of the parade-ground; on one side "extending from the corner of the Chancellor of the Exchequer's garden to the Egyptian gun"; on the opposite side, "from the Admiralty towards the Park." To right and left of the archway under the Horse Guards leading to Whitehall were drawn up the "recruiting parties stationed in the Home District."

At a quarter to ten came on the scene the first of the actors in the day's proceedings, the "King's Guard" of the day, "in their best uniforms, and with sprigs of oak and laurel in their hats." Marching up, headed by the combined bands of the First Guards and the Coldstreamers, with the regimental colour of the First Guards, they formed on the right, along the open side of the square, facing towards the Horse Guards. Following them, a few moments later, came the picked detachment appointed as the "trophy-escort," furnished jointly by the grenadier companies of the First Guards and the Coldstreamers.

All were in review-order full dress, "wearing long white gaiters, with oak and laurel leaves in their hats." A captain of the First Guards was in command; and the detachment was made up of two subalterns, four sergeants, and ninety-six rank and file. They took post on the left of the King's Guard. As the trophy-escort halted, up came another detachment of Guards, a hundred strong, with the Life Guards; marching across the square and through the Horse Guards archway to line the way thence to the doors of the Chapel Royal.

Towards ten o'clock privileged spectators were admitted within the square, "to stand at an appointed spot": several veteran generals, "in their best uniforms and powdered," as a newspaper reporter remarks; Lord Liverpool the War Minister; the Earl Marshal; the Speaker; the Spanish and Portuguese Ambassadors, both gorgeously attired; and "a number of beautiful and elegant ladies of distinction."

The Horse Guards clock struck ten, and as the last clanging stroke died away "the authorities" came clattering on to the ground on horseback: Sir David Dundas, commander-in-chief of the Army and governor of Chelsea Hospital, at the head of a number of other plumed and cocked-hatted generals in full uniform, together with the Headquarters Staff at the Horse Guards. Prominent in the glittering array of gold-laced red coats, "mounted on a cream-coloured Arab," was General Sir John Doyle, Colonel of the 87th Royal Irish Fusiliers; the regiment whose prowess at Barrosa had won the great trophy of the day—"the Eagle with the Golden Wreath."

With royal punctuality, as the clock chimed the half-hour, amid cheers from the crowd and the spectators filling the windows of the Horse Guards and Admiralty and other Government offices overlooking the ground, came riding up the three princes who were to preside at the ceremony—the Dukes of York, Cambridge, and Gloucester.

The display began forthwith.

Preceded by the two Guards' bands playing the "Grenadiers' March," the trophy-escort of grenadiers crossed the Parade at a slow step, and marched in four divisions, or "platoons," to the old Tilt Yard orderly-room under the Horse Guards. There the trophies had been taken beforehand to be in readiness for the ceremony. The grenadiers halted before the doors, and the trophies, twelve in number, were brought out by Lifeguardsmen from the Tilt Yard Guard and committed to the charge of twelve picked sergeants—six of the First Guards, six of the Coldstreamers—selected to bear them to the Chapel Royal.

The trophy-bearers carrying the Eagles then took post according to the date of the capture of each trophy; the earliest taken of the Eagles leading. In advance of all, immediately after the band, marched the three officers with swords drawn; the captain and the two subalterns. Then, with their flanking grenadiers as escort, a file to each trophy, came, one after the other, three Battalion Eagles of Napoleon's 82nd of the Line, surrendered at the capitulation of Martinique in 1809.

Immediately in rear marched No. 1 platoon of grenadiers; in the interval between the first trophy-group and the second. That consisted of the Regimental Eagle of the French 26th of the Line, surrendered at Martinique at the same time as the Eagles of the 82nd, and then that of the 66th of the Line, surrendered at the capitulation of Guadaloupe in 1810, with, just behind them, the all-important trophy of the day, the first Napoleonic Eagle captured—or, at any rate, taken possession of—by British soldiers on the battlefield: "the Eagle with the Golden Wreath"—that Eagle of Napoleon's 8th Regiment of the Line, won in hand-to-hand fight by the 87th Royal Irish Fusiliers at Barrosa.

Five of the Eagles had their silken tricolour flags still attached to the poles. The Barrosa Eagle had none: it showed simply a bare pole topped by the wreathed Eagle. The wreath, according to a newspaper reporter present, was:

> An honour conferred on the regiment for fine conduct at the Battle of Talavera, where they were opposed to the 87th; and, by a singular coincidence of circumstances, these regiments met in conflict at Barrosa and recognised each other.

As we shall see, the statement was a freak of journalistic imagination, without a scrap of fact behind the story, although, strangely, the legend holds to this day and reappears periodically in print. Adds the reporter, as to the appearance of the Eagle, recording this time what he actually saw:

> The Eagle is fixed on a square pedestal, and standing erect on one foot; the other raised as if grasping something; its wings expanded. It is about the size of a small pigeon, and appears to be made of bronze, or of some composition like pinchbeck, gold-gilt.

The "something" which the talons of the Eagle appeared to be grasping was the "thunderbolt," which was missing, having been either knocked out of its place in the scuffle on the battlefield, or stolen later by somebody for a relic. The wreath was really of gold. A couple of its leaves picked up on the field after the battle and given to Major Hugh Gough, the gallant commander of the 87th at Barrosa, are now in possession of one of that officer's descendants.

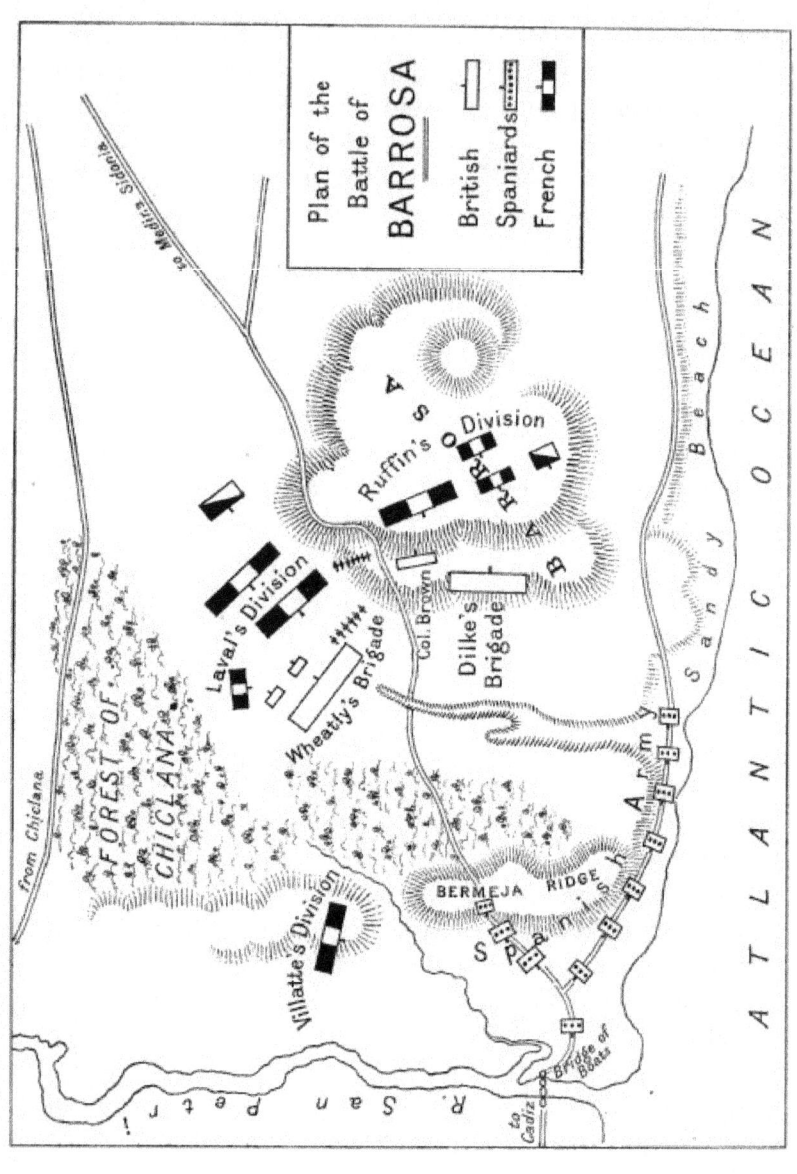

The second grenadier platoon divided the Eagles from the first three of the flag-trophies, borne in file, one by one, in the same way as the Eagles. The first in date of capture led; a French Republican standard taken in fight at Sir Ralph Abercrombie's victory at Alexandria, ten years before, and kept ever since at the War Office: "the Invincible's standard."

"As it is falsely called," adds the reporter; right for once. "So tattered is it," he continues, "that the mottoes are not legible; a bugle in the centre was the only figure we could distinguish." Two flags taken by Wellington's men in the Peninsula accompanied the Alexandria flag: "a Fort Standard," as it is described, and the battalion colour, or "*fanion*," of the Second Battalion of Napoleon's 5th of the Line. [1]

In rear of the colour of the 5th marched the third grenadier platoon, and the last three trophies sent to England by Wellington. Two were a pair of tattered German standards, the flags of the two battalions of a Prussian regiment in Napoleon's service, composed of unfortunate soldiers levied compulsorily during the French occupation of their country, and tramped off to Spain to meet their fate under British bullets. Each flag bore the legend "*L'Empereur des Français au Régiment Prussien*" on one side, and "*Valeur et Discipline*" on the other, and was mounted on a staff with a steel pike-head instead of an Eagle. They were silken flags of the ordinary Napoleonic pattern. The third flag of the group was that of a "provisional regiment"; also with a steel pike-head to its staff.

---

1. As to this last trophy, it was unfortunate from our point of view—since Fate willed that the 5th of the Line should lose its colours to an enemy—that one of the original Battalion Eagles of the corps had previously, in accordance with Napoleon's order of 1808, been returned to Paris. The half-winged Eagle of the 5th would have made a notable trophy for Chelsea Hospital. While heading an attack on an Austrian field-work in Masséna's battle at Caldiero on the Venetian frontier in November 1805, the Eagle was smashed from its staff by a grape-shot and dashed violently to the ground, with one wing shattered. At the same time the battalion recoiled before the terrific fire with which its charge was met. The Eagle saved the honour of the corps. Picking its battered remains up and waving it at arm's-length above his head, with a shout of "Come on, comrades! follow the Eagle," one of the officers rushed with it through the *mêlée* to the front and led the forlorn-hope onset that stormed the post. After that, the Eagle, lashed to the stump of its broken pole, went through the battle to the end, doing its part in rallying the battalion round it, to keep at bay greatly superior numbers of the enemy until relief arrived. There had been almost a mutiny in the 5th in 1808 when they were ordered to return their battle-scarred ensign to the Invalides, but the order was obeyed. Otherwise the half-winged Eagle would have been at Chelsea now.

From the Tilt Yard orderly-room the trophies and their escort-guard set off, as before, in slow time, the bands playing "God save the King!" The sergeants, carrying the Eagles and flags between the files of grenadiers, marched in the intervals between the four divisions "in double open-order with arms advanced." Right round the square they now passed, close along the lines of the troops drawn up, "the immense multitude rending the air with huzzas." In front of the First Guards, in front of the recruiting parties, in front of the long line of Coldstreamers, along each of the three sides of the square, paced the procession with martial pomp to the stately music of the two bands as they led the way. Then it proceeded along the fourth side of the square until it came face to face with the King's Guard, all standing with ordered arms, not at the present. There was a brief pause in front of the Colour of the King's Guard.

That was the supreme moment of the display. Now took place the formal act of obeisance to the victors; the formal act of abasement and humiliation for the vanquished. Amid redoubled cheering from all sides, the Eagles and the other flags were, one and all, formally dipped and prostrated. "The captured standards saluted and were lowered to the ground in token of submission."

The procession turned away in front of the King's Guard and led round in front of the three royal dukes, seated on their chargers, a little in advance of the commander-in-chief and Horse Guards Staff, at the centre of the parade-ground. Again, as they now passed before the royal trio, the hapless Eagles of Napoleon and the other French flags in turn were one by one made to pay homage, bowed grovelling to the dust; the crowd of onlookers shouting themselves hoarse "with," as we are told, "truly British huzzas."

After that the trophy procession marched across to the Horse Guards archway, and through to Whitehall and the Chapel Royal; between Life Guards on one side and more Foot Guards on the other, drawn up to keep a lane open through the immense crowd of people who had gathered there, and thronged the wide roadway. Our reporter says:

> The procession moved off the Parade amid the acclamations of many thousand spectators and entered the chapel as the clock was striking eleven, which (*sic*) was crowded by all the beauty and fashion in town.

Another reporter speaks of the Chapel Royal as being "exceedingly crowded in all parts with nobility and gentlemen and ladies of distinction."

"The religious part of the ceremony," we are told, "was solemn and impressive." It comprised Morning Prayer and a sermon by the Sub-Dean.

> Previous to the commencement of the *Te Deum*, a pause was made, when three grenadier sergeants entered at each door by the sides of the altar with the Eagles on black poles about 8 feet high. They took their stations in front of the altar. Each party was guarded by a file of grenadiers, commanded by two officers; the whole of them with laurel-leaves in their caps as emblems of victory. At the same instant the five French flags and Bonaparte's honourable standard entered the upper gallery at the back of the altar, all carried by grenadier sergeants.
>
> The whole remained presented for some time for the gratification of the beholders, after which the Eagles were placed in brass sockets on each side of the altar, suspended by brass chains. The five flags were suspended from the front of the second gallery, and Bonaparte's honourable standard placed over the door of the second gallery, behind the others.

The trophies, with others won at Salamanca and Waterloo, and subsequently laid up in the Chapel Royal, were removed later to Chelsea Royal Hospital, where all, except "the Eagle with the Golden Wreath," are now kept treasured amid befitting surroundings .

"The Eagle with the Golden Wreath" disappeared from Chelsea Hospital in broad daylight. It was displayed in the chapel, affixed in front of the organ-loft over the doorway, until it suddenly vanished from there a little after midday on Friday, April 16, 1852, in the absence of the pensioner-custodian of the chapel during the Hospital dinner-hour. How it was stolen was apparent; but the thief was never traced. The thief, attracted undoubtedly by the widely told story that the wreath was of gold, made his way into the chapel by the roof, which was under-going repairs at the time, to which he got access by a workman's ladder.

He got inside by the trapdoor on the leads above the organ-loft. There, with a saw, he cut through the Eagle-pole near where it was fastened to the organ-loft, and, secreting it under his coat, made his escape by the way he had come, unseen by anybody. The Eagle-pole was found outside, in front of the building, with the Eagle and wreath wrenched off.

For some reason the Royal Hospital authorities of the day offered a reward of only a sovereign, and though the London police did their best, the malefactor was never discovered.[2] At Barrosa Napoleon's 8th of the Line was in the French column that made its attack on the right. It was one of the regiments that charged forward across the plain at the foot of Barrosa ridge, to break through General Graham's second brigade and drive it back to the edge of the cliffs by the seashore, while the French left attack seized the ridge itself, and beat back the British first brigade in the act of hastening to regain that unwisely abandoned position. The Eagle went down in the fierce counter-attack with which Graham's men on the plain, the 87th Royal Irish Fusiliers in the front line, met the French onset.

What befell the 8th of the Line is told by one of their own officers in his *Journal de Guerre*—Lieutenant-Colonel Vigo-Roussillon, in command of the First Battalion, with which was the Eagle. Colonel Roussill says:

> Just before the critical moment, the 8th, who were on the flank of the French second line, lost touch with the regiment next them, and had in consequence to meet the 87th by themselves. They fired their hardest as the British troops came on, but could not stop them, ever advancing to a bayonet attack.

They came on silently, steadily, irresistibly. Adds one of Victor's staff:

> Their officers kept up all the time the old custom of striking with their canes those of the men who fell out of the ranks. Our own non-commissioned officers, placed as a supernumerary rank, crossed their muskets behind the squads, thus forming buttresses which kept the ranks from giving way. Several of the French officers, also, picked up the muskets of the wounded,

---

2. The present imitation Eagle at Chelsea was specially cast in brass from a mould of one of other trophies; one of the Eagles of the 82nd being used as the model. The imitation wreath was made from a sketch by an old officer of the Hospital staff. The Eagle and wreath were specially reproduced in order that the Barrosa Eagle trophy should be represented among the Peninsular and Waterloo Eagles displayed together at the head of the *catafalque* on the occasion of the lying-in-state at Chelsea of the remains of the Duke of Wellington, seven months after the theft. The dummy is in the Chapel at Chelsea now, with a brass tablet beneath it notifying that it is not the original Eagle, set up where the Barrosa Eagle used to be, in front of the organ-loft. The existing staff, however, is genuine. It is the Eagle-pole that the thief threw away in his fright; the staff actually borne by the *Porte-Aigle* of Napoleon's 8th of the Line under fire at Austerlitz and Friedland; the identical staff inclined in salute with the Eagle to Napoleon on the throne on the Day of the Eagles on the Field of Mars.

and flung themselves into the gaps made in the ranks of the men.

Colonel Roussillon describes again:

> I saw the English line at sixty paces continuing to advance at a slow step without firing. It seemed impossible to stop them; we had not sufficient men.

Apparently he then caught sight of General Graham, leading the British line.

> Under the influence of a sort of despair, I urged forward my charger, a strong Polish horse, against an English mounted officer who seemed to be the colonel of the nearest regiment coming on at us. I got up to him, and was about to run him through with my sword, when I was held back by a sense of compassion and abandoned the murderous thought. He was an officer with white hair and a fine figure, and had his hat in his hand, and was cheering on his men. His calmness and noble air of dignity irresistibly arrested my arm.

Such is the lieutenant-colonel's own account. But did he really get quite close to the general? Graham was the last man in the world to let him get back unfought!

> I then, (*as Vigo-Roussillon continues,*) quickly galloped back to my own men, and was riding along the line, telling them to meet the enemy with our bayonets, and drive them back, when a bullet from an English marksman broke my right leg.
> I managed to dismount and tried to pass through in rear of the line, but it was impossible to walk. The ground was covered with thick bushes, and I was crippled and in great pain. All I could do was to sit down where I was, calling on the men to fire again. A moment later I was enveloped in smoke; and at the same instant the English charged in among us.
> I called out my loudest, cheering on my men; and now two soldiers tried to lift me up and carry me. But both were shot down.
> For the time we held our own, and kept the enemy back; but some of the English got round us. Seeing themselves outflanked, the battalion began to give ground. Then came a second furious charge from the English, and that broke us.
> The fight, man to man, went on desperately for several minutes-

some of the British soldiers, as yet another French officers relates, fighting with their fists.

Many of the Englishmen broke their weapons in striking with the butts or bayonets; but they never seemed to think of using the swords they wore at their sides. They went on fighting with their fists.

It was in the final *mêlée* that "the Eagle with the Golden Wreath" was taken; after a sharp and fierce hand-to-hand fight round it.

Colonel Roussillon himself was at almost the same moment struck down, and lay insensible for a space among the dead nearby. He was recovering his senses and trying to stand up, when, as he tells, a British sergeant saw him and ran at him with his halberd. He parried the thrust, and kept the sergeant off, and then a British officer came up. To him the *commandant* of the First Battalion of the 8th surrendered his sword.

The fight for the Eagle—on one hand to take it, on the other to keep it—was furious; desperately and heroically contested by both sides.

First, a gallant Irish boy, from Kilkenny, Ensign Edward Keogh of the 87th, caught sight of it, borne on high above the fray. There had been no unscrewing of the Eagle of the 8th, no trying to break it from its pole. "See that Eagle, sergeant!" called Keogh to Sergeant Masterton, among the foremost, close by his officer; and then he dashed straight into the thick of the party round the Eagle, sword in hand. The brave lad cut his way through, with Masterton and four or five privates close behind him. He got close up to the "*Porte-Aigle*," crossed swords with him, and got a grip of the Eagle-pole. But he could not wrench it from the no less brave Frenchman's hands before he went down with half a dozen musket bullets and bayonet stabs in his body.

Porte-Aigle Guillemin, as the gallant French Eagle-bearer of the 8th was named, fell dead at the same moment, shot through the head by one of the British privates.

Instantly other Frenchmen rushed up to save the Eagle, and formed round it hastily. One of the British privates who seized hold of the staff was slashed to death, and the French recovered it. The fight round the Eagle went on for some minutes. In that time no fewer than seven French officers and sub-officers fell dead in defence of the Eagle. An eighth officer, Lieutenant Gazan, clung to the pole to the last, regardless of wounds that nearly hacked him to pieces. Finally the Eagle was torn from his grasp by Sergeant Masterton, at the end the sole unwounded survivor of the attacking British party. Gazan "survived miraculously," and lived to be decorated by Napoleon for his devoted courage. Masterton seized the Eagle and kept it. So "the Eagle with the Golden Wreath" became a British trophy.

From the crossing of the bayonets in the final charge to the taking of the Eagle, the *mêlée* lasted about fifteen minutes.

The remnant of the 8th were saved by a rally to the spot by the French 54th, after another regiment, the 47th, had attempted its rescue in vain. The 47th lost their Eagle in the *mêlée*, but recovered it. "The man who had charge of it was obliged to throw it away, from excessive fatigue and a wound," explains a British officer. The 8th lost at Barrosa their Colonel (Autie) and the Lieutenant-Colonel of the Second Battalion, killed; Vigo-Roussillon, of the First Battalion, wounded; and 17 other officers and 934 of the rank and file killed or wounded. The *Moniteur*, the official Paris newspaper under the Napoleonic *régime*, in reporting the battle of April 5, referred to the loss of the Eagle in these terms:

> A battalion of the 8th, having been charged in wood-covered ground, and the Eagle-bearer being killed, his Eagle has not been found since.

The battalion that fared so hardly had to pay the regulation penalty. Napoleon gave the 8th no other Eagle. He held rigidly to his rule, and set his face relentlessly against a second presentation. They must present him first with a standard taken on the battlefield from the enemy. But with Wellington's men opposed to them to the end, the 8th got few chances in that direction. They had to fight without an Eagle to the close of the Peninsular War.

Two days after Barrosa, when General Graham re-entered Cadiz with the Spanish army, "the Eagle with the Golden Wreath" was publicly paraded through the crowded streets, "between the regimental colours," as the 87th marched to barracks, the church bells ringing triumphantly, and amid exultant shouts and cheers of the populace, and cries of "Long live Spain! Death to our oppressors!" At the barracks "we presented the Eagle to our gallant commander," says one of the officers.

The Eagle was then sent to England in the custody of the officer carrying General Graham's despatch. Its capture is commemorated to this day by the Royal Irish Fusiliers, who wear "an Eagle with a Wreath of Laurel" as a regimental badge, while a similar Eagle is embroidered in gold on the regimental colour. Also, a representation of the wreathed Barrosa Eagle was granted later on as a special augmentation to the family arms of the officer who commanded the 87th in the battle, Major Hugh Gough, on his being raised to the Peerage while commander-in-chief in India after the first Sikh War. "The Algiers" was always the regiment's *sobriquet* after Barrosa among their comrades in Wellington's army; a *sobriquet* that has endured since then in the form of "the *Aigle*-Takers," although our modern recruits are said to prefer calling themselves "the Bird-Catchers."[3]

It was in this way that the Barrosa trophy Eagle came by its golden wreath. The decoration, as has been said, had nothing to do with Talavera.

The wreath was one of those voted by the City of Paris to the regiments that had gone through the Jena and Polish frontier campaigns, the first of which was presented to the Imperial Guard. First of all, in the outburst of patriotic enthusiasm in France at the news of Jena, wreaths had been voted as decorations for the Eagles, by way of popular tribute to the regiments which had helped in dealing that staggering blow to the famous Prussian Army. After the crowning victory of Friedland which ended the war, in a fresh outburst of enthusiasm, golden wreaths were voted wholesale for the Eagles of all the corps that had taken part in the fighting that followed Jena, during the nine months of war, down to the final day of Friedland. It was a costly guerdon, and their proposed generosity staggered the Paris municipality when the estimate was presented. No fewer than 378 wreaths—according to the official return—had to be provided.

But the vote had been carried by acclamation on its first proposal, and trumpeted all over France. Also, the Emperor had taken up with the idea warmly. The Paris authorities dared not back out, and had to go on with it in spite of the cost. They carried it out with so good a grace that, as the sequel, a suggestion came from the Tuileries that the Austerlitz battalions of the Grand Army which had not had the fortune to be in the Jena-Friedland campaign should receive wreaths as well, an Imperial hint that the authorities, shrinking from the extra expense, were so slow to fall in with, that in the end it had to be forced on them, by means of a bluntly worded letter through the Ministry of

---

3. In a letter from an officer of the 87th, published in the London papers, it is stated that the regiment also captured the Eagle of the French 47th, but "the man who had charge of it was obliged to throw it away, from excessive fatigue and a wound. We had been under arms for thirty-two hours before the action began."

War. Napoleon wrote to the War Minister,:

> Tell the Prefect of the Seine, that I expect wreaths of gold, similar to those given for Jena and Friedland, to be provided on behalf of the City of Paris for all the regiments at Austerlitz!

The 8th was presented with its wreath in Paris, while on the way to take part in the Peninsular War. It was one of the regiments of the First Corps of the Grand Army, which Napoleon hastily recalled from Germany in the spring of 1808, and hurried across Europe to reinforce the troops in Spain on the first news of serious trouble being on foot in that quarter. The whole First Army Corps was recalled; starting from Berlin, where it had been quartered, and journeying by Magdeburg and Coblentz. Along the route the unfortunate German burgomasters and village authorities had to provide, not only provisions day by day, but transport vehicles for 30,000 soldiers; mostly farm-carts and wagons, each taking from four to sixteen men.

The troops travelled by night and day, with only two stoppages of fifty minutes each in the twenty-four hours, for meals, and the authorities of the villages and towns named as halting-places were compelled to have hot food kept ready so that the men might fall to instantly on arrival. It was a journey the soldiers never forgot. The weather was rough and wet, the roads in places were almost impassable, and the carts continually broke down, in addition to which the peasant-drivers requisitioned for the conveyances deserted at every opportunity, usually going off at night with the horses after cutting the traces, leaving their wagon-loads of sleeping soldiers stranded by the roadside.

The 8th received its wreath at the Barrier of Pantin, on the outskirts of Paris. It arrived with the Second Division of the corps, and the troops were met by the Prefect of the Seine and the Municipal Council in State, while Marshal Victor, the commander of the army corps, attended the ceremony in full-dress uniform. He replied to the Prefect's complimentary address by declaring that "these golden crowns hence-forward decorating the Eagles of the First Corps will to them ever be additional incentives to victory." One by one the regiments passed before the prefect, who hung round each Eagle's neck "a wreath of gold, shaped as two branches of laurel." A triumphal march into Paris and an open-air banquet to all ranks in the Tivoli Gardens, with free tickets to the theatres after it, wound up the day.

All along the line of march through France to the Spanish frontier, banquets and elaborate festivities welcomed the regiments—and at the same time, it would appear, gave some of their entertainers more than they bargained for. The triumphal progress, from all accounts, proved such hard work for the ladies in the country towns, where public balls were in the programme every night, that at some places for the later comers—the 8th and other regiments in the Second Division of Marshal Victor's corps—the balls had to be abandoned, "because the ladies were too tired to dance anymore." It was explained, with apologies, that they had practically been danced off their feet by the regiments of the First Division, which had preceded the Second, incessantly passing through during the previous three weeks, and that "most of the ladies, through sheer fatigue, had taken to their beds!"

At Talavera, the 8th, as part of a brigade of three regiments, had a passage of arms on the battlefield, first with the British 83rd; and then with the Guards; lastly with the 48th, before whose magnificent charge in the final phase of the fight they had to give ground. They did not meet the 87th Royal Irish Fusiliers at all in the battle.[4]

---

[4]. The successor to the 8th of the Line of the Grand Army in the Army of the Third Napoleon was, in its turn, no less unfortunate than its predecessor. The Eagle of the 8th of the Line of the Army of the Second Empire is now at Potsdam, one of the spoils of the war of 1870-1. It was carried through the streets of Berlin in the triumphal parade of the Prussian troops on their return home after the war, and after that, was deposited over the vault of Frederick the Great in the Church at Potsdam in the presence of the old Kaiser Wilhelm, Moltke, Von Roon, and other leaders of the victorious host. It bears these "battle-honours," inscribed on its silken flag, among them "Talavera":
Austerlitz 1805.
Friedland 1807.
Talavera 1809.
Anvers 1832.
Zaatcha 1849.
Solferino 1859.

Chapter 9

Other Eagles in England From Battlefields of Spain

Napoleon's Eagles made a second appearance before the London populace in the following year. That was on September 30, 1812, and the Horse Guards Parade was again the scene of the display—this time with more elaborate ceremonial, and with the added presence of yet greater personages. Queen Charlotte herself this time witnessed the reception ceremony, with four of the princesses; and the prince regent in person, "mounted on a white charger," attended, to be publicly done obeisance to by the humbled standards of the enemy. Four of his Royal brothers, the Dukes of Clarence, York, Cambridge, and Sussex, accompanied the prince regent. Only the poor old king, blind and insane, was absent of the Royal family, remaining in his seclusion at Windsor Castle.

The queen and princesses watched the scene from the windows of the Levée Room at the Horse Guards, looking down over the Parade; the prince regent was on the ground and took the salute. The Eagles this time were five in number; and four French flags, one of exceptional interest, the garrison-standard of Badajoz, were with them in the procession.

The military display was on the grandest scale possible; the *ensemble* making up, as we are told, "a spectacle grand and impressive beyond anything ever beheld." The First and Second Life Guards were present, "drawn up in a line reaching from the Foreign Office nearly to Carlton House," with their bands in State dress and their standards. All three regiments of Foot Guards took part, with the State Colour of the First Guards, and three bands. Horse and Foot Artillery from Woolwich were also there; forming by themselves one side of the great hollow square which occupied the wide space of the ground, the scene of the reception of "the Eagle with the Golden Wreath."

Ninety grenadiers, drawn from the three regiments of Foot Guards, thirty from each, formed the trophy-escort, which, as before, accompanied the Eagles and captured standards round the square at a slow march—the five Eagles in advance by themselves, borne by as many Guards' sergeants between files of grenadiers with fixed bayonets.

Again the trophies of Napoleon were spared nothing in the humiliation that they had to undergo. Twice were they lowered to the, dust before the queen; twice to the prince regent; eight times before the standards of the Life Guards; three times before the standards of the Guards and the King's Colour of the First Guards, "the immense concourse of spectators rending the air with their huzzas" every time the trophies went down. Then, as before, the trophies were paraded across Whitehall to the Chapel Royal, and solemnly "churched "and hung up there, before the royal family and "all the Cabinet Ministers and the leading members of the nobility in London."

They were this time all Wellington's trophies. Two of the Eagles were spoils from the Battle of Salamanca—"dreadfully mutilated and disfigured in the conflict," according to a newspaper reporter's account, "one of them having lost its head, part of the neck, one leg, half the thunderbolt, and the distinctive number; the other without one leg and the thunderbolt." Two had been taken in Madrid "in more perfect state and without their flags." The last of the five had been "found on the way to Ciudad Rodrigo, in the bed of a river, dried up in summer, having been thrown away some months before during Masséna's retreat." The four Eagles which still bore distinctive numbers were, we are told, "those of the 22nd, 13th, and 51st and the 39th." Of the standards, the garrison flag of Badajoz looked "like a sieve, a great part of it quite red with human blood"; the four other colours "were so mutilated that not a letter or device was legible."

How we came by the trophies so displayed in London on that Wednesday forenoon is our story.

The two Salamanca Eagles were—and are, for they have a place today among our Chelsea Hospital trophies—mementoes of one of the most dramatic episodes of a battle in which there were many.

Salamanca, it may be said incidentally—the battle, like Waterloo, was fought on a Sunday, on July 22, 1812—was, in Wellington's own eyes, his *chef d'œuvre*, his masterpiece, although it may be rather overlooked now perhaps by most of us and the world at large, eclipsed in the dazzling splendour of the last crowning victory of Waterloo. It was at Salamanca that Wellington, in the words of a French officer, speaking, of course, in general terms, "defeated 40,000 men in forty minutes." The victory was held in such estimation by Wellington himself that he selected it in preference to all his other victories to be displayed over again in a sham fight on the Plain of Saint-Denis in the presence of the three Allied Sovereigns during the occupation of Paris in 1815 after Waterloo. Of it he wrote at the time:

I never saw an army receive such a beating.

Upwards of 6,000 prisoners were taken, including one general and 136 other officers. Six thousand of the enemy, at the lowest computation, were left dead or wounded on the field of battle. Three French generals were killed and three wounded. Marshal Marmont himself, the enemy's commander-in-chief, was among the wounded; grievously maimed by a bursting shell as he galloped to rally one of his broken columns. "Spurring furiously to the point of danger, he was struck by the fragment of a shell, which shattered his left arm and tore open his side." Marmont bore the arm in a sling for the rest of his life. He was carried off the field under fire, on a stretcher made of a soldier's great-coat with a couple of muskets thrust through the armholes to give it shape, under the escort of a squad of grenadiers. Eleven cannon—melted down at Woolwich Arsenal in 1820 as a cheap way of making new field-guns for the British Army—with the two Eagles and six stand of colours, were the trophies of the day.

The two Salamanca trophy Eagles at Chelsea Hospital are the spoils of the fiercest cavalry charge that British horsemen ever delivered on a battlefield; the death-ride—for 1,200 of Napoleon's infantry—of the Heavy Brigade, which annihilated an entire French division in less than a quarter of an hour. It came about as one of the results of that opening false move on the part of the French commander which cost France in the end the loss of the battle.

Marmont, after a series of ably conducted manoeuvres in the neighbourhood of Salamanca, had forced Wellington, on July 22, into a position so unfavourable that the British commander decided to retire towards the Portuguese frontier under cover of darkness during the following night. But at the last moment the French marshal overreached himself. Taking in the difficulties that confronted his opponent he attempted to anticipate him and cut him off from his base by barring the one line of retreat that was open to Wellington. In doing that, Marmont gave his game away. He rashly divided his force in the presence of the enemy, separating his left wing to a distance from the main body and marching off a whole division of infantry, cavalry, and artillery to occupy the road to Ciudad Rodrigo.

The fault was flagrant, and Wellington seized eagerly at the chance all unexpectedly offered him. He was at breakfast when Marmont's troops began their false move and the *aide de camp* whom he had posted on the lookout hurriedly came to him with the news. "I think they are extending to the left—" the young officer began. He did not finish the sentence.

"The devil they are!" interposed Wellington hastily, with his mouth full. "Give me the glass!"

He took it, and for nearly a minute scanned the movements of the enemy with fixed attention.

"By God!" he ejaculated abruptly as he lowered the glass. "That'll do!"

He turned to another *aide de camp*.

"Ride off and tell Clinton and Leith to return to their former ground." These were the generals commanding the Fifth and Sixth Divisions, on the right and right-centre of the British position. Then Wellington ordered up his horse. Closing his spy-glass with a snap, he turned with these words to his Spanish *attaché*, Colonel Alava: "*Mon cher Alava, Marmont est perdu!*": A moment later Wellington was on horseback and his staff also, all galloping off.

Wellington grasped the meaning of Marmont's move. He saw his chance of falling on in force and overpowering the detached French wing before help could reach it.

He made his way as fast as his charger could carry him to the British Third Division—Picton's men, temporarily commanded by Wellington's brother-in-law, General Sir Edward Pakenham.

"As he rode up to Pakenham," says an officer whose regiment was close by, "every eye was turned on him. He looked paler than usual, but was quite unruffled in his manner, and as calm as if the battle to be fought was nothing more than an ordinary assemblage of troops for a field-day."

"Ned," said Wellington, as he drew rein beside Pakenham, tapping him on the shoulder and pointing in the direction of the separated French column as its leading troops were beginning to move towards their distant position, "Ned, d'ye see those fellows on the hill? Throw your division in column, and at 'em and drive 'em to the Devil"

"I will, my lord, by God!" was Pakenham's laconic reply, and he turned away to give the necessary orders.

The two Eagles were taken in the course of Pakenham's attack, when the Third Division, with the Fifth advancing on one flank, was moving forward to meet the fierce counter-attack with which the enemy, after the first collision, attempted to make amends for their commander's blunder.

> We were assailed, (*describes a British officer in the Third Division,*) by a multitude who, reinforced, again rallied and turned upon us with fury. The peals of musketry along the centre continued without intermission, the smoke was so thick that nothing to our left was distinguishable; some men of the Fifth Division got intermingled with ours; the dry grass was set on fire by the numerous cartridge-papers that strewed the battlefield; the air was scorching; and the smoke rolling onwards in huge volumes, nearly suffocated us.

In the midst of the din and turmoil the Heavy Cavalry came suddenly on the scene.

> A loud cheering was heard in our rear; the brigade half turned round, supposing themselves about to be attacked by the French cavalry. A few seconds passed, the trampling of horses was heard, the smoke cleared away, and the Heavy Brigade of Le Marchant was seen coming forward in line at a canter. 'Open right and left!' was an order quickly obeyed; the line opened, and the cavalry passed through the intervals, and, forming rapidly in our front, prepared for their work.

Catastrophe for the French assailants followed at once; swift, overwhelming, irremediable. The enemy in front had practically ceased to exist within the next twelve minutes. The entire French division and its supporting troops were struck down and shattered; broken to fragments and annihilated.

There was a:

> ... whirling cloud of dust, moving swiftly forward and carrying within its womb the trampling sound of a charging multitude. As it passed the left of the Third Division, Le Marchant's heavy horsemen, flanked by Anson's Light Cavalry, broke out at full speed, and the next instant 1,200 French infantry, formed in several lines, were trampled down with terrible clangour and tumult. Bewildered and blinded they cast away their arms and ran through the openings of the British squadron, stooping

and demanding quarter, while the dragoons, big men on big horses, rode on hard, smiting with their long, glittering swords in uncontrollable power, and the Third Division, following at speed, shouted as the French masses fell in succession before this dreadful charge.

So Napier describes the onset.

Startled and aghast at what they saw coming at them, the French attempted hastily to form squares. But Le Marchant's impetuous squadrons were too quick for them. They came swooping down, the troopers galloping their hardest, with loosened reins, all racing forward, charging down with the irresistible sweep of an avalanche, and crashed into the midst of the ill-fated infantrymen before the squares could be formed.

Down on the enemy the cavalry thundered, 1,200 flashing British sabres. Three of the finest regiments of the British Army formed the brigade—the 3rd Dragoons, the "King's Own"; the 4th, "Queen's Own"; the 5th Dragoon Guards strong and burly men on big-boned horses, and with sharp-edged swords. "*Nec aspera terrent*" was—and is—the fearless motto of the gallant "King's Own," who showed the way; and they flinched at nothing that day. "*Vestigia nulla retrorsum*" was—and is—the motto of the 5th, who closed the column; and dead and wounded and prisoners were the vestiges they left in rear on that stricken field.

General Edward Le Marchant, a daring and capable soldier—"a most noble officer," was what Wellington called him—led them.

A French regiment a little in advance, the ill-fated 62nd of the Line, was the first to face the British, and to go down. They did not attempt to form square. They had, indeed, no time to do so. Yet they were in a formation sufficiently formidable. The 62nd was a regiment of three battalions, and stood formed up in a column of half-battalions, presenting six successive lines closely massed one behind the other. Their front ranks opened fire just before the leading horsemen reached them, but it did not check the British onset even for a moment. The cavalry bore vigorously forward at a gallop and burst into and through their column, riding it down on the spot. Nearly the whole regiment was killed, wounded, or taken; leaving the broken remnants to be carried off as prisoners by the infantry of the Third Division as these raced up in rear, clearing the ground before them.

The 62nd were disposed of by the cavalry in less than two minutes. According to French official returns, the unlucky regiment, out of a total strength that morning of 2,800 of all ranks in its three battalions, lost 20 officers and 1,100 men in killed alone; the survivors who escaped capture not being sufficient to form half a battalion.

Cheering triumphantly, the charging squadrons dashed on. They came full tilt on a second French regiment, the 22nd, catching it in the act of forming square. The front face of the square was already drawn up and met the troopers with a hasty volley which brought down some of the men and horses. But that made little difference. The next moment the cavalry were on them. The mass of the square in rear made but a weak effort at resistance. They swayed back, broke their ranks, and fell apart in utter confusion. Slashed down right and left, as had been the case with the 62nd, in little more than a minute only groups of fugitives were left, to be made prisoners by the British infantry, following in rear of the horsemen.

The cavalry raced on then to attack a third French regiment. In turn it attempted to make a stand, but only to be dealt with in like manner. It, too, was caught before its square could be formed, and was ridden down.

Yet another French battalion confronted the British troopers after that. It had had time to take advantage of a small copse, an open wood of evergreen oaks, where it formed its ranks in *colonne serrée*, to await attack, and make a stand.

> The men reserved their fire with much coolness, until the cavalry came within twenty yards. Then they poured it in on the concentrated mass of men and horses with deadly effect. Nearly a third of the dragoons came to the ground, but the remainder had sufficient command of their horses to dash forward. They succeeded in breaking the French ranks and dispersing them in utter confusion over the field.

All the time the infantry in rear were racing on with exultant cheers, finishing off the horsemen's work as fast as they came up. It was an easy task. Further fight had been scared out of the French under the stress of the fearful experience they had gone through.

> Such as got away from the sabres of the horsemen, (*says one of the British officers,*) sought safety amongst the ranks of our infantry; and, scrambling under their horses, ran to us for protection, like men who, having escaped the first shock of a wreck, will cling to any broken spar, no matter how little to be depended on. Hundreds of beings, frightfully disfigured, in whom

the human face and form were almost obliterated black with dust, worn down with fatigue, and covered with sabre-cuts and blood—threw themselves among us for safety. Not a man was bayoneted—not one even molested or plundered. The invincible old Third on this day surpassed themselves; for they not only defeated their terrible enemies in a fair stand-up fight, but saved them when total annihilation seemed the only thing.

The two Salamanca Eagles were taken now. They fell to two infantry officers as their actual captors: one to an officer of a regiment of the Third Division, and the other to an officer of the Fifth Division, which had come into the fight, and were following the cavalry, partly mingled with Pakenham's men.

The first Eagle—that of the hapless French 62nd, whose fate has been told—fell to Lieutenant Pierce of the 44th, a regiment in the Fifth Division. He came on the Eagle-bearer while in the act of unscrewing the Eagle from its pole in order to hide it under his long overcoat and get away with it. Pierce sprang on the Frenchman, and tussled with him for the Eagle. The second *Porte-Aigle* joined in the fight, where-upon three men of the 44th ran to their officer's assistance. A third Frenchman, a private, added himself to the combatants, and was in the act of bayoneting the British lieutenant, when one of the men of the 44th, Private Finlay, shot him through the head and saved the officer's life. Both the *Porte-Aigles* were killed a moment later—one by Lieutenant Pierce, who snatched the Eagle from its dead bearer's hands.

In his excitement over the prize Pierce rewarded the privates who had helped him by emptying his pockets on the spot, and dividing what money he had on him amongst them—twenty dollars. A sergeant's halberd was then procured, on which the Eagle was stuck and carried triumphantly through the remainder of the battle. Lieutenant Pierce presented it next morning to General Leith, the commander of the Fifth Division, who directed him to carry it to Wellington. In honour of the exploit the 44th, now the Essex Regiment, bear the badge of a Napoleonic Eagle on the regimental colour, and the officers wear a similar badge on their mess-jackets.

The second Eagle taken was that of the 22nd of the Line. It was captured by a British officer of the 30th, Ensign Pratt, attached for duty to Major Cruikshank's 7th Portuguese, a Light Infantry (or *Caçadores*) battalion, serving with the Third Division. He took it to General Pakenham, whose mounted orderly displayed the Eagle of the 22nd publicly after the battle, "carrying it about wherever the general went for the next two days."

Two more Eagles, it was widely reported in the Army, came into the possession of other regiments of the Third and Fifth Divisions. One of them is said to have "wanted its head and number"; but what became of them is unknown. Possibly the existence of these particular trophies was merely camp gossip. According to one story, an officer picked up one of the Eagles during the battle and "carried it about in his cap for some days." No Eagles, however, reached headquarters after Salamanca except those of the 62nd and 22nd, which in due course were sent to England.[1]

One Eagle narrowly evaded capture at the hands of the Hanoverian Dragoons of the King's German Legion in the pursuit after Salamanca. It escaped—to find its way to Chelsea Hospital on a later day, as the famous trophy of our own 1st Dragoons, the "Royals," at Waterloo. What took place when the Eagle of the 105th of the Line so nearly fell into the enemy's hands after Salamanca is a story that in its incidents stands by itself.

General Anson's cavalry brigade, made up of British Light Dragoons and the Hanoverians, was sent in chase to follow and break up the wreck of the defeated army. It came upon the French rearguard in the act of taking post at a place called Garcia Hernandez. In front were several squadrons of cavalry; in rear the 105th of the Line. The three battalions of the regiment were moving in column, with guns in the intervals. Not seeing the French infantry and guns at first, owing to an intervening ridge, Anson rode for the cavalry and drove them in.

---

1. Southey, in his *History of the Peninsular War*, makes this ugly suggestion in regard to the Eagle trophies of Salamanca: "It is said that more than ten were captured, but that there were men base enough to conceal them and sell them to persons in Salamanca who deemed it good policy, as well as a profit-able speculation, to purchase them for the French." It may be, as to that, that Marmont's army lost more than the two Eagles now at Chelsea. It is of course possible that camp followers and Spanish peasants of the locality, wandering over the battle-field to strip and plunder the dead on the day after the battle, when Wellington and the army were miles away, picked up Eagles on the scene of so tremendous a disaster for the French. They might easily traffic in them with French agents at Salamanca, well aware of their value if they could be secretly restored to their regiments. It is, however, inconceivable that British soldiers could have acted as alleged and been guilty of the dastardly crime that Southey hints at. Four Eagle-poles, with screw tops and the Eagles gone, were found on the field by British burying-parties; but those were all, and one of the four may have been the pole of the Eagle of the 62nd.

Their squadrons fled from Anson's troopers, abandoning three battalions of infantry, who in separate columns were making up a hollow slope, hoping to gain the crest of some heights before the pursuing cavalry could fall on, and the two foremost did reach higher ground, and there formed in squares.

The squares at once opened fire on the horsemen, and for a moment checked them.

The Hanoverian Dragoons were the nearest of the pursuers to the rearmost of the French squares, and there was no way to ride past without exposing their flank at close range. Captain Von Decken, who was leading the dragoons, on the spur of the moment took the daring decision to attack the square with the single squadron he had with him, then and there. Without an instant's hesitation the gallant captain charged, regardless of the fierce fusillade that met him at once, from which his men went down all round. They dropped fast under fire. By twos, by threes, by tens, all round they fell; yet the rest of them, surmounting the difficulties of the ground, hurled themselves in a mass on the column and went clean through it.

The gallant Von Decken was among the first to go down, shot dead a hundred yards from the square. But a leader no less heroic was at hand. Instantly Captain Von Uslar Gleichen, in charge of the left troop, dashed to the front. He rode out to the head of the squadron, inciting his men by voice and gesture and example. Another French volley smote hard on the squadron, but the intrepid troopers galloped through it, and, bringing up their right flank, swept on towards the enemy's bayonets, making to attack the square on two sides. The two foremost ranks of the French were on the knee with bayonets to the front, presenting a deadly double row of steel. In rear the steady muskets of four standing ranks were levelled at the horsemen. The dragoons pressed on close up, and some were trying, in vain, to beat aside the bayonets before them, and make a gap through, when an accident at the critical moment gave the opportunity.

A shot from the kneeling ranks, apparently fired unintentionally, as it is said, killed a horse, and caused it with its rider to fall forward, right across and on top of the bayonets. Thus a lane was unexpectedly laid open to the cavalry. They seized the chance instantly and crowded in through. The square was broken. It was cleft apart: its ranks were scattered and dispersed. All was over in a few moments. Within three minutes the entire battalion had been either cut down under the slaughtering swords of the dragoons or had been made prisoners.

Immediately on that another Hanoverian captain, Von Reitzenstein, came sweeping by with the second squadron, riding for the second French square. These met the charge with a bold front and rapid volley, but their *moral* had been shaken by the startling and horrible scene they had just beheld. The front face of the second square gave way as the horsemen got close, and four-fifths of that battalion were either sabred on the spot or made prisoners.

There was yet, nearby, the third battalion in its square. Its numbers had been added to by such fugitive survivors from the first and second squares as had been able to reach the place and get inside. The third squadron of the dragoons dealt with the third square in the same way, riding boldly at it, and breaking in with deadly results, as before.

How the Eagle of the 105th was saved—it was with the first battalion in the square first broken—is not on record. It did, however, somehow, evade capture hidden hastily perhaps beneath the coat of somebody in the handful of men who got away in the *mêlée*. Only the broken Eaglepole was left, to be picked up among the dead after the fight. A British officer who went over the ground after the fight described:

> The contest ended in a dreadful massacre of the French infantry. The 105th bravely stood their ground, but the ponderous weight of the heavy cavalry broke down all resistance; and arms lopped off, heads cloven to the spine, or gashes across the breast and shoulders showed the fearful encounter that had taken place.

The third of the trophy Eagles paraded in London before the prince regent was that of Napoleon's 39th of the Line. It had been picked up in the dried-up bed of the River Ceira, one of the tributaries of the Douro. Apparently the Eagle had been dropped, owing to the fall of its bearer during the night action of Foz d'Aronce on June 15, 1811, when Ney's corps of Masséna's army, then retreating from Torres Vedras, was roughly handled and driven across the river by Wellington's Third and Light Divisions.

The fourth and fifth of the Eagles were found at Madrid on Wellington's occupation of the city after Salamanca—stored away in the French arsenal and army *dépôt* there, to which uses the ancient Royal Palace of the Buen Retiro, just outside the walls of Madrid, had been converted.[2] Seventeen hundred men held the Retiro, and the ap-

---

2. As to Napoleon's opinion in regard to the preservation of trophies so acquired, see his memo to Ney at Magdeburg, quoted in Chapter 5, as footnote 4.

proaches to the arsenal had been fortified by order of Napoleon, but the garrison surrendered without firing a shot. They gave up to the victors 180 brass cannon, 900 barrels of powder, 20,000 stand of arms, muskets and bayonets, together with the Eagles of the 13th and 51st of the Line, which had been laid up at the Retiro for safe custody while the two regiments were operating in a wild part of the country against the Spanish guerrillas.[3]

The last Eagles taken by Wellington in the Peninsular War came into our hands in the battles of the Pyrenees.[4] Neither of them is now in existence. One was taken by our 28th in the combat of the Pass of Maya. The 28th, supporting the 92nd Highlanders in the fighting, overwhelmed with a series of fierce volleys an unfortunate French regiment, which was after-wards discovered to be the French 28th—a curious coincidence. The Eagle of the 28th, the senior corps of its brigade, was found on the battlefield, and was brought to England and hung in the Chapel Royal, Whitehall. It disappeared from there in circumstances already related. The second French Eagle was that of the 52nd of the Line, presented by Wellington, as has been told, to the Spanish Cortes. That also has since been entirely lost sight of.

This also may be added. Early in 1813 a special order was issued by Napoleon to the army in Spain requiring the Eagles of most of the regiments to be sent back to France. Napoleon at that time was in Paris, engaged in getting together a new Grand Army to replace that destroyed in Russia. The regiments in Spain, he said, would be so weakened by the intended withdrawal of their third, fourth, and fifth battalions (which he was recalling in order to send them to Germany for the coming campaign there), that the Eagles—in charge of the first battalions which were remaining in Spain—would be exposed to undue risk. He wrote:

---

3. Napoleon had given permission to his marshals in Spain to grant colonels of regiments, in certain circumstances, discretionary powers as to the disposal of their Eagles. Colonels were authorised, when their regiments were proceeding on what might be considered "exceptionally hazardous service," or when operating in difficult country, to keep the Eagles back, and leave them in camp or in a fortress. That is how Wellington in 1812 came to find the Eagles of the 13th and 51st of the Line at Madrid.

4. On July 28, 1813, in a skirmish in the Pyrenees, the 40th (now the 2nd Somersetshire Regiment) surrounded and captured the French 32nd of the Line, rounding its First Battalion up in a valley and charging it with the bayonet, 24 officers and 700 men being taken. The Eagle had been thrown into a rapid mountain torrent in sight of our men, during the retreat of the 32nd, but it was impossible to prevent it, or to recover the Eagle afterwards.

In future there will in Spain be only one Eagle to each brigade, that of the senior regiment of the brigade." The Eagles withdrawn from Spain, added the order, would "in the end rejoin the battalions with the Grand Army in Germany, as soon as these had been reconstituted afresh as regiments, with a sufficient force of men to ensure the safety of the Eagles.

All the cavalry Eagles were recalled:

No regiment of cavalry in Spain is to retain its Eagle. Those who have not done so are immediately to send theirs to the *dépôt*.

It was due to this order mainly that at Vittoria, after the overwhelming rout of the French Army, only one Eagle-pole—with its Eagle gone—fell into British hands, although there had been on the field upwards of 70,000 French soldiers (of whom 55,000 were infantry), and the French lost everything—in the words of one of their own generals (Gazan), "all their equipages, all their guns, all their treasure, all their stores, all their papers." [5]

---

5. Others of the Eagles had narrow escapes during the Peninsular War. In the fighting south of the Douro, near Grijon, on the day before Wellington's passage of the river at Oporto, the 31st Light Infantry all but lost their Eagle on being charged by the British 14th and 20th Light Dragoons. The 31st broke in confusion before the British onset, and only rallied some miles from the battlefield. "Our losses," described one of the officers, "were very heavy, but our Eagle, which had been in extreme peril in the encounter, was happily saved." Again, in the pursuit up the mountain side after the defeat of Girard's Division at Arroyo dos Molinos, the Eagles of the 34th and 40th of the Line escaped capture—although both regiments were all but annihilated—to Marshal Soult's expressed relief. In reporting the reverse to Napoleon, Soult added this by way of *solatium*: "*L'honneur des armes est sauvé; les Aigles ne sont pas tombés au pouvoir de l'ennemi.*" After Talavera, the Eagle of the 25th of the Line was picked up on the battlefield by a party of the King's German Legion—it was sent to Hanover and is now in Berlin; also, during the battle, the British 29th took two Eagle-poles in a charge, but with the Eagles unscrewed from the tops and removed by the Eagle-bearers at the last moment and carried out of the fight under their coats.

CHAPTER 10: IN THE HOUR OF DARKEST DISASTER

After Moscow: How the Eagles Faced Their Fate

There are seventy-five standards of Napoleon's Grand Army of 1812 now in Russia, trophies of the Moscow disaster. Rather more than half of the number are Eagles. The remainder of the trophies are battalion and cavalry flags; some French, some the ensigns of allied contingents and the troops of vassal states of the Napoleonic Empire, compelled to take a part in the campaign. All the European armies of the period are represented among the trophies: green and white Saxon flags; blue and white Bavarian flags; violet and white Polish ensigns; Spanish, Dutch, and Portuguese colours; Swiss flags; Westphalian and Baden flags of the Confederation of the Rhine; the red and black of Würtemburg; the yellow and black of Austria; the white and black of Prussia; the green, white, and red tricolour of Italy.

They are preserved at St. Petersburg, in the Kazan Cathedral and in the cathedral of St. Peter and St. Paul. Those in the Kazan Cathedral are grouped over and round the tomb of the septuagenarian hero, Kutusoff, who lies buried on the spot where he knelt in prayer before setting out to take command as *generalissimo* of the national army. Nearby, suspended against the pillars, are the marshal's baton of Davout, and the keys of Hamburg, Leipsic, Dresden, Rheims, Breda, and Utrecht, similarly spoils of the Napoleonic war. (*See note following.*)

> *Note*:—Elsewhere are other permanent trophies of the campaign, spoils of another kind. Nine hundred and twenty-nine of Napoleon's cannon fell into Russian hands, mostly abandoned during the retreat, without attempt at defence. Of these, most are fittingly kept at Moscow; they number 875, and are exhibited in the arsenal, or mounted as trophies in the public squares

in the Holy City. As with the flags, they are not all French. Those bearing the French Imperial cipher, the letter "N" surmounted by the Eagle and Napoleonic crown, number less than a half of the total. The French guns number 365; the bulk of the collection being made up of artillery from allied and *vassal* states: 189 Austrian cannon, 123 Prussian, 70 Italian, 40 Neapolitan, 34 Bavarian, 22 Dutch, 12 Saxon, 8 Spanish, 5 Polish, with 7 Westphalian, Würtemburg, and Hanoverian pieces.

The Prussian and Austrian guns, most of them, it is fair to say, were not captured from the contingents serving with the Grand Army in Russia: they formed part of the artillery marching with Napoleon's main column; they belonged to the French army, and were manned by French gunners, being spoils from the Austerlitz, Wagram, and Jena campaigns, turned to account to form field batteries for the French army. Innumerable other reminders of the fate of the Grand Army are preserved all over Russia: soldiers' arms and accoutrements, personal belongings and decorations of French officers and men, fragments of uniforms, helmets, swords and lances, pistols and muskets; relics mostly picked up on battlefields or by the wayside along the route of the retreat.

The muskets serve to illustrate incidentally, in the variety of the woods used for their stocks, the makeshifts to which, some time before 1812, the demands of Napoleon's armaments had reduced France: the musket-stocks of oak, chestnut, elm, beech, maple, of even poplar and deal, tell a tale of exhausted supplies of the walnut and ash woods ordinarily used in the manufacture of firearms.

The total of 75 Eagles and other standards is no extravagantly large array of trophies, remembering the overwhelming nature of the catastrophe to the Grand Army in Russia. Of the 600,000 soldiers who mustered round their regimental colours at the crossing of the Niemen at the outset of the campaign, 125,000 were killed in fight, and 193,048, according to the Russian official returns, were taken prisoners. In round numbers 250,000 died on the line of march during the retreat, from cold, hardships, and starvation, or were killed as stragglers by the *Cossacks* and peasants.

The mementoes also of their grim fate exist today in Russia. The graves of most of them may be seen all along the railway line from Wilna to Moscow, which follows closely the route of Napoleon and the Grand Army, over country the same in appearance now as then; a dreary, windswept, lonesome plain, broken only by vast stretches of dark, monotonous birch and pine forests, with here and there narrow ravines, and strips of hilly ground, amid which wind chill and sluggish rivers.

At intervals huge mounds, looking like embankments or ancient barrows of enormous size, rise over the flat expanse of plain. They are the graves of the French dead. It took three months to destroy the remains of the dead soldiers and of some 150,000 horses which perished in the campaign. The ghastly task was carried out locally by the peasantry, under an urgent Government order, so as to prevent the outbreak of pestilence in the spring from the vast numbers of unburied corpses that strewed the track of the ill-fated host.

The bodies, when the snow thawed, were dragged together and collected in heaps each "half a *verst* long and two fathoms high," over 500 yards long and some 14 feet high. At first, efforts were made to burn them, but the supply of firewood failed, and the stench all over the country was unbearable. The corpses were then hauled into shallow trenches alongside, and quicklime and earth heaped over them, making the mounds now to be seen along the railway, on either side of the old post-road from Wilna to Moscow, the route of Napoleon's retreat.

In the province of Moscow, 50,000 dead soldiers and 29,000 dead horses were so disposed of before the middle of February; in the province of Smolensk, by the end of the month, 72,000 dead soldiers and 52,000 horses; in the province of Minsk, 40,000 human corpses and 28,000 horses; to which, later on, when the ice had melted, 12,000 more dead soldiers were added, the bodies found in the Beresina; in the province of Wilna, also by the end of February, 73,000 dead soldiers, with 10,000 dead horses. There were, in addition, very many never accounted for: dead stragglers who had perished in the forests, their remains being devoured by the wolves; and those who were massacred—beaten to death, or buried alive, or burned alive—by the peasants in places away from the line of march. Such was the appalling loss of life that attended the Moscow campaign, and which the trophies represent. In the circumstances, in proportion, the toll is hardly a large one.

The actual Eagle trophies number all told between forty and fifty:

less than a third of the total array of Eagles that crossed the Niemen at the head of their regiments on the outbreak of the war. The majority of the Eagles of the Grand Army were saved from falling into the hands of the Russians through the devoted heroism of those responsible for their safe-keeping amid the horrors of the retreat. Of those at St. Petersburg, not more than half at most were taken in actual combat, and they were only yielded up by their bearers with life, being picked up from among the dead bodies, and carried off by the Russians on going over the field after the fight was over. Five Eagles only were surrendered by capitulation.

The others were brought in by the *Cossacks*, who came upon them while prowling in rear of the retreating army. They were found, some in hollow trees, where their despairing bearers had tried to conceal them; some in holes dug with bayonets in the frozen ground underneath the snow. Others were dragged to light, broken from their staves, from beneath the coats or from the knapsacks of officers and men, who had fallen by the way at night and been frozen to death, during the final stage of the retreat between Wilna and the Niemen. It is in remembrance of how, to the last, during the Moscow retreat, in many a dark and hopeless hour, there yet remained detachments of devoted men, the last remnants of regiments, at all times ready to stand at bay and sacrifice themselves for the honour of their Eagles, amidst hordes of disorganised fugitives all round—in remembrance of that, the army of modern France commemorates on the colours of certain regiments, as representing corps that bore the same numbers in Napoleon's Grand Army in Russia, the names, among others, of "Marojaroslav," "Polotz," "Wiasma," "Krasnoi," "La Berezène," defeats and disasters though these were.

The Eagles were under fire for the first time in Russia on July 17, in the attack on Smolensk on the Dnieper, the ancient Lithuanian capital, where took place the first important battle of the war. There the Eagles of Ney's and Davout's corps did their part in inciting the men to add fresh laurels to the fame of their regiments; ever prominent in the attack, leading charge after charge as the columns made repeated efforts to storm the fortified suburbs and lofty ramparts of the citadel. The soldiers did all that intrepidity and desperate valour might attempt, but in vain. No valour could prevail against the stubborn endurance of the Russians, who also occupied a strongly walled position that was practically impregnable. The fierce contest went on all through a whole day, until nightfall, and then, under cover of darkness, the defenders silently drew off and retreated beyond the city, leaving Smolensk in flames. No fewer than 15,000 French and 10,000 Russians fell in the merciless encounter.

Next morning there followed a spectacle hardly ever perhaps paralleled: the march of the Grand Army through the streets between the still blazing houses, "the martial columns advancing in the finest order to the sound of military music." As an officer puts it:

> We traversed between furnaces, tramping over the hot and smouldering ashes, in all the pomp of military splendour, bands playing and each Eagle leading its men.

At Smolensk one regiment won its Eagle, which Napoleon presented at five o'clock in the morning on July 19, before the paraded battalions of Davout's corps. It was the 127th of the Line; a regiment, it is curious to note, enrolled a few months before, from former Hanoverian subjects of our own King George the Third, and commanded by French officers as a regular corps of the French Line. By Napoleon's latest ordinance, issued just before the Emperor quitted Paris in May, the regiments newly raised for the Russian War, of which there were several, were in each case to win their Eagles on the battlefield. The Eagle for each regiment was to be provided in advance, but would be held back, locked up in the regimental chest, until it "should be won by distinguished conduct."

The 127th won their Eagle at Smolensk, their brilliant service being specially brought before Napoleon by Marshal Davout, who, of his own initiative, claimed the Eagle for them from Napoleon. The regiment bore it with distinction through the hottest of the fighting at Borodino, carried it all through the disastrous retreat from Moscow, and preserved it to the end to go through the later campaign in Germany, and face the enemy after that in the last stand before Paris in 1814. The Eagle was eventually destroyed by order of the restored Bourbon Government.

The second great battle-day of the Eagles in the Russian War was at Borodino, on September 7. There a quarter of a million and more combatants faced each other: on one side, 132,000 Russians with 640 guns; on the other, 133,000 French with 590 guns. The battle of Borodino was perhaps the most sanguinary and the most obstinately contested in history. The opening shots were fired at sunrise. When at sunset both sides drew sullenly apart, exhausted after twelve hours of carnage, neither army was victorious. Each held the ground on which it had begun the battle; 25,000 men lay dead on the field, and 68,000 more lay wounded, an appalling massacre that staggered even Napoleon.

Amidst the ferocious savagery of the hand-to-hand fighting that characterised Borodino all over the field, many of the Eagles were in desperate peril. Several were cut off in the terrible havoc that the ferocious Russian counter-charges wrought in the French ranks, and were only saved by the stern fortitude of the soldiers, fighting at times back to back round the Eagles, keeping off the enemy with bayonet thrusts till help should come. In one part of the field the 9th of the Line was isolated and for a time broken up and scattered. The Eagle-bearer was cut off by himself and surrounded. He saved the Eagle, as he fell wounded.

> Amidst the confusion, wounded by two bayonet thrusts, I fell, but I was able to make an effort to prevent the Eagle falling into the hands of the enemy. Some of them rushed at me and closed round, but, getting to my feet, I managed to fling the Eagle, staff and all, over their heads towards some of our men, whom I had caught sight of, fortunately nearby, trying to charge through and rescue the Eagle. This was all I could do before I fell again and was made prisoner.

The brave fellow returned to France two years later, at the Peace of 1814, and made his way to the regimental *dépôt*, where he found barely twenty of his comrades at Borodino left. The rest had succumbed during the retreat from Moscow. The survivors had brought back the Eagle to France; only, however, to have to give it up to the new Minister of War for destruction.

The 18th of the Line, broken in a Russian counter-attack, after storming one of the Russian redoubts erected to defend part of the position, rallied with their Eagle in their midst and held their ground in spite of repeated attacks until help could get through to them. At the roll-call next morning, 40 officers out of 50, and 800 men out of 2,000 were reported as missing; left dead or wounded on the field. Another regiment lost its colonel and half one battalion dead on the field; the Eagle-Guard were all shot down or bayoneted round the Eagle, which in the end was saved and brought out of the battle by a corporal, who was awarded a commission by Napoleon in the presence of the remains of the regiment next day.

The Eagle of the 61st of the Line again was only kept out of Russian hands by the devotion of the men round it. Napoleon rode past the regiment next day while being paraded for the roll to be called. Only two battalions were there, and he asked the colonel where the third battalion was. "It is in the redoubt, Sire!" was the officer's reply, pointing in the direction of the Great Redoubt, round which some of the hardest fighting of the day had taken place. The battalion had literally been annihilated: not an officer or a man of the 1,100 in the third battalion of the 61st had returned from the fight.

A regiment of *Cuirassiers* lost its Eagle at Borodino: the Eagle had disappeared in the midst of a fierce *mêlée*, in which the Eagle-bearer had gone down. The loss was not discovered till later. All, however, refused to believe that it had been captured: that was incredible. The dead Eagle-bearer's body was found after the battle, but no Eagle was there. Overwhelmed with shame, the regiment had to admit that the impossible had happened, and during the weeks that they were at Moscow "they remained plunged in a profound dolour."

The Eagle reappeared in an extraordinary way. In the retreat, when passing the scene of the battle, a ghastly and horrible spectacle with its unburied corpses and the carcasses of horses strewn thickly and heaped up all over the field, a sudden thought struck one of the officers. Late that night, he and a brother officer, taking the risk of capture by *Cossacks* on the prowl in rear of the retreating army, rode back and found their way by moonlight to where the *Cuirassiers* had had their fight and the Eagle-bearer had fallen. They found the Eagle inside the carcass of the Eagle-bearer's horse. It had been thrust in there by the dying Eagle-bearer through the gaping wound that had killed the horse, as the only means to conceal it in the midst of the enemy.

The Eagles made their last triumphant entry into a conquered capital at Moscow on September 14, the Eagle of the Old Guard leading the way at the head of the grenadiers of the Guard, all wearing for the day their full-dress parade uniform. As has been said, every officer and soldier of the Guard, by Napoleon's standing order, carried a suit of full-dress uniform in his kit or knapsack on campaign in readiness for such occasions—"*en tenue de parade comme si elle eut défiler au Carrousel.*" They had marched like that with music and full military pomp twice through Vienna, and through the streets of Berlin and Madrid; but there was at Moscow a disconcerting and ominous difference, both in their surroundings and in the reception that they met.

Elsewhere, alike in Vienna, Berlin, and Madrid, the parade march of the victorious Eagles passed through densely crowded streets of onlookers, silently gazing with dejected mien at the scene. At Moscow not a soul was in the streets, at the windows, anywhere; on every side were emptiness and desolation. The inhabitants had fled the city, and only deserted houses remained. The first incendiary fires at Moscow broke out at midnight, within twelve hours of Napoleon taking up his residence in the Kremlin.

The spell after that was broken. Henceforward victory deserted the Eagles; the hour of fate was at hand for Napoleon and the Grand Army. The Fortune of War, indeed, turned against the Eagles even before Napoleon had quitted Moscow.

Early on October 18, Napoleon, while at breakfast in the Kremlin, suddenly heard distant cannonading away to the south. He learned what had happened that afternoon while holding a review of the Italian Royal Guard.

We hastily regained our quarters, packed up our parade-uniforms, put on our service kit ... and to the sound of our drums and bands threaded our way through the streets of Moscow at five in the afternoon.

During the past five weeks, while all had been outwardly quiet, the Russian armies had been manoeuvring to close in along the only road of retreat open to Napoleon.

The nearest of the Russian armies, concentrated to the south-west of Moscow, struck the first blow on October 18 at daybreak, by surprising Murat's cavalry camp near Vinkovo. The results to the French were disastrous. Two thousand of Murat's men were killed and as many more were taken prisoners. Between thirty and forty guns were lost, and Murat's personal camp-baggage train, which included "his silver canteens and cooking utensils, in which cats' and horse flesh were found prepared for food"—a discovery that opened the eyes of the Russians to the precarious position of affairs in Napoleon's army. Murat himself, according to one story, "rode off on the first alarm in his shirt."

He only got away, according to another, by cutting his way through the Russians sword in hand, at the head of his personal escort of carabineers. Two Eagles were spoils of the surprise; the first to fall into Russian hands in the war. They were lost in the general scrimmage, their bearers being sabred at the outset of the Russian onslaught. The Eagles were at once sent off to St. Petersburg to be presented to the Czar Alexander.

On the other hand nine Eagles were saved, their escorts fighting their way successfully through the Russians.

Many stories are recorded in memoirs of survivors of the Grand Army of heroic endeavours made repeatedly by officers and men to save their Eagles from the enemy amid the disasters and horrors of the retreat. Their devotion and self-sacrifice had their reward in the preservation of seven Eagles in every ten.

Two Eagles were lost fourteen days after leaving Moscow, in the disastrous battle at Wiasma on November 2, halfway on the road back to Smolensk, where the advanced columns of the pursuing Russians attacked and all but cut the retreating French Army in two. The rearguard of the Grand Army, Marshal Davout's corps, with the Italian corps of the Viceroy Eugène Beauharnais, was overpowered and driven in and broken up; crushed under the overpowering artillery fire of the Russians. They left behind 6,000 dead, 2,000 prisoners, and 27 guns.

Two Eagles were taken, their regiments being virtually annihilated, but twenty-one were saved. They were safeguarded through the rout by groups of brave-hearted officers and men, who beat off the rushes made at them by the Russian cavalry and the *Cossacks*. They fought their way through until they met Ney's troops, who had heard the firing and turned back, arriving in time to stem and check the Russian pursuit and enable what was left of the two shattered army corps to rally under their protection.

One infantry regiment at Wiasma perished on the battlefield to a man, but saved its Eagle. It was the rearmost of all, and was isolated and surrounded beyond reach of help. In vain its men formed square and tried to fight their way after the rest through the surging masses of the Russians. They made their way for a time until the enemy brought up artillery. A Russian battery galloped up, unlimbered close to them, and opened fire with murderous effect. The Frenchmen tried desperately to charge the guns, but were beaten back by a rush of cavalry. At last, in despair, they formed square and faced the cruel slaughter that the guns made in their ranks, in the hope that help might reach them. Terms were offered them and refused. They would not surrender, and fought on till dusk, when their ammunition gave out.

The Russians were closing round for a final decisive charge on the small handful of survivors, when the wounded colonel, seeing all was over, made the attempt that saved the Eagle. The scanty remnant of what had that morning been a regiment of 3,000 men formed round in a ring, facing towards the enemy with bayonets levelled. The Eagle-staff was broken up and the fragments thrust under the ground. With flint and steel a match was lighted and the silken tricolour consumed. The Eagle was then tied up in a *havresac* and entrusted to an old soldier who was known to be a good rider. The colonel, giving up his own charger to the man, bade him watch his chance and, as the enemy came on in the dark, dash through them and ride his hardest.

"Carry the Eagle to His Majesty," were the colonel's words. "Deliver it to him, and tell him that we have done our duty!" The man rode off. He was able to get through the nearest Russians under cover of the darkness, having to fight his way before he got clear, and receiving several wounds. Then his horse fell dead from its injuries. On foot he stumbled on, and before midnight reached, not Napoleon, but Marshal Ney, to whom he gave up his precious charge.

No officer or man of the others of the luckless regiment was ever heard of in France again. No prisoners from it ever returned—only the Eagle survived.

Three days after Wiasma the Russian winter suddenly set in on the doomed host. It brought about at once the disintegration and disorganisation of the Grand Army. Already, demoralised by their privation, hundreds of men had fallen out of the ranks, flinging away their muskets and knapsacks, and straggling along in disorderly groups. A third practically of the Army ceased to exist as a fighting force within the first fortnight of the retreat, before the first snows fell.

The others, though, still kept to their duty. Marching in the ranks day after day, they strove their hardest to beat back the incessant attacks of the swarms of *Cossacks*, hovering round on the watch to raid the baggage-convoys at every block or stoppage on the road. With the coming of the snow the doom of the Grand Army was sealed. It was impossible to maintain discipline with the thermometer at twenty degrees below zero. Men dropped dead from cold by the score every half-mile.

On November 6 the sun disappeared; a grey fog enshrouded everything; the frost set in; and a bitter north wind in howling gusts swept over the face of the land; with it came down the snow, falling hour after hour by day and night without ceasing.

> From that day the army lost its courage and its military instinct. The soldier no longer obeyed his officer. The officer separated himself from his general. The disbanded regiments marched in disorder. In their frantic search for food they spread themselves over the plain, pillaging and destroying whatever fell in their

way. (So a survivor wrote).

The snow came down in large broad flakes, which at once chilled and blinded the soldiers: the marchers, however, stumbled forward, men often struggling and at last sinking in holes and ravines that were concealed from them by the new and disguised appearance of the country. Those who yet retained discipline and kept their ranks stood some chance of receiving assistance; but amid the mass of stragglers, the men's hearts, intent only on self-preservation, became hardened and closed against every feeling of sympathy and compassion. The stormwind lifted the snow from the earth, as well as that steadily pelting down from above, into dizzy eddies round the soldiers. Many were hurled to the ground in this manner, while the same snow furnished them with an instant grave, under which they were concealed until the next summer came, to display their ghastly remains in the open air.

The *Cossacks* redoubled their attacks on the retreating army after Wiasma. They had harassed the French incessantly from the day after Napoleon passed Mojaisk, but after Wiasma their audacity increased a hundredfold. They captured prisoners hourly, from among the stragglers mostly; in droves, by fifties and hundreds at a time. Day after day they hung on the flanks, swooping down with loud shouts on the unfortunate wretches, rounding them up like sheep, and driving them before them towards their own camps at the points of their long lances. Many they killed on the spot, or stripped naked to perish in the snow. Others they drove along to the nearest camp of Kutusoff's regulars for the sake of the money reward offered for prisoners brought in alive.

Others again, to save themselves the trouble of driving them all the way to the army camp, they handed over to peasants in the villages, selling them at a rouble a head, for the peasants to make sport of and maltreat or kill. The brutalities and ruthless devastations that the French army had committed in its advance to Moscow had infuriated the Russian peasantry. Intent on vengeance they now made use of their opportunity to the full.

They burned alive some of their captives, by tossing them into pits half filled with blazing pine-logs. Seventy were done to death in this horrible way in one village. Others they buried up to their necks in the ground and left to die; or else tied them to trees for the wolves to tear to pieces. ² Others they clubbed or flogged to death, tying down the wretched Frenchmen to logs on the ground, hounding on the women and children to hammer their heads to pieces with thick sticks. A common method of *Cossacks* and peasants alike for making prisoners was to light great watch-fires at night, a little way off from the retreating column, and as the frozen and starving stragglers came crowding up to the blaze they surrounded them and carried them off wholesale.

After the snow set in, guns and baggage-wagons were abandoned to the *Cossacks* at almost every hundred yards. It was impossible for the weakened and dying horses to drag them along; even to keep their footing on the frozen ground. Within the first week after Wiasma the appalling number of 30,000 horses either died of starvation, there being no way of getting fodder for them because of the snow, or were frozen to death.

In spite of everything, some of the regiments still kept together and marched in military formation, with their Eagles at their head; those in particular of Marshal Ney's corps. They formed the rearguard and chief protection to the army from Wiasma onwards; held together by the heroic example and personality of their indefatigable leader, ever present where there was fighting, ever calm and confident, and ready with words of encouragement. Not an Eagle was lost along the line of march between Moscow and Smolensk by Ney's men; rallying round them to beat off the *Cossack* attacks time and again with the cry, "*Aux Aigles! Voici les Cosaques!*"

This incident, not unlike the *cuirassier* ride to recover the Eagle left on the field at Borodino, is said to have taken place between Wiasma and Smolensk. One regiment of Ney's cavalry missed its Eagle after a sharp fight on the road, the Eagle-bearer having apparently fallen during the encounter, unseen by the survivors. That night round the bivouac fire lots were drawn, and two officers rode back amid blinding snow squalls to try to find the Eagle. They successfully evaded the Cossacks and made their way ten miles back to the scene of the combat, where, after scaring off some wolves, they searched in the snow

---

2. The wolves killed many of the stragglers as they wandered in search of food or shelter from the cold, away from the retreating columns. They followed in the track of the Grand Army to the last, across Germany to the Rhine. It is the fact, indeed, that the presence of wolves today in the forest lands of Central Europe is largely due to the tremendous incursion of ravenous brutes from Russia which swept in huge swarms in rear of Napoleon's ill-fated host.

Marshal Ney with the rearguard in the retreat from Moscow

and found the dead officer's body with the Eagle by its side. They brought it back safely to the regiment and restored it to their comrades. Their limbs were frost-bitten and rigid from cold, so that they had to be lifted off their horses, but the brave men were content—they had saved their Eagle.

At Krasnoi, on November 19, between Smolensk and the Beresina, Napoleon underwent another severe defeat from the pursuing Russians, 10,000 prisoners and 70 guns falling into the victors' hands. Two Eagles were carried off from the battlefield and despatched to St. Petersburg by special courier, together with Kutusoff's report to the *Czar*. Twenty-seven Eagles, however, got past the Russians, fighting their way through, thanks to the endurance of brave men who rallied round them. Krasnoi it was that gave the death-blow to Napoleon's last hope of rallying the Grand Army. After it less than 30,000 men remained under arms with the main column, including the 8,000 survivors of the Imperial Guard.

Up to then, according to the Russian official returns, 80,000 prisoners, 500 guns, and "40 standards and flags of all kinds" had fallen into the hands of the pursuers. Not more than ten, however, of the forty standards taken were Eagles: the two taken at Murat's surprise at Vinkovo; the two taken at Wiasma; the two taken at Krasnoi; also two taken before Napoleon reached Smolensk, from a brigade sent from Smolensk to help him on the road, which blundered into the middle of the Russian army and had to surrender; and two captured elsewhere, from the French flanking armies of Marshal Macdonald and Marshal St. Cyr. An eleventh Eagle was taken in the second battle at Krasnoi, from Ney's rearguard; the only Eagle that Ney actually lost in fight throughout the 600 miles' march between Moscow and the frontier.

At Krasnoi, Ney's rearguard, following at a day's march behind the rest of the army, found its way barred. The Russians, after defeating Napoleon's main column, a day's march in advance, had waited on the scene of the former fighting for Ney. They held a position that it was practically impossible for Ney's comparatively small force to get past. After vainly attempting to break through, Ney had to draw back, and make a forlorn-hope effort to avoid destruction by a long detour, in the course of which he had to abandon guns, baggage, and horses, and cross the Dnieper on ice hardly thick enough to bear the weight of a man.

On the eve of Krasnoi, indeed, the rearguard found itself in so desperate a position, that Ney ordered all its Eagles to be destroyed. His regiments had suffered so severely in their continuous fighting, that it was impossible adequately to safeguard the Eagles. Every musket and bayonet was wanted in the fighting line. It was impossible to supply sufficient Eagle-escorts. So far, in spite of the dreadful straits to which some of the regiments had been reduced, all had marched openly with their Eagles, and fought round them, guarding them sedulously by night and day. Colonel De Fesenzac of the 4th of the Line describes:

> When excess of fatigue constrained us to take a few moments of repose, we (what was left of the regiment able to carry arms—not 100 men) assembled together in any place where we could find shelter, a few of the men standing by to mount guard for the protection of the regimental Eagle.
>
> Then, came the order that all the Eagles should be broken up and buried. As I could not make up my mind to this. I directed that the staff should be burned, and that the Eagle of the 4th Regiment should be stowed in the knapsack of one of the Eagle-bearers, by whose side I kept my post on the march.

The Eagle of the 4th, it may be added by the way, was the identical Eagle that Napoleon had presented to the regiment in place of that lost at Austerlitz, in exchange for, as has been told, two captured Austrian flags. Other officers did the same as Colonel De Fesenzac. One officer, however, the colonel of the 18th of the Line, flatly refused to have his regimental Eagle either broken up or hidden away. He says in his journal, which still exists:

> The Eagle had throughout, until then, been carried at the head of the regiment, and I declined to obey the order on behalf of the 18th. It seemed to us a monstrous ignominy. Our Eagles were not given us to be made away with or hidden: they ought to perish with us.

The Eagle of the 18th did actually perish with the regiment. In the rearguard repulse at Krasnoi the entire regiment was destroyed, except for some twenty survivors, including the colonel, severely wounded. "Our Eagle," says the gallant colonel, proudly recording its fate, "remained among our dead on the field of battle."

That Eagle of the 18th was the only one of Marshal Ney's Eagles to fall into the hands of the Russians in battle. Some ten of the Eagles now at St. Petersburg were found on the bodies of officers and men who had been either frozen to death or had fallen dead on the march during Ney's retreat after Krasnoi; they were not taken in fight.

Ney rejoined Napoleon with only 1,500 men left out of 12,000, of which the rearguard had consisted when it left Smolensk. It was while making his last effort to get past the Russians after his attempt to break through at Krasnoi had failed, that Ney, overtaken on the banks of the half-frozen Dnieper on the evening before he risked his perilous crossing, and summoned by the Russians to surrender, made that proudly defiant reply which has ever since been a treasured memory to the French Army: "*A Marshal of France never surrenders!*": Six hours later he had evaded capture and, with the remnant of his corps, was across the river. All the world has heard how Napoleon, hopeless of seeing him again, welcomed Ney with the words:

> I have three hundred millions of *francs* in the vaults of the Tuileries; I would have given them all for Marshal Ney!

The remaining Eagles had by now been assembled for preservation under the protection of what troops of the main column, which Napoleon accompanied, still continued under arms. Further effort to rally the shattered host was beyond possibility. Only portions of the two army corps of Marshals Victor and Oudinot, called in from holding the line of communications, still retained military formation, together with the reduced battalions of the Old Guard which had kept near Napoleon throughout. To save the remaining Eagles, the officers of broken-up and disbanded regiments, with some devoted soldiers who stood by them, took personal charge of the Eagles, and carried them with their own hands. Banding together and marching in company side by side, they tramped on, plodding through the snow day and night for 200 miles; the collected Eagles all massed in the centre. They attached themselves to the column of the Old Guard, and kept their way close by Napoleon.

A survivor of the retreat from Moscow, in his memoirs, describes how he saw Napoleon and the Eagles pass by him on the way to the Beresina on the morning of November 25:

> Those in advance seemed to be generals, a few on horseback, but the greater part on foot. There was also a great number of other officers, the remnant of the doomed squadron and battalion, formed on the 22nd and barely existing at the end of three days. Those on foot dragged themselves painfully along, almost all of them having their feet frozen and wrapped in rags or in bits of sheep's-skin, and all nearly dying of hunger. Afterwards came the small remains of the Cavalry of the Guard. The Emperor came next, on foot, and carrying a staff. He wore a large cloak

lined with fur, and had a red velvet cap with black-fox fur on his head. Murat walked on foot at his right, and on his left the Prince Eugène, Viceroy of Italy. Next came the Marshals Berthier—Prince of Neufchatel—Ney, Mortier, Lefebvre, with other marshals and generals whose corps had been annihilated.

The Emperor mounted a horse as soon as he had passed; so did a few of those with him: the greater part of them had no horses to ride. Seven or eight hundred officers and non-commissioned officers followed, walking in order and perfect silence, and carrying the Eagles of their different regiments, which had so often led them to victory. This was all that remained of 60,000 men. After them came the Imperial Guard on foot, marching also in order.

Four Eagles were lost in the fighting at the passage of the Beresina, where a whole division of Marshal Victor's corps (General Partonneaux's) was cut off and compelled to surrender. On the last night, when either massacre under the Russian guns or laying down their arms was all that was left to them, they broke up and buried their Eagles in the ground underneath the snow. The officers of one regiment, it is told, broke up their Eagle before burying it, burned the flag at their last bivouac fire, mixed the ashes with thawed snow, and swallowed the concoction.

The little column of officers with their Eagles passed the Beresina with the Guard, and thus escaped that last catastrophe, the crowning horror of the bridge disaster, when 24,000 ill-fated human beings were sent to their account; either killed in the fighting with the Russians, or drowned in the river, jammed together on the burning bridge, while the Russian guns from the rear thundered on them with shot and shell.

The officer-escort with the Eagles tramped on until Wilna was reached; until after Napoleon had left the army and set off for Paris. Then, on the final falling apart of the remnants of the stricken host, the officers themselves dispersed, to escape as best they could individually and get to the Niemen; breaking up the Eagle-poles and concealing the Eagles and flags in knapsacks or under their uniforms. The dispersal, says one officer, was at Napoleon's own instance.

He ordered all the officers who had no troops to make the best of their way at once to the Niemen, considering that their services had best be saved for the future army he was going to

Napoleon and the "Sacred Squadron" on the way to the Beresina

Paris to raise and organise.

That is one story. According to another officer, utter despair at their frightful position, abandoned by their chief, was the cause of the breakup at Wilna and the final *débâcle*.

Until then a few armed soldiers, led by their officers, had still rallied round the Eagles. Now, however, the officers began to break away, and the soldiers became fewer and fewer, and those left were finally reduced, of necessity, some to conceal the Eagles in knapsacks, others to make away with them.

Some of the officers fell dead on the way to the Niemen, struck down suddenly by the cold, and their Eagles remained with them. Others who died, with their last strength tried to put their charges beyond reach of the enemy by scraping or digging holes in the frozen ground, and burying the Eagles.[3]

The Eagle of the Old Guard recrossed the Niemen at Kovno, while Ney was making his final stand, defending the gate of the town;

---

3. Coignet, then a lieutenant of the Old Guard, thus speaks of the horrors of those latter days immediately following the Beresina: "The cold continued to grow more intense; the horses in the bivouacs died of hunger and cold. Every day some were left where we had passed the night. The roads were like glass. The horses fell down, and could not get up. Our worn-out soldiers no longer had strength to carry their arms. The barrels of their guns were so cold that they stuck to their hands. It was twenty-eight degrees below zero. But the Guard gave up their knapsacks and guns only with their lives. In order to save our lives, we had to eat the horses that fell upon the ice. The soldiers opened the skin with their knives, and took out the entrails, which they roasted on the coals, if they had time to make a fire; and, if not, they ate them raw. They devoured the horses before they died. I also ate this food as long as the horses lasted. As far as Wilna we travelled by short stages with the Emperor. His whole staff marched along the sides of the road. The men of the demoralised army marched along like prisoners, without arms and without knapsacks. There was no longer any discipline or any human feeling for one another. Each man looked out for himself. Every sentiment of humanity was extinguished. No one would have reached out his hand to his father; and that can easily be understood. For he who stooped down to help his fellow would not be able to rise again. We had to march right on, making faces to pre-vent our noses and ears from freezing. The men became insensible to every human feeling. No one even murmured against our misfortunes. The men fell, frozen stiff, all along the road. If, by chance, any of them came upon a bivouac of other unfortunate creatures who were thawing themselves, the newcomers pitilessly pushed them aside, and took possession of their fire. The poor creatures would then lie down to die upon the snow. One must have seen these horrors in order to believe them. . . . But it was at Wilna that we suffered most. The weather was so severe that the men could no longer endure it: even the ravens froze."

the marshal fighting musket in hand at the last, with less than twenty soldiers. That Eagle was still carried openly—the only one still so displayed—carried defiantly aloft on its staff, borne to the last with its escort in military formation, in the midst of the ranks of the 400 men of the Old Guard who were all that were able to reach the frontier.

At Bay in Northern Germany 1813

There were yet dark days in store for the Eagles after the retreat from Moscow was over. The tale of their misfortunes was not yet ended. There was yet to be the sequel to the great catastrophe; further humiliations in the War in Germany of 1813, and the Winter Campaign of 1814 in Eastern France, which followed as the consequence and result of the overthrow in Russia.

No fewer than fifteen of the Eagles that the devotion of their officers brought through the retreat from Moscow are now—making allowance for difficulties of identification, owing to defective records—among the trophies of victory to be seen at Berlin and Potsdam, in Vienna, and also at St. Petersburg. Those in Germany are mostly kept in the Garrison Church of Potsdam, suspended triumphantly above the vault in which lies the sarcophagus of Frederick the Great. They were placed there of set purpose as an act of retribution, as a votive offering to the *manes* of the Great Frederick; as a Prussian rejoinder to Napoleon's act of wanton desecration after Jena. The four trophy Eagles at Vienna are in the Imperial Arsenal Museum there. Two of them are the spoils of Kulm; displayed together with the keys of Lyons, Langres, Troyes, and the fortress of Mayence, which were surrendered during the march of the Allies on Paris.

The Russian trophy Eagles of 1813 are at St. Petersburg, displayed with the Eagles which fell into Russian hands in the retreat from Moscow. What the annihilation of the Grand Army in Russia meant for Europe, with what dramatic rapidity its import for the vassal states of Napoleon was realised and turned to account, is a familiar story. Prussia led the revolt at once, and all Northern Germany rose in arms *en masse* to commence the "War of Liberation," joining hands with Russia as the pursuing armies of the *Czar* crossed the frontier. Then Austria, after negotiations rendered abortive at the last by Napoleon's infatuated pride and overweening self-confidence, threw her sword into the balance and turned the scale decisively against France. Napoleon's hastily raised conscript levies, out-numbered and outmanoeuvred, were defeated on battlefield after battlefield, and driven in rout across the Rhine to their final surrender at the gates of Paris; and then came the abdication of Fontainebleau.

Yet, with all that, in those dark hours of their fate the Eagles died hard. The trophy-collections of Berlin, Vienna, and St. Petersburg testify to that. Only a percentage of the Eagles which faced their fate on the battlefield became spoils to the victors. Marshal Macdonald's army, routed by Blücher on the Katzbach, thanks to the devotion of the regimental officers and some of their men, saved all its Eagles from the enemy except three. Ney's army, no less roughly handled at Dennewitz, managed to retain in like manner all its Eagles except three. Vandamme's army, annihilated and dispersed at Kulm, saved its Eagles all but two. Oudinot was routed at Gross Beeren, with the loss of guns and many prisoners; Gérard underwent the same fate near Magdeburg; Bertrand was surprised and defeated with heavier losses still; but not one Eagle was left as spoil of these disasters in the hands of the victorious foe.

In one battle the Eagle of Napoleon's Irish Legion was only just kept from being today among the trophies displayed in the Garrison Church of Potsdam over the tomb of Frederick the Great. It was immediately after Macdonald's defeat on the Katzbach. The Irish Legion was one of the regiments in one of Macdonald's divisions, that of General Puthod. They had had a hard fight of it, and their retreat was barred by the River Bober in flood. Under stress of the continuous attacks of the Prussians in ever-increasing force, the 12,000 men of Puthod's Division had been reduced to barely 5,000. They had used up their last cartridges, and had been driven back to the riverbank, where the Prussian army closed in on them "in a half-moon." The Prussians halted for one moment until they realised that the troops before them had no more ammunition. Then, aware that they had their foe at their mercy, they rushed forward, cheering exultantly, to deliver the *coup de grâce*. An Irish officer describes:

> All of a sudden 30,000 men ran forward on their prey, of whom none but those who knew how to swim could attempt to escape.

The greater number of the French, all the same, jumped into the river, and took the risk of drowning rather than surrender. Less than five hundred got across the stream, and after that they had to wade waist-deep for half a mile over flooded marshes under a pitiless fire from the Prussian batteries. In the end only 150 men reached dry ground alive. Among the survivors were just 40 men of the Irish Legion, with their Eagle—Colonel Ware, eight officers, the Eagle-bearer, and thirty privates. The Irish remnant made their way eventually to Dresden, and reported themselves to Napoleon.

That adventure, by the way, was the Irish Eagle's second escape from falling into an enemy's hands since Napoleon presented it to the Legion on the Field of Mars. On the first occasion it came within an ace of being now among our British trophy Eagles at Chelsea; of, indeed, being the first Napoleonic Eagle to be brought as spoil of war to England. The Irish Legion was in garrison at Flushing in 1809, when the fortress surrendered to the British Walcheren Expedition. On the night before the final capitulation, Major Lawless of the Irish Legion took charge of the Eagle, and in a rowing-boat made a risky passage among the British ships of war in front of the batteries. He escaped up the Scheldt to Antwerp, where he delivered the Eagle personally to Marshal Bernadotte. Napoleon sent for the major to Paris, decorated him for saving the Eagle, with the Cross of the Legion of Honour, and promoted him lieutenant-colonel.

In the disaster on the Bober also, a soldier of the 134th of the Line saved the Eagle of another regiment, the 147th. The two regiments, as the Prussians charged down on them after their cartridges gave out, in desperation rushed to meet their assailants with the bayonet. They were overpowered and hurled back in confusion to the bank of the river, all intermingled in the *mêlée*. The Eagle-bearer of the 147th fell dead, shot down, and a Prussian officer made for the Eagle. A soldier of the 134th bayoneted the officer as he got to it, picked up the Eagle, and, seeing only more Prussians round him, flung himself, still holding on to the Eagle, into the river. The man could not swim, and was fired at as he floundered in the water, but he was not hit.

Unable to reach the other side, he somehow got on to a shallow patch, and, still holding fast to the Eagle, kept his footing there, until, to get away from the hail of bullets all round him, he again risked drowning by trying to drift downstream. He managed to keep his head above water, and got over to a bed of rushes, fringing the farther bank. Creeping in there, still holding on closely to the Eagle, the brave fellow hid for six hours until dark, embedded in mud to his armpits most of the time. After nightfall he worked his way through and crawled ashore. Finally, after wandering across country for eight days, feeding on berries and what he could pick up, in constant peril of discovery among the hostile peasants and parties of Prussian dragoons scouring the district, the heroic soldier at length found his way to Dresden. There he was brought before Marshal Berthier, to whom he delivered the Eagle.

At the Battle of the Katzbach the colonel of the 132nd of the Line threw away his life under the mistaken impression that he saw the Eagle of his regiment captured by the enemy. He was short-sighted, and suddenly missed it in the middle of a charge. Thinking he saw the Eagle being carried off by a party of Prussians he rode straight through the enemy at them, to fall mortally wounded halfway, with his horse shot beneath him. Some of the men saw the colonel fall, and charged after him. They got to him and carried him off the field, and in the retreat until a place of safety was reached, where the survivors of the regiment had rallied.

There the officers came round to bid farewell to their dying chief. The Eagle-bearer of the regiment was among them, and he, to the amazement of all, produced the Eagle from his *havresac*, broken from its staff, and held it up before the eyes of the dying colonel. No enemy's hand, he declared, had contaminated it. Finding himself and the Eagle, he explained, in imminent danger of capture, he had wrenched the Eagle off the staff and hidden it—his act causing the disappearance which the colonel had marked, and which had resulted in his fatal dash among the enemy.

The 17th of the Line saved their Eagle and themselves after Vandamme's defeat at Kulm, and made their way to safety, as one of the officers relates, after an extraordinary series of adventures. They had joined Vandamme's army at the beginning of the first day's fighting-the battle lasted three days—coming in after a week's march from Dresden, through pouring rain most of the time. They numbered four battalions, 4,000 men in all. Vandamme was successful on the first two days and the 17th by themselves routed an Austrian regiment and captured a gun.

On the evening of the second day the French advanced again, driving the enemy before them into the valley of Kulm. They bivouacked on the ground they had won, anticipating a final triumph on the morrow. But during that night two Russian and Prussian army corps reinforced the Austrian columns unknown to the French.

One of the officers of the 17th, Major Fantin des Odoards, during the night had his suspicions aroused about the enemy, and made a discovery; but Vandamme would not listen to him. Major Fantin says:

He was unable to sleep, and, learning from a patrol that mysterious sounds were being heard in the direction in which the Austrians had retreated, he left the bivouac and went out alone beyond the outposts, to creep in the dark towards the Austrian watch-fires. At times, as he crawled forward, he lay flat and listened with his ear to the ground. In the end he felt certain that he heard the tramp and stir of a vast number of men, and also the rumble of artillery wheels moving across the front.

Apparently, from the direction the unseen troops were taking, they were marching to cut off the retreat of the army from Dresden, Napoleon's base of operations throughout the campaign.

Major Fantin returned to the bivouac and went at once to report to the general, finding him asleep. He aroused Vandamme and told what he had heard and suspected; only, however, to be rebuffed and rudely answered that he was quite mistaken. Vandamme, a surly and ill-conditioned boor to deal with at all times, awoke in a vile temper. "You are a fool!" was what he said in reply. "If the enemy are on the move at all, they are in retreat, trying to escape me. Tomorrow will see them flying, or my prisoners." With that Vandamme terminated the interview, and turned over and went to sleep again.

He found out his mistake all too soon. Daylight disclosed dense swarms of Austrians, Prussians, and Russians in front of Vandamme, on his flanks, and closing on his rear; outnumbering him nearly four to one. It was a desperate position, for the only road by which Vandamme might retreat was held by the enemy. Little time was left to him to deliberate what to do. He was in the act of forming up his columns in a mass to try to fight his way through, when the enemy attacked in overpowering force.

Before noon that day, out of 30,000 men, 10,000 had fallen. Seven thousand more were wounded or prisoners. The rest were fugitives, flying for shelter and hiding-places in the woods round the battlefield. All the French guns and baggage had been taken, and Vandamme himself was a prisoner, together with many officers of rank. The "annals of modern warfare record few instances of defeat more complete than that of Vandamme at Kulm."

The only regiment that kept its order was the 17th, and it before the crisis had lost heavily. Its colonel and two of the *chefs de bataillon* had been killed; the two others were wounded. Only some 1,700 of the 4,000 men remained. It rested with Major Fantin, as senior officer, to save those that were left and the Eagle.

The 17th were on the extreme right of the battle, where they had been posted as support to Vandamme's artillery. They held their ground as long as possible, but the enemy closed in on them, overlapping them on both flanks, and then stormed and captured the guns. The 17th were isolated and in imminent peril—surrender or destruction were the only alternatives before them.

Looking round, the major, as he describes, marked a wooded hill some little way off, and decided to make for that. There was just time to get away before the enemy closed in on them. He sent off all his *tirailleurs*, about 400 men, to skirmish and hold in check the advancing Austrians. As they went off he shouted to the rest: "*En haut l'Aigle! Ralliement au drapeau!*" ("Display the Eagle! All rally to the standard!") The men of the regiment formed round him quickly, and the major pointed out the wooded hill to them with his sword. "All of you disperse at once," he told them, "and make your way there as quickly as you can. You will find the Eagle of the regiment there, and me with it."

The 17th broke up and scattered, and, under the protection of the skirmishers, aided by the opportune mist which hung low over the ground after the heavy rains of the past week, they made off in groups in the direction pointed out. All just got past the enemy in time, Major Fantin and two officers accompanying the Eagle.

An hour later, "*nos débris*," as the major puts it, were straggling up the hill, where they again rallied round the Eagle. The skirmishers, cleverly withdrawn at the right moment, evaded the enemy also, and most of them joined their comrades on the hill, where all silently drew together. They then moved off, to halt for concealment in a wooded glade behind. They stayed there, keeping quiet and lying down beside their arms, for several hours; off the track of the pursuit, and undiscovered by the enemy. "We were all very hungry and without anything but what cartridges we had still left."

At nightfall they moved away in the direction in which Dresden was judged to be, without having a single map or anything to guide them. They marched all night, mostly by a forest road, and keeping their direction by means of occasional glimpses of the stars seen through rifts in the cloudy sky overhead. More than once they had to halt as the enemy were heard on the move not far off. They groped their way forward with extreme caution, not a light being struck, and the necessary words of command being spoken in an undertone, until after midnight. Then they suddenly came into the open round a bend of the road, and discovered, not half a mile off in front, the numerous watch-fires of a large body of troops.

The column halted at the sight like one man and stood in absolute silence. Who were those in front of us? Friends or the enemy?

Two scouts were sent forward to try to find out. They were away for half an hour; an interval of intense suspense and anxiety to the others. At the end of the time the two scouts came rushing back. They brought unexpectedly good news. It was a French bivouac: that of the 14th Army Corps—Marshal St. Cyr's. So the 17th and their Eagle were saved.

Other Eagles that got away from the rout at Kulm and rejoined the army owed their safety to the determination of small groups of officers and men who cut their way through the enemy.

Officers fought with their swords, privates with their bayonets and the butts of their muskets: and as the struggle was to escape and not to destroy, a push and wrestle, or a blow, which might suffice to throw the individual struck out of the way of the striker, prevented in many instances the more deadly thrust.

Finally, as the 17th had done, they found shelter among the woods and ravines of the neighbourhood, and lay low there until the enemy had moved off towards Töplitz, whereupon they made their way to Dresden. The cavalry saved their Eagles by cutting their way through the enemy. They suffered heavy losses, but succeeded in their effort. Their commander, General Corbineau, "presented himself, wounded and covered with blood, before Napoleon"; it was his arrival that announced the disaster. The Eagles of the 33rd and the 106th of the Line taken at Kulm are at Vienna.

The three days of battle at Leipsic, between October 16 and 19, 1813, cost Napoleon 60,000 men in killed, wounded, and prisoners, and 300 guns; but not more than 6 Eagles were among the trophies of battalion-flags and squadron-colours taken or found on the field, now at Berlin, Vienna, and St. Petersburg.

One Eagle was lost during the first day's fighting at Leipsic—taken on the 16th by Blücher from Ney's corps; but no others were lost until the end. The 80,000 men who were able to make good their retreat with Napoleon across the bridge over the Elster before it was prematurely blown up, through a non-commissioned officer's blunder, carried their Eagles with them. What colour-trophies came into the possession of the Allies were taken amid the final scenes of carnage; from cut-off battalions of the three divisions left behind on the right bank of the river, victims of the destruction of the bridge. They were mostly captured in the ferocious hand-to-hand fighting which marked the closing phase of the battle in the suburbs of Leipsic. The French defended themselves there to the last with the courage of despair among the fortified villas and loopholed garden walls.

Pressed upon by superior numbers, and fighting, now in the streets, now in the houses, now through gardens or other enclosures, the single end which they could accomplish or which in point of fact they seemed to desire, was that they might sell their lives at the dearest rate possible.

Two at least of the Eagles now at Berlin were hastily buried in gardens during the last stand, and were dug up there later when the ground was being turned over.

Forced to give back before their ever-increasing enemies, not a few of the French:

.... preferred death to captivity, and fought to the last. These, retiring through by-lanes and covered passages, made their way to the river, some where the ruins of the bridge covered its banks, some above and others below that point, and, plunging into the deep water, endeavoured to gain the opposite shore by swimming, an attempt in which comparatively few succeeded.

The three doomed divisions of Lauriston, Regnier, and Poniatowski, who were cut off by the blowing up of the bridge, had, as it happened, not many Eagles among them to lose. They were largely made up of newly raised conscript regiments to whom Napoleon had not yet awarded Eagles; regiments not yet entitled to carry Eagles, according to the later regulations that Napoleon had laid down. Only four of the newly raised regiments altogether, so far during the campaign in Germany, had qualified for the honour. They had received their Eagles with the customary ceremony at the hands of Napoleon: three of them on October 15, the day before the battle of Leipsic opened. The fourth had received its Eagle at Dresden a month earlier. Two of these four Eagles only were lost to the enemy at Leipsic.

The Eagle-bearers of four or five other regiments among those cut off by the bridge disaster tried to swim across the Elster with their Eagles. Their fate is unknown; probably they were drowned in the attempt. Other Eagle-bearers, before surrendering, were seen to fling their Eagles into the river to sink there.

How one Eagle, during the battle on the 18th, was momentarily lost, and then regained by a splendid act of valour, is told by Caulaincourt, who was on Napoleon's staff, and witnessed the gallant deed that won the Eagle back. In the midst of the fighting, a number of Saxon regiments abandoned Napoleon's cause and went over *en masse* to the enemy. To signalise their defection they turned on the nearest French regiment and mobbed it; attacking it at close quarters with the bayonet. Thrown into confusion by the unexpected onslaught, the French were for the moment broken and forced back, whereupon the Saxons, making for the Eagle, got possession of it.

> A young officer of Hussars, (*relates Caulaincourt,*) whose name I forget, rushed headlong into the enemies' ranks. In the charge some of the miserable renegades had carried off one of our Eagles. The gallant young officer rescued it, but at the cost of his life. He threw the Eagle at the Emperor's feet, and then he himself fell, mortally wounded and bathed in blood. The Emperor was deeply moved. 'With such men,' he exclaimed, 'what resources does not France possess!'

The regiments left by Napoleon to garrison the fortresses in Germany, at Stettin, at Magdeburg, Torgau, Dantzic, and elsewhere, previous to surrendering took steps to prevent their Eagles falling into the hands of their adversaries. In every case they destroyed them, smashing the Eagles into small fragments, which were either distributed among officers and men, or else thrown into the ditch of the fortress. In more than one case they melted the Eagles down, and broke up and buried the metal, while the flags were burned.

At Dresden, where Marshal St. Cyr had to surrender, a month after Leipsic, the terms granted by the Austrian general conducting the siege allowed the troops to return to France with their arms, their baggage, and their Eagles, seven in number. Superior authority, however, cancelled the privilege. The garrison had already started on their march when, to their utter consternation, the capitulation was abruptly annulled by the Austrian *generalissimo*, Schwartzenberg, with the result that the hapless troops were compelled to yield themselves prisoners at discretion.

The soldiers were defenceless and could only submit to their hard fate. They did not, however, let their seven Eagles pass into the enemy's hands. Five of the seven were broken up, and the flags torn to pieces and divided among the regiments. Two of the Eagles, those of the 25th of the Line and the 85th, were concealed intact by two officers, who kept them from discovery for months, while they were prisoners in Hungary. After the Peace, in the following year, they brought them back to France—to meet there the doom that awaited all the Eagles of Napoleon of which the officials of the Bourbon *régime* got possession.

One memento of the Winter Campaign in Eastern France is now at the Invalides—the Eagle of the 5th of the Line. It was found in the river Aube at Arcis after the battle there, which, in its result, decided the fate of Napoleon; its outcome being the immediate march of the Allied armies on Paris. The 5th was one of the regiments of the rearguard column, under Oudinot, half of which was drowned in the river in trying to get across at night, after stubbornly holding out in the town all the afternoon in order to enable Napoleon to cross the river in safety. The 5th was one of the regiments that sacrificed themselves. Its Eagle-bearer was among the drowned, and his Eagle sank with him. It remained in the bed of the stream until long afterwards, when it was accidentally discovered, and fished up.

The 132nd of the Line of the modern army of France commemorates on its flag a feat of arms done under the Eagle of the old 132nd of Napoleon's Army, after having been saved from the Prussians at the Katzbach, and again at Leipsic. It was in one of the fights in the closing campaign in Eastern France. The proud legend inscribed in golden letters, "*Rosny, 1814: Un contre huit,*" commemorates how the regiment, single-handed, held at bay and beat off an enemy eight times its force, saving itself for the third time, and its Eagle.

The surviving Eagles of the war, the last to face the enemy in the north of those presented on the Field of Mars, paid their last salute to the War Lord at Napoleon's final review of the remnants of the Grand Army at Rheims on March 15, 1814.

A pitiful, a moving, sight was that hapless military spectacle: the closing parade before Napoleon of his last remaining soldiers.

This is how Alison describes it:

> How different from the splendid military spectacles of the Tuileres or Chammartin, which had so often dazzled his sight with the pomp of apparently irresistible power! Wasted away to half the numbers which they possessed when they crossed the Marne a fortnight before, the greater part of the regiments exhibited only the skeletons of military array. In some, more officers than privates were to be seen in the ranks; in all, the appearance of the troops, the haggard air of the men, their worn-out uniforms, and the strange motley of which they were com-

posed, bespoke the total exhaustion of the Empire.

It was evident to all that Napoleon was expending his last resources. Besides the veterans of the Guard—the iron men whom nothing could daunt, but whose tattered garments and soiled accoutrements bespoke the dreadful fatigue to which they had been subjected—were to be seen young conscripts, but recently torn from the embraces of maternal love, and whose wan visages and faltering steps told but too clearly that they were unequal to the weight of the arms they bore. The gaunt figures and woeful aspect of the horses, the broken carriages and blackened mouths of the guns, the crazy and fractured artillery wagons which denied past, the general confusion of arms, battalions, and uniforms, even in the best appointed corps, spoke of the mere remains of the vast military army which had so long stood triumphant against the world in arms.

The soldiers exhibited none of their ancient enthusiasm as they denied past the Emperor; silent and sad they took their way before him: the stern realities of war had chased away its enthusiastic ardour. All felt that in this dreadful contest they themselves would perish, happy if they had not previously witnessed the degradation of France![4]

What is indeed the most interesting of all the Eagles, the most famous battle-standard in the world, which for a time was at the Invalides, is at present preserved in private hands in Paris—the Eagle of Napoleon's Old Guard, the Eagle of the "*Adieu* of Fontainebleau." It is treasured with devoted care in the family of the officer who commanded the Grenadiers of the Guard in the retreat from Moscow, at Fontainebleau, and at Waterloo—General Petit. It is kept in the house, in Paris, in which the old general died, in the room he used as his *salon*. General Petit refused to be parted from the Eagle of his regiment during his lifetime; he kept it with him where-ever he went, always in his personal care. It was at the Invalides while General Petit was in residence there as governor of the hospital.

---

4. One of those who presented arms before Napoleon at the Rheims review died, just twenty years ago, as the last French survivor of Trafalgar—André Manuel Cartigny. At Trafalgar he had been a powder-boy on board the celebrated *Redoubtable*, from the mizen-top of which the bullet was fired which killed Nelson. He paraded at Rheims among the remnant of survivors of Napoleon's last battalion left of the Seamen of the Guard, and was present a month later at the historic farewell at Fontainebleau.

On that never-to-be-forgotten April forenoon of 1814, in the Court of the White Horse of the Château of Fontainebleau, Napoleon embraced the standard, and taking the Eagle in his hands, kissed it in front of the veteran Grenadiers of the Old Guard. His travelling carriage, to convey the fallen Emperor on the first stage of his journey to Elba, was in waiting, close by, ready to start. Twelve hundred Grenadiers of the Guard stood with presented arms all round the courtyard; drawn up in a great hollow square as a guard of honour to render to the master they adored the parting salute.

Napoleon passed slowly round the square and inspected the ranks, man by man, looking intently into the scarred and war-worn, weather-beaten old faces, each one of which was familiar to him. Their station on every battlefield had been close at hand to where he took up his post. Night after night, in every campaign from Austerlitz to those last dreadful weeks, he had slept in their midst; his tent always pitched in the centre of the camp of the Imperial Guard. That had been Napoleon's invariable custom in war. They had shared with him that last forlorn-hope march to save Paris, until, completely worn out and footsore, exhausted nature forbade their attempting to go farther. With tears streaming from their eyes the old soldiers, before whose bayonets in the charge no Continental foe had ever stood, mutely returned Napoleon's last wistful, pathetic look of farewell.

He addressed a few touching words to them, standing in the centre of the square. Next he turned to General Petit, near at hand, and before them he took the general in his arms, as representing all, and kissed him on the cheek. "I cannot embrace you all," exclaimed Napoleon in a voice broken with emotion, yet which all could hear distinctly, "so I embrace your General!" Then he motioned to the *Porte-Aigle*, standing all the while before him, with the Eagle held in the attitude of salute.

"Bring me the Eagle," he said, "that I may embrace it also!" "*Que m'apporte l'Aigle, que je l'embrasse aussi!*" were Napoleon's words.

The *Porte-Aigle* advanced and again inclined the Eagle forward to the Emperor. Napoleon took hold of it, embraced and kissed it three times, tears in his eyes, and displaying the deepest emotion.

"Ah, chère Aigle," he exclaimed, "*que les baisers que je te donne retentissent dans la postérité.*"

The Eagle-bearer then stepped back a pace.

"*Adieu, mes enfants! Adieu, mes braves! Entourez moi encore une fois!*" were Napoleon's closing words as the historic scene terminated.

Napoleon's farewell to the Old Guard at Fontainebleau

The old soldiers all stood utterly broken down, weeping bitter tears, overcome with grief, as Napoleon made his way to the carriage; the members of the Household bowing low as he passed, and kissing his hand, were all also in tears.

Finally, amid a mournful cry of "*Vive l'Empereur!*": Napoleon drove away.

As soon as Napoleon's carriage was beyond the precincts, the Grenadiers of the Guard solemnly lowered the Imperial Standard, flying above the *château*. There, in the courtyard, they burned it. Then, mixing the ashes in a barrel of wine that was brought out, they handed round the liquor in bowls and drank off the draught, pledging Napoleon with cries of "*Vive l'Empereur!*" So it is related by one who was an eyewitness and a partaker; one of the officers of the Old Guard.

Kept safely in concealment for ten months by General Petit, during the Bourbon Restoration period in 1814, the Eagle of the Old Guard appeared once more after the return from Elba. It faced the enemy for the last time at Waterloo. Something of that will be said further on. General Petit kept close beside it all through the retreat, during that night of horror after Waterloo; a faithful band of devoted veterans accompanying him and surrounding the Eagle. So it made its final return to France, to be preserved for the rest of his life by the man who, above all others, had most right to be custodian of the Eagle of the Old Guard.

The Bourbon War Minister ordered it to be given up, to be burned at the artillery *dépôt* at Vincennes with the other Eagles that the Restoration officials were able to get hold of. General Petit flatly and indignantly refused to part with the Eagle of the Old Guard. He was able, as before, to conceal it successfully, in spite of every effort to discover its whereabouts, until after the Revolution of 1830. Then, at the last, it was safe.

Faded and frayed away in parts, the gold embroidery on it dulled and tarnished from the lapse of years, and torn here and there round the jagged bullet-holes in the silk, is now, in its old age, the Flag of the Old Guard. As it was at first—as it was when it made its debut at the opening of its career, on that December afternoon on the Field of Mars—the flag is of rich crimson silk, fringed with gold, sprinkled over on both sides with golden bees, and with, at the corners, encircled in golden laurel-wreaths, the Imperial cipher, the letter "N," In shape it was—and of course is still—almost a square: a metre deep, vertically, on the staff, and some half-dozen inches more than that lengthwise, horizontally, in the fly. On one side, in the centre, the Napoleonic Eagle is displayed, a gold embroidered Eagle poised on a thunder-bolt. Inscribed round the Eagle in letters of gold is the legend:

Garde Impériale
L'Empereur Napoléon
Au 1er Regiment des
Grenadiers à Pied.

On the other side are inscribed these fifteen names of Napoleon's great days in war, also in golden letters: "Marengo; Ulm; Austerlitz; Jena; Berlin; Eylau; Friedland; Madrid; Eckmühl; Essling; Wagram; Vienna; Smolensk; Moskowa; Moscow."

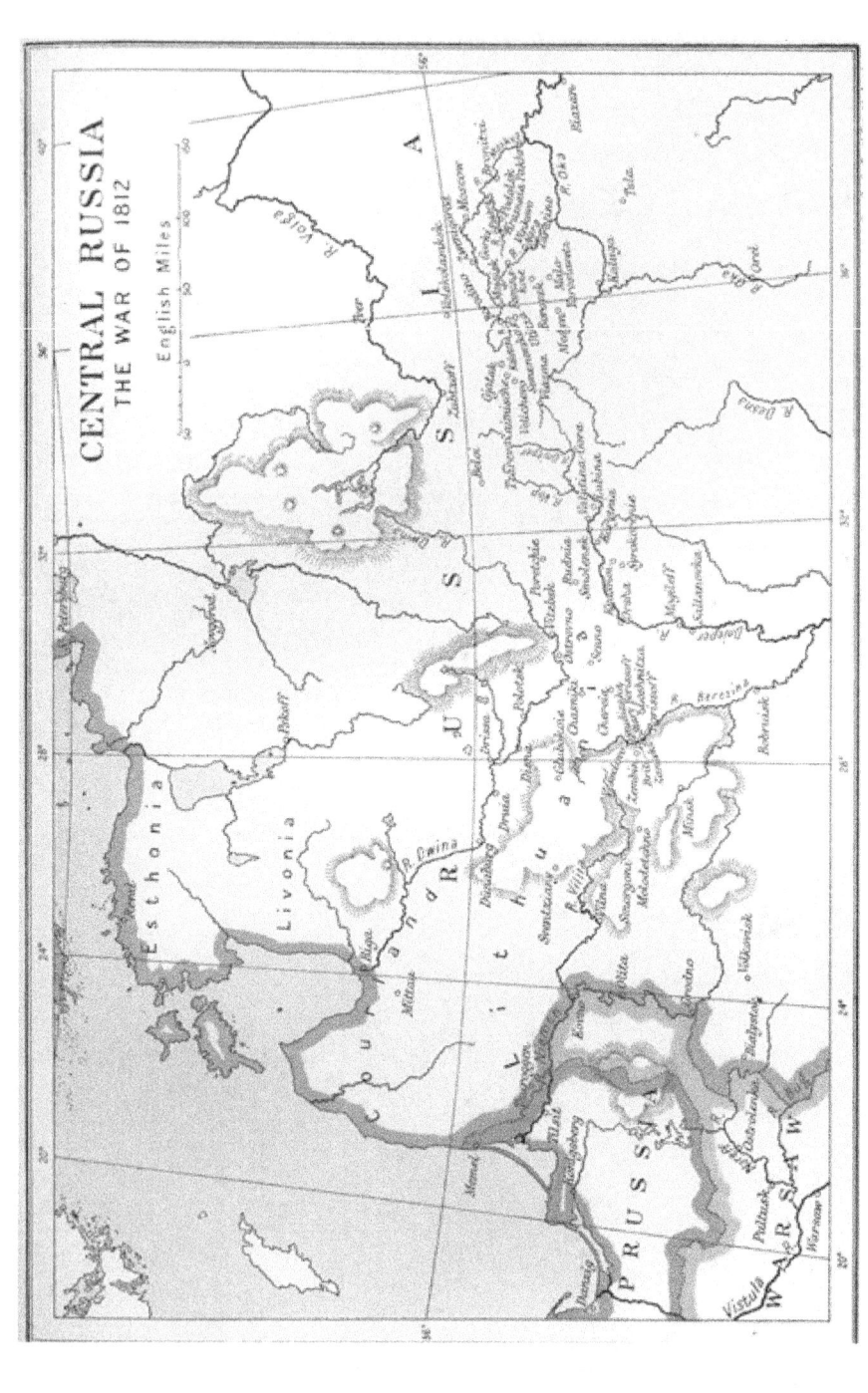

CHAPTER 11

That Terrible Midnight at the Invalides

The Battalion Eagles of 1804, those of the second and third battalions withdrawn by the decree of 1808, together with the Light Cavalry (Hussar, Chasseur, and Dragoon) Eagles recalled in the autumn of 1805, and a number of Light Infantry Eagles returned to the Ministry of War at the end of 1807, perished in the flames of the great holocaust of trophy-flags at the Invalides on the night of March 30, 1814, the night of the surrender of Paris to the Allies.

It was on that tragic Wednesday night that the great sacrifice was made, amid the bowed and weeping old soldiers of France, the veterans of a hundred battlefields, on the most terrible and mournful occasion in the wide-ranging annals of the great institution which the *Grand Monarque*, in the full pride of his power, at the topmost pinnacle of his renown, founded and opened in person with grandiose martial pomp and State display. All was over for France on that night

Around a slaughtered army lay,
No more to conquer and to bleed:
The power and glory of the war
Had passed to the victorious Czar.

The two marshals charged with the defence of Paris, Marmont and Mortier, had on that afternoon placed the submission of the capital in the hands of Alexander of Russia on the heights of Montmartre, whence, and from the Buttes Chaumont and the other northern heights from right to left, 300 loaded cannon pointed threateningly down over the vanquished and panic-stricken city, supported by the bayonets and sabres of 120,000 men, Russians and Prussians, Bavarians, Würtemburgers, and Austrians, flushed and exultant in their hour of supreme triumph, the soldiers of all the nations of the Continent at war with Napoleon.

It was at ten o'clock on that fateful night for France that the great destruction of trophies at the Invalides took place. Napoleon had set his last stake, had attempted his desperate last manoeuvre, and had failed. He had been foiled and baffled when within reach almost of his goal. At that very hour indeed, only twelve miles away, he had just been stopped in his wild midnight gallop, his final forlorn-hope effort to reach the capital, by the news that all hope was past, that the worst had happened, that Paris had fallen.

Only forty-eight hours before, on Monday night, at Saint-Dizier, a small town 170 miles away, had Napoleon suddenly realised the gravity of the catastrophe impending over Paris. He was at that moment in the act of dealing the Allies a counter-stroke which he confidently believed would save the situation and bring the enemy's advance to a general stand. Just a week before, he had abruptly turned back in his retreat towards the capital and had boldly started to march across the rear of the Allies in the direction of the Rhine. He would sever their communications; he would cut the enemy off from their base. Calling out the *levée en masse* of the peasantry all over Eastern France, and at the same time rallying to him the garrisons of the French fortresses in Alsace and Lorraine, with 100,000 men at his disposal, led by Ney, Macdonald, Victor, and Oudinot, while two other marshals, Marmont and Mortier, held the enemy at bay in front of Paris, he was looking forward to checkmate the Allies at the last moment and paralyse their advance on the capital.

It was a daring and masterly project; but the Fortune of War was against Napoleon. He had sent word of his plans to Marie Louise at the Tuileries, together with instructions to his brother Joseph, Governor of Paris, but on the way a *cossack* patrol captured the bearer of the vitally important documents. Napoleon's despatch for once was not in cipher, and its full import was apparent instantly. It was carried to the Czar Alexander, and forthwith laid before a hastily convened Russian council of war. Another letter, taken at the same time, laid bare the critical condition of affairs inside Paris itself, describing how all was in confusion there, and that treachery to the cause of the Empire was at work within the city.

The council of war decided to pay no heed to Napoleon's counter-stroke, and, instead, to march at once on Paris in full force. Marmont and Mortier, it was known, could barely muster 6,000 regulars. With Blücher's Prussians, at that moment on the point of joining them, the Allies could bring into line not far short of 150,000 men. This final plan was agreed to on the afternoon of Friday, March 24, and the general advance began at once.

Napoleon knew nothing of what was happening until late on the night of the 27th, the following Monday. Then he was suddenly made aware of the full position. "Nothing," exclaimed the doomed Emperor in blank dismay, "but a thunderbolt can save us now." The Allies then had not turned back! The enemy nearest him, whom he had planned to attack next day, believing them to be the Russian main army, was only—he discovered at the last moment—a cavalry division, sent back to delude him and prevent his finding out what was really going on. And the troops advancing on Paris were already three clear days ahead of him! Napoleon counter-marched his whole force at once to hasten to the rescue of the capital. They would take the route by Sens, Troyes, and Fontainebleau, making a sweep to keep clear of the enemy's columns, and approach Paris by the south bank of the Seine. It was a long march of fully 180 miles, but there was no other way open. Marmont and Mortier, to whom the news of Napoleon's intended approach was sent off immediately, must manage to hold out in front of the city on the north bank until the Emperor arrived.

Fresh news, however, and yet more serious, as to the imminence of the grave peril threatening Paris, reached Napoleon during Tuesday night. Leaving the army to follow, he pressed forward ahead of the troops by himself in his travelling-carriage, escorted only by the Old Guard. They hurried forward with feverish eagerness all that night and the next day, the men of the Guard panting along at the double in their effort to keep up. With hardly a halt, they struggled along, famishing—most of the men had tasted no cooked food for the past five days—shoeless most of them, plodding and splashing barefoot through the mud, ankle deep; under a pitiless downpour of rain all the time. By Wednesday evening, the 30th, they had reached Troyes, after a forty miles march without a stop. There, still worse news reached Napoleon. Marmont and Mortier had been disastrously defeated at Meaux, and in consequence their defence of the northern heights outside the city was all but hopeless.

Napoleon, on that, abandoned his travelling-carriage for a light post-chaise, which set off at a gallop. He must now risk a ride practically unattended, in the desperate hope of being able to evade hostile patrols and get by stealth into the city. Once there, he would himself take charge of the defence. The men of the Old Guard were left behind at Troyes. They were worn out and unable, from sheer exhaustion, to go a step farther. Only a troop of *cuirassiers* rode with the post-chaise, and most of these had to give up and drop back as the chaise raced forward, Napoleon himself from time to time calling from the windows to the postillions to keep on flogging the horses and go faster and faster.

At every stopping-place to change horses the Emperor sent off a courier to tell Paris to hold out; and at each post-house he received still more alarming messages from the city. Now he heard that the Empress and his little son had had to fly from Paris. Then he learned that the whole city was in a state of complete panic, with affrighted peasants from all round crowding in; the shops and banks all shut; the theatres closed, a thing that had not happened even at the height of the Reign of Terror; everywhere chaos and hopeless despair. After that came the news that the enemy were advancing so fast that they were expected at any moment before the City barriers.

At ten o'clock Napoleon arrived at the village of Fromenteau, near the Fountains of Juvisy, twelve and a half miles from Paris. The post-chaise had to stop there again for a relay of fresh horses. As it drew up, a party of soldiers passed by, coming from the direction of the capital. Not knowing who was in the chaise, some of them shouted out to the occupants, Napoleon, and Caulaincourt, who had been riding with the Emperor: "Paris has surrendered!"

The dread news struck Napoleon like a bullet between the eyes. "It is impossible! The men are mad!" he hissed out, gripping at the cushions of his seat. Then he turned to his companion: "Find an officer and bring him to me!"

One rode up, as it happened, at that moment, a General Belliard. Napoleon questioned him eagerly, and he gave the Emperor sufficient details to leave no doubt of what had befallen. Great drops of sweat stood on Napoleon's forehead. He turned, quivering with excitement, to Caulaincourt. "Do you hear that?" he ejaculated hoarsely, fixing a gaze on his companion under the light of the lamps, the bare memory of which made Caulaincourt shudder ever after to his dying day.

They left the chaise, and looking across the Seine Napoleon saw to the north and east, in the direction of Villeneuve Saint-Georges, the glare of the enemy's watch-fires. Marshal Berthier now came up in a second post-chaise which had been following the Emperor's. Speaking excitedly, Napoleon declared that he would go on to Paris. He set off walking rapidly along the road in the dark, leaving the horses to be put to and the post-chaise to pick him up. Berthier and Caulaincourt attended him, and General Belliard and some dragoons followed at a few paces behind. Napoleon rejected every remonstrance and refused to turn back. Napoleon, talking half to himself, half to his companions, exclaimed:

> I asked them to hold out for only twenty-four hours! Miserable wretches! Marmont swore that he would be cut to pieces rather than yield! And Joseph ran away: my own brother! To surrender the capital to the enemy: what poltroons!

So he went on in a breathless torrent of words. He added finally:

> They have capitulated: betrayed their country; betrayed their Emperor; degraded France! It is too terrible! Everyone has lost his head! When I am not there they do nothing but add blunder to blunder.

But to go on, with Paris in the hands of an army of 150,000 men, was out of the question. Napoleon had to bow to the inevitable. He at length yielded to the protests of the others. He stopped beside the Fountains of Juvisy. Labédoyère, an eyewitness, described:

> He sat down on the parapet of one of the fountains, and remained above a quarter of an hour with his head resting on his hands, lost in the most painful reflections.

Then he rose, went back to the post-chaise, and, telling General Belliard to rally all the men he could at Essonne, set off to drive to Fontainebleau. He reached there at six next morning.

Between ten o'clock on Wednesday night and six o'clock on Thursday morning the tragedy at the Invalides was enacted. Its opening scene took place just as Napoleon's post-chaise was drawing up in the village of Fromenteau. Its final scene took place just as the post-chaise was entering the courtyard of Fontainebleau.

The Capitulation of Paris was signed before the Barrier of La Villette at five in the afternoon. Its first article laid down that the French army must evacuate Paris within twelve hours: before five o'clock next morning. The last clause recommended the city to the mercy of the Allied Sovereigns, and of the Czar Alexander in particular.

All day long the booming of cannon and rattle of musketry had dinned in the ears of the trembling and terrified Parisians, ever steadily drawing nearer. The marshals, Marmont and Mortier, had made their last stand, and, resisting desperately to the last, in a struggle in which the Allies lost two to every one of the defenders, so ferocious was the contest, had been beaten back into the city. They carried back with them, so gallantly had they counter-attacked at one point, the standard of the Second Squadron of the Russian *Garde du Corps* now a trophy in the present collection at the Invalides.

The outnumbered and exhausted troops could make no further fight, although, to the end, many of the soldiers were for holding out to the last cartridge. The *générale* had beaten to arms at two in the morning; at six, with sunrise, the enemy's guns opened fire; from then until late in the afternoon the fighting had gone on incessantly.

All was over by four o'clock. From east to west, from Charenton and Belleville, right round to Neuilly, the Allies, the Russians, Blücher's Prussians, and the Austrians, had captured every position capable of defence, one after the other, by sheer weight of numbers, and had carried at the point of the bayonet every place of vantage held by the French. Woronzeff and the Prince of Würtemburg had stormed Romainville, La Villette, and La Chapelle. Langeron and the Russian Imperial Guard were masters of the heights of Montmartre and the Buttes Chaumont, looking down directly on Paris.

Eighty-six guns had been taken from the marshals since the morning; nearly six thousand soldiers and National Guards had fallen, killed or wounded, facing the foe. A six-miles long line of batteries and battalions on the side of the Allies had closed in to within short musket range of the Paris barriers. Already the Russian cannon were opening fire on the city, and their shells were bursting over the central streets of Paris; falling, some in the Chaussée d'Antin and on the Boulevard des Italiens.

At four o'clock Marmont, who had been the soul of the defence, fighting, now on horseback, now on foot, using his sword at times:

> The marshal was seen everywhere in the thickest of the fight, a dozen or more soldiers were bayoneted at his side, and his hat was riddled with bullets.

At four o'clock Marmont repassed within the barriers to announce that further defence was impossible. He was scarcely recognisable, we are told—

> He had a beard of eight days' growth; the great-coat which covered his uniform was in tatters; from head to foot he was blackened with powder-smoke.

Then had to be done the only thing that was left to do. Marmont and Mortier held a hasty conference, and after it a trumpeter and an *aide de camp* carrying a white flag rode out through the firing line to the nearest advanced post of the Allies. The officer was taken before the Czar Alexander on the plateau of Chaumont, and Paris surrendered. The last sounds that were heard on the French side as the firing ceased came from a battalion of the Imperial Guard which had been serving under Marmont, from a scanty remnant of veterans stubbornly resisting at bay to the last—shouts of "*Vive l'Empereur!*"

The old pensioners of the Invalides manfully did their duty, and bore their part in the defence all day, as well as they were able. All who could carry a musket had gone out to the barriers; others did their best by helping to bring up ammunition. Most of them fought at the Barrière du Trône on the Vincennes road, assisting the brave lads of the Polytechnic School to hold the post and man a battery of eight-and-twenty cannon in front of the barrier; until a headlong charge of Russian cavalry, Pahlen's dragoons with some *cossacks*, swooped down from the flank, annihilating the devoted band of gunners. Those of the boys who were left, however, saved the school flag, presented to the Polytechnic just ten years before by the Emperor with his own hand, on the Day of the Eagles on the Field of Mars.

With the Invalides' veterans and some of the National Guards, the survivors held the barrier throughout the day to the end, beating back repeated attempts of the Russians to storm the gate. The lads, finally, after learning that Marmont had capitulated, made their way back to the school, and there burned their precious standard to save it from falling into the enemy's hands. Those who were left of the veterans hastened back to the Invalides at the same time, overcome with anxiety to learn what was to happen to their own priceless treasures within the Hospital, the trophy flags. There were at the Invalides at that time, by one account, 1417 trophy flags; according to another account—which included apparently in the total the returned Battalion and Light Infantry and Cavalry Eagles—altogether 1,800 standards.

Within the walls of the Invalides all was deep gloom and hopeless despondency among those in charge. Even at nightfall, as it would appear, the authorities had not made up their minds how the trophies were to be disposed of.

It is a hapless and pitiful story from first to last. Some time previously, while the Allied armies were still being kept at bay on the plains of Champagne, the Governor of the Invalides, old Marshal Serrurier, a distinguished veteran of the Revolutionary Army, had applied to the

Minister of War for instructions as to the disposal of the trophies at the Invalides in the event of the enemy advancing on Paris. The only answer he received was a formal letter to the effect that the matter would have to go before the Emperor. At that time Napoleon was in the midst of his last forlorn-hope attempt to stem the tide of invasion; in the midst of a life-and-death struggle, fighting desperately day after day at one place or another. The Ministry of War apparently pigeon-holed the application after that, and forgot all about the trophies at the Invalides until the actual day of the attack on Paris—until that Wednesday forenoon.

Then, when already Marmont's outer line of defence had been forced, and the last fight for the inner heights overlooking the city was raging furiously, almost within sight from the Invalides, a letter from the War Minister was handed to Serrurier. It "trusted that the Marshal had taken steps for the safety of the trophies; especially for the preservation of Frederick the Great's sword. The flags," continued the letter, "had best be detached from their staves, and rolled up carefully. The War Minister is sure that your Excellency will do all that is possible. The road to the Loire is open." Such were the instructions sent to the Invalides after the eleventh hour!

Then, during the afternoon, when the enemy's bombshells, fired from the plateau of Chaumont, were falling in the heart of the city, a single artillery wagon, or *fourgon*, a vehicle barely large enough to remove a small percentage of what there was to carry away, drew up at the main gates of the Invalides. It brought also ten more trophy flags, collected from somewhere in Paris. In the general con-fusion nobody, it would seem, even inquired what they were or where they came from. The driver's instructions were merely that "they were to go away with the Invalides trophies." The ten flags were taken out and stacked in a corridor for the time being, while the *fourgon* waited unheeded at the gate until after dark.

What steps Marshal Serrurier took during the afternoon to secure adequate transport is unknown; or, indeed, what he did with himself all that time. The Governor was seen just before the dinner-hour in the Corridor d'Avignon, in an out-of-the-way part of the building, in conference with the lieutenant-governor and an adjutant-major. Another officer, Adjutant Vollerand, was with them, holding in his hands Frederick the Great's sword and sash. Apparently they did not want to be observed, and were discussing how to hide the relics or bury them within the precincts of the Invalides.

After that nothing more was seen of Serrurier at the Invalides until between nine and ten at night, some hours after the Capitulation, and when it had become known that the Allies intended to occupy Paris in force, and that their troops would enter and take possession of the city early next morning. Then the governor reappeared.

A few minutes after nine o'clock the veterans of the Invalides, who had been restlessly pacing about the halls and corridors during the evening, or standing about in dejected groups in the court-yards, not knowing what they were to do, were suddenly summoned to muster at once in the Grand Court, or *Cour d'Honneur*. All turned out from the wards and paraded, forming up by the light of lanterns. All but those who were bedridden were brought out, the maimed and cripples being led out, or hobbling out on their crutches, together with the survivors of those who had fought so gallantly at the barriers during the day, their faces still begrimed with powder-smoke, their clothes torn and stained, some without their hats, their arms in slings, or with bandages over recent wounds.

Then the tall, spare figure of the governor, a grim, hard-featured old warrior, white-haired, over seventy years of age, was seen emerging from his quarters, with the senior staff-officers of the hospital following in rear. Serrurier harangued the pensioners briefly. He told them that the enemy would enter the city next day and would present themselves at the Invalides to enforce the giving up of the trophies. What did the men of the Invalides desire should be done?

There was a pause for a moment; a dead silence, as the old soldiers gazed dumbfoundedly at one another. Then one man stepped out to the front and spoke up for the rest. A battle-scarred old sergeant-pensioner of the Grenadiers of the Old Guard answered the governor on behalf of his comrades, his reply, greeted as it was by vociferous shouts of approval on every side, voicing the unanimous wish of the veterans. "If they will not let us keep our banners, let us burn them here! We will swallow the ashes!" The order to make a bonfire of the trophies then and there was issued forthwith.

Anything that came to hand for fuel was eagerly seized, and a great pile speedily made of broken-up stools and mess-tables and forms, hauled out from the barrack-rooms withindoors. They were stacked in a heap just in front of the pedestal on which it had been intended to erect an equestrian statue of the heroic Marshal Lannes, who died from his wounds at Aspern in the arms of Napoleon. Meanwhile, parties of men ran inside with ladders, and set to work to strip the dining-halls and the chapel of the rows of flags hanging up there. They bore them outside, roughly bundled together in their arms; some, silently, with frowning, stern-set faces and set teeth; others beside themselves with rage, and cursing savagely aloud; others sullenly muttering oaths; not a few of the old fellows with tears streaming down their cheeks.

They carried the trophies out and heaped them up into an immense funeral pyre. The battalion and other Eagles shared the fate of the captured trophies—standards, some of these, that had been borne under fire in the thick of triumphant battle at Austerlitz, and Jena, at Auerstadt and Friedland—to save them on the morrow from falling into the hands of those in whose defeat and humiliation they had had their part. The fire was lighted and the masses of tattered silk blazed up furiously. When the flames were at their fiercest, Marshal Serrurier stepped forward and with his own hand flung into the midst of the fiery mass the sword of Frederick the Great.

For half the night the veterans stood round and watched the flames complete the work of destruction. They stood massed round in a densely packed throng of sullen, gloomy, broken-hearted men. They stayed there until long after mid-night, gazing, in a state of dull despair, at the fire; while some now and again stirred up the glowing fuel and made the flames leap up afresh, roaring and crackling and casting a dull red throbbing glare over the old walls and rows of windows all round, and gleaming on the lofty gilded dome of the Invalides, in itself an intended memento of victory.

On first seeing the golden domes of the Kremlin as he approached Moscow, Napoleon had sent orders to Paris to have the dome of the Invalides gilded as a memorial of his achievement of the goal of the campaign! Most of the veterans stood there throughout the greater part of that cold March night, watching until the fire had died down and only a great heap of smouldering cinders remained; all that was left of the trophies of victorious France.

Among the vast array of foreign trophies at the Invalides that perished on that night were English flags nearly two centuries old, the remains of the spoil of some forty-four English banners of Charles the First's soldiers, triumphantly carried to Paris from the Ile de Rhéin November 1627 and hung in Notre Dame. Others flags destroyed there, too, dated from the wars of the *Grand Monarque*; spoils won on the battlefield by the famous Condé and Turenne; also trophies taken from William the Third at Steenkirk and Landen and elsewhere; the British and Dutch and Danish and Bavarian ensigns won by Turenne's great successor, Marshal Luxembourg, "*le Tapissier de Notre Dame*," as they dubbed him at Versailles, for the almost innumerable trophies sent by Luxembourg to be hung up in the Cathedral of Paris, with State processions and *Te Deums* in the presence of the king.

Other British battle-spoils, the trophies of France, which passed out of existence at the Invalides on that night were these: a flag taken at Fontenoy by the Irish Brigade; the regimental colours surrendered by the garrison of Minorca which Admiral Byng failed to rescue; those of another British garrison of Minorca of the time of the Great Siege of Gibraltar, when France, for the second time, wrested the island from England; four British and Hessian regimental flags surrendered to Washington at Yorktown and sent by Congress as a gift to the King of France; flags taken by the French from British West India garrisons in the same war; besides British naval ensigns also taken during the American War, with other British ship-flags, some of which indeed dated from the earlier battle times of Duguay Trouin and Jean Bart.

Destroyed at the Invalides also on that Wednesday night was a British naval ensign from Trafalgar. It had been hoisted on board one of Nelson's prizes, the *Algéciras*. In the storm after the battle the ship was in imminent peril of wreck, and the French prisoners on board were liberated in order to help to save her. They used their freedom to overpower the small British prize-crew and carried the vessel off into Cadiz, whence the British ensign, hoisted originally in triumph over the French tricolour during the battle of two days before, on the *Algéciras* being captured, was sent as a trophy to Paris. There were also destroyed at the Invalides at the same time the ensign of Lord Cochrane's famous brig-of-war, the *Speedy*, captured in the Mediterranean in 1801, and those of three British line-of-battle ships, the *Berwick*, the *Swiftsure*, and the *Hannibal*, taken within the previous twenty years.

Most of the trophies won by Napoleon and the Grand Army all over Europe, and by the Armies of the Republic and Consulate before that, perished in the holocaust: the spoils of Valmy and Fleurus and Jemmapes; of Hohenlinden; of Dego and Mondovi; of Rivoli and Montenotte; of Castiglione, Lodi, and Arcola; of Zurich and Marengo, and other victories. On that night, too, passed out of existence the famous flag of the Army of Italy presented by Napoleon, and bearing inscribed on it the names of eighty triumphs on the battlefield and the detailed record of the taking of 150,000 prisoners, 170 standards, 550 siege-guns, and 600 pieces of field artillery; the Horsetail banners of the Mamelukes, taken by Napoleon at the Battle of the Pyramids;

the historic standard of the Knights of St. John, won in hand-to-hand fight outside the main gate of Valetta.

Most of the 340 Prussian standards Napoleon sent to Paris after the Jena campaign, together with the sword and Black Eagle sash of Frederick the Great, as well as the recovered French trophies of the Seven Years' War, originally won by Frederick at Rosbach, the standards of Frederick the Great's Guards, and Austrian spoils taken by the Prussians at Leuthen, Kolin, and Hohenfriedburg, all of which had been carried off to Paris by Napoleon—these were among the war-treasures destroyed at the Invalides on that night. With them went into the flames the Grand Army's Russian trophies from Eylau and Friedland, the Austrian trophies from Eckmühl and Wagram, besides many Spanish and Portuguese trophies taken before Wellington landed in the Peninsula to turn the tide of war.

One French Eagle which perished on that night was the survivor of a disaster: Dupont's surrender at Bailen in Andalusia in 1808, (*see note following*,) at the outset of the Spanish insurrection; that cruel humiliation for the arms of France, the news of which came on Europe with all the startling effect of a thunderclap, and drove Napoleon nearly frantic in his furious indignation. It had been one of three Eagles taken by the Spaniards, that of the 24me Légère, and had been recovered by the daring of an officer of the regiment, one of the prisoners, Captain Lanusse. Confined in a prison-hulk at Cadiz, he escaped to shore one night, managed to find out where his regiment's flag was kept, displayed as a Spanish trophy, got hold of it, and then made his way outside the city into the lines of the besieging French army. There he presented the Eagle to Marshal Soult, who forwarded it direct to Napoleon. Lanusse, as his reward, was promoted a *chef de bataillon* of the 8th of the Line, and fell to the bayonet of a British soldier of the 87th Royal Irish Fusiliers at Barrosa. The recovered Eagle Napoleon sent to the Invalides.

> *Note:*—General Dupont, an officer of the highest promise and with an exceptionally brilliant record, Ney's right-hand man, and chief divisional leader on many battlefields, a special favourite also with Napoleon ("a man I loved and was rearing up to be a marshal," were Napoleon's words of him), while on the expedition which was to win him the *bâton*, at the head of 25,000 men, let himself be surrounded and cut off; trapped among the gorges of the Sierra Morena by a horde of peasants backed up by Spanish regulars; and then, in spite of a final chance that

offered for him to force his way through, surrendered to the enemy. He had committed *"une chose sans exculpe; une lacheté insultante"* declared Napoleon in savage fury on hearing of the surrender. Those who had had part in it, declared the Emperor, should "die on the scaffold"—*"ils porteront sur l'échaffaud la peine de ce grand crime national!"*

He had Brigadier Legendre, Dupont's Chief of the Staff, who had been released on parole, brought before him at Valladolid, and heaped on the wretched, broken man the bitterest reproaches and revilings; beside himself in his wrath. Not a word in reply, in explanation, would he listen to. Before the Imperial Guard on parade, and the assembled Imperial Staff, Napoleon finally gripped the general by the wrist and shook it passionately. An onlooker, another officer, describes the scene: "A nervous contraction of the muscles seemed to seize the Emperor. 'What, General!' he ejaculated, his voice quivering with fury. 'Why did not your hand wither when it signed that infamous capitulation!' Legendre was cashiered: Dupont (who had been ill and was wounded during the battle) was cashiered, degraded from the Legion of Honour, and kept under police *surveillance* as long as the Empire lasted.

What became of the other two Eagles, those of the "*Garde de Paris*" and of the Second Battalion of the 5th Light Infantry, and the fourteen Reserve Battalion flags that were taken at Bailen is unknown. They are not in Spain, although one trophy indirectly associated with the disaster is now at Madrid, the admiral's flag of Admiral Rosily, who was at Cadiz with the French squadron which Dupont was marching to rescue. It is kept as a trophy in the Museo Naval of Madrid. Rosily had charge of the five French ships of the line which escaped into Cadiz after Trafalgar.

When Spain rose against Napoleon, they were placed in danger from the garrison of Cadiz; being at the same time unable to put to sea because a British fleet blockaded the port. Dupont's army was specially sent to bring away the 4,000 soldiers and sailors on board, who were then to abandon the ships. Just before Dupont reached Bailen, the Spaniards attacked Rosily, bombarding his ships with heavy cannon, and mortars and a gunboat flotilla, and he had to surrender, his admiral's flag being carried off by the Spaniards, ultimately to find its way to its present resting-place.

By morning all that remained of the proud trophies of France at the Invalides was a heap of grey ashes, fragments of charred flag-poles, and scraps of partly molten metal. The *débris* was raked up at daylight, and shovelled into the artillery *fourgon* of the previous afternoon, which had been standing all night outside the main gate of the Invalides. The artillery wagon drove off with it to the Seine nearby and emptied the heap into the river. That was the end of the night's destruction.

Some portion of the *débris* was recovered from the Seine a year afterwards, and is preserved in the Chapel of the Invalides now. In June 1815 a workman, doing some repairs by the riverside, discovered a portion of a flag under water, and on hearing of that, two patriotic young Frenchmen, an engineer and a journalist, privately set to work soon afterwards to see if they could fish up anything that might be worth preserving. At the time the Allies were in possession of Paris, during the second occupation, after Waterloo, and the two young men had to proceed cautiously.

They were successful in the end in recovering portions of 183 trophies, metal spear-head ornaments, from ensign-staves mostly. Seventy-eight were later identified as of Austrian origin; one as part of a British flag; two as having belonged to Russian standards; various fragments as the remains of thirty-nine Prussian standards; four from Spanish flags with Bourbon *fleurs-de-lis*; and two fragments of Turkish standards from Egypt. The remainder of the salvage it was impossible to identify.

That the great sacrifice had not been made in vain, was speedily apparent. In the course of the morning after the bonfire, a little before noon on Thursday, March 31, within two hours of the entry into Paris of the vanguard of the Allied armies, a Russian *aide de camp* presented himself at the Invalides, and, in the name of the Allied sovereigns, demanded a statement of the trophies kept there. The officer came up on horseback, accompanied by a mounted man of the National Guard, and an armed escort of Russian dragoons. The main gate was open as usual, and the Russian officer rode through without taking notice of the gate-sentry's challenge. He was only stopped by a rush of the pensioners' day-guard, called out by the sentry's shout of alarm—"*Aux armes!*" The guard turned out and faced the aide de camp with lowered halberds.

The Russian colonel protested, but the officer on duty refused to let him pass without orders from his own chief, and General Darnaud, the lieutenant-governor, was sent for. That officer came, and the Russian dismounted and explained his mission. He had orders, he said, to "take cognisance "of the trophies of the Invalides. General Darnaud replied bluntly: "Very good, I will permit you to visit the Hotel. Come with me!"

The general added: "As to the trophies, sir, we have dealt with them according to the laws of war!" "*On en avait agi suivant les lois de guerre!*" were his words. The Russian did not seem to grasp the general's meaning, and stood still for a moment, staring blankly at him.

On that, Madame Darnaud, the lieutenant-governor's wife, who had followed into the courtyard immediately after her husband, interposed. She addressed the officer, speaking volubly and angrily, but only to draw down on herself from the Russian the uncivil rejoinder that he had not come there to talk to a woman!

After that, the general, accompanied by some of the men of the main guard with shouldered halberds, formally conducted the officer inside the Invalides, the party taking their way along the colonnade round the Court of Honour, in the midst of which could be seen the wide burnt-out space where the fire had been, the pungent smell of the fumes from which still hung about the place, and so into the Chapel of St. Louis.

There the scene that met the Russian *aide de camp's* eyes seemed to stagger him: bare blank walls, the gallery stripped and defaced; with empty and broken metal sockets here and there to show where the flags had been fastened up. The interior had been entirely cleared from end to end along the sides. It was absolutely unrecognisable to any who had seen it before. The Russian officer, who had visited the Invalides six or seven years previously, after Tilsit, could only gaze round dumbly, utterly taken aback. He muttered something, but did not speak aloud.

Then, glaring round savagely into the eyes of those about him, he turned away abruptly, and was conducted to the Outer Court, where he remounted his horse, and rode off hastily in the direction whence he had come. All Napoleon's trophies, however, did not perish at the Invalides. Some of the Grand Army's captured flags, as it so chanced, escaped destruction on that night, and are at the Invalides now. They are in the chapel and in the Salle Turenne, besides half a hundred in the crypt, grouped round Napoleon's tomb.

The forty-five Austrian flags taken at Ulm are beside Napoleon's tomb, with nine other flags. Presented by the Emperor to the Senate, as has been told, the Ulm trophies, during the night of March 30, were hastily taken down from where they had been hung in the Grand Salon for the past nine years, and hidden in a vault below. They made a second public appearance on the occasion of Napoleon's funeral at the Invalides in 1840, when they were placed at the head of the coffin. They have ever since been kept beside the tomb.

The Austerlitz trophies met another fate. Kept at Notre Dame, they disappeared mysteriously from there in the early morning of the day of the entry of the Allies into Paris. At three in the morning of March 31 an urgent message from the Prefect of the Seine was delivered at Notre Dame, calling on the cathedral authorities to take down and conceal the Austerlitz trophies at once. The chapter met hastily in the archbishop's room, and the flags were all down within half an hour. They have never been seen since, nor was their fate ever accounted for.

At the Luxembourg Palace were displayed 110 trophies, the spoils of the Eagles, won from all the nations of Europe and presented to the *Corps Legislatif* by Napoleon. They were safely removed on the night of March 30, and were hidden securely. Brought out and set up again a year later, on Napoleon's return from Elba, the authorities forgot about hiding them again in the confusion after Waterloo. As the result more than half of them are now in Berlin.

Blücher sent a party of staff officers to seize the entire collection, but a sharp-witted functionary hoodwinked the Prussians on their arrival. They went back to get written orders, and before they returned, as many as possible of the trophies had been pulled down and got out of the way.

One of the attendants managed the affair on his own initiative, a hall-porter named Mathieu. He was able to save and hide as many as fifty-one of the flags, and they have since been forwarded to the Invalides.

The other fifty-nine trophies the Prussians seized and carried off. Two Austrian standards taken by Napoleon at Marengo escaped destruction by having been previously lent from the Invalides to an artist, Charles Vernet, for a battle-picture he had been commissioned to paint for Napoleon. They were in Vernet's studio in March 1814. His son, Horace Vernet, returned them in later days to the Invalides, where they now are.

In addition, it would seem, at least a moiety of the Invalides trophies were kept back at the last moment by some of the veterans themselves. Several of the old soldiers, it would appear, after stripping down the flags from the walls, instead of carrying all out into the courtyard to the bonfire, retained and hid a few of them on their own account, to smuggle them outside afterwards and keep them in concealment.⁶

---

6. Years later these trophies were again brought to light, and by degrees, one at a time, or two or three together, found their way once more to the *hôtel*, where they form part of the present collection. Among those now in the Invalides are six of Frederick the Great's trophies annexed at Berlin by Napoleon in 1806; six Austrian and Bavarian flags, also of the Seven Years' War period, removed by Napoleon from Vienna; an old German flag taken by Marshal Turenne, and in earlier times hung in Notre Dame; five Austrian colours of unknown origin; one Russian flag-trophy from Austerlitz; one Prussian standard from Jena; and a number of Spanish and Portuguese flags from the Peninsular War.
Three British regimental flags, originally captured by Napoleon's Polish lancers at Albuera, found their way back in this manner to the Invalides. They were taken at Albuera in the first part of the battle, when, under cover of mist and rain squalls, the French cavalry, circling round one flank, swooped down on the leading British brigade before its regiments could form in square. Of the five other British flags at present in the Invalides, four were taken on March 8, 1814, just three weeks before the burning of the trophies, and had not yet reached Paris. They were taken from us in very tragic circumstances—at the disastrous attempt to storm the fortress of Bergen-op-Zoom; but the details of that painful story nor the identification of the flags do not concern us here. One of the four flags is kept beside Napoleon's tomb. The fifth flag purports to have been a British sloop-of-war's red ensign and to have been captured in the Baltic in December 1813, in an action of which the British Admiralty has no record, and the French account is only a tradition. It again, apparently, had not reached Paris by March 1814.

CHAPTER 12

The Eagles of the Last Army

The Eagles came back to France with the return of Napoleon from Elba; to lead the last Army to the campaign of the Hundred Days.

They "flew from steeple to steeple across France," in Napoleon's expressive phrase, 14 from the shores of Fréjus until they alighted on the towers of Notre Dame." The enthusiasm that greeted their reappearance spread like wildfire; it blazed up like an exploding magazine. The rapturous acclamation and enthusiasm with which the Eagles were welcomed back was the measure of the prevailing discontent and resentment among the soldiers at the harsh and unworthy treatment they had received during the ten months of the restored *régime*.

The army had come off badly by its change of masters. The Bourbons had done all in their power to alienate its regard; as much through malice in not a few cases, as through downright stupidity.

Of all the institutions of France the most thoroughly national and the most thoroughly democratic was the Army; it was accordingly against the Army that the *noblesse* directed its first efforts. Financial difficulties made a large reduction in the forces necessary. Fourteen thousand officers and sergeants were accordingly dismissed on half-pay; but no sooner had this measure of economy been effected than a multitude of emigrants who had served against the Republic in the army of the Prince of Condé or in La Vendee were rewarded with all degrees of military rank. . . . The tricolour, under which every battle of France had been fought from Jemmapes to Montmartre, was superseded by the white flag of the House of Bourbon, under which no living soldier had marched to victory. . . . The Imperial Guard was removed from service at the Palace, and the so-called Military Household of the old Bourbon monarchy revived, with the privileges and the insignia belonging to the period before 1775.

The abolition of the Eagles was the preliminary step of all. A justifiable measure, no doubt, from a political point of view, it touched to the quick the military instinct of the nation. And on that followed the abolition of the national tricolour in favour of the old Bourbon white flag.

Within three weeks of the Farewell of Fontainebleau the Eagles of the Army, with the tricolour standards, were officially proscribed; the order went forth to send them to Paris forthwith for destruction in the furnaces of the artillery *dépôt* at Vincennes. On May 12 it was notified that the white Bourbon flag was again to be the standard of the Army, with a brass *fleur-de-lis* at the head of the colour-staff in place of the Eagle.

Every regiment was required to send its Eagle to the Ministry of War in Paris on receipt of the order. No allowances or exceptions were made; although in several instances officers urgently petitioned to be allowed to retain their Eagles with the corps, if only as mementoes of feats of arms achieved by the regiments in battle. Every request was rejected, whatever the circumstances. There were reasons of State policy no doubt, as has been said, against the general retention as regimental standards of military insignia so intimately associated with Napoleon; but in certain instances, at least, indulgence might reasonably have been extended to the applications. There were personal and romantic associations connected with some of the Eagles, specially endearing them to the soldiers, for which privilege might well have been accorded. One very hard case may be cited as typical of others: that of the Eagle of the 25th of the Line.

The Eagle of the 25th had been carried under fire in some twenty battles and all through the Moscow campaign; and had notable battle-scars to show for its distinguished services. One leg and one wing of the Eagle had been shot away in action, and there were five bullet-holes in its metal body. Its maimed appearance, indeed, had attracted Napoleon's attention at a review, and he had stopped while riding past the regiment and taken the Eagle into his hands, examining it with extreme interest and putting his fingers into the bullet-holes, finally returning it to the *Porte-Aigle* with a deep bow of respect. The regiment almost worshipped their Eagle on its own account, for what it had gone through; but it had further undergone yet more surprising adventures. The 25th had been in the garrison of Dresden in 1813 when Marshal St. Cyr had to capitulate to the Austrians.

On the night before the surrender the Eagle-staff was broken up and burned, and the few strips of ragged silk that remained of the shot-torn regimental tricolour flag were tied under an officer's uniform for secret conveyance out of the city. The shattered Eagle broke in two while being removed from its staff, and its two fragments were concealed under the petticoats of two *vivandieres* who were to convey it in that manner to the regimental *dépôt* in France. Under the capitulation the garrison was granted the honours of war and a safe-conduct back to France.

The terms, however, were annulled by the Allied Sovereigns then advancing, after Leipsic, to invade France, and in the outcome all the regiments, after they had started for France, were made prisoners and marched away to be interned in Hungary. The major of the 25th got back the two fragments of the Eagle, stowed them away under his uniform, and kept them about him by day and night for five months; until finally, on his release after Napoleon's abdication, he brought the Eagle back across the Rhine, "wrapped up like contraband."

On the 25th receiving the order to send in its Eagle for destruction, he wrote personally to the Minister of War—General Dupont, of Bailen notoriety, as has been said—who had never forgiven Napoleon's harsh usage of him, and now took every opportunity of paying back old scores on the heads of his former comrades in arms. The major wrote setting forth in detail the story of the regimental Eagle, relating its exception-ally interesting career and its battle damages, also how he had preserved it after Dresden, and implored the War Minister, in the name of the regiment, that they might retain the two fragments to be kept in the regimental "*Salle d'Honneur*" as an honoured relic.

The reply was a peremptorily worded command to send the Eagle to Paris forthwith for destruction with the other Eagles of the army. The major, in the circumstances, considered himself compelled to comply. He summoned the officers to his quarters, where they "paid their last *adieux* to the object of veneration, and then, in their presence, the Eagle fragments were packed in a box, and despatched to the Ministry of War."

The story, with others to the same effect, went the round of every barrack-room in France, and wherever it was told, there were angry murmurings and increased discontent.

By no means all the Eagles of the army, it would appear, were given up to the authorities in Paris. Not a few colonels flatly refused to comply with Dupont's order, taking the risk of prosecution or of being turned out of the service summarily—a certainty in any event under the new *régime*, as the majority of the senior regimental officers anticipated, and as actually came to pass. General Petit of the Grenadiers of the Old Guard, as has already been said, refused to give up that famous Eagle, and concealed it successfully; and not a few other officers did the same with the Eagles of their corps. Others destroyed their regimental Eagles and either burned the silken tricolour flags, or cut them up; dividing the ashes or fragments among their comrades.

Their Eagles taken away, it was next made known to the army, that the "battle honours" and war distinctions of the various corps, won under Napoleon, would not appear on the new regimental flags when issued. "Austerlitz," "Jena," "Friedland," and the other names of pride to the Grand Army, were henceforward to be erased from military recognition. The new flags, when publicly distributed in September 1814, showed each a blank white field, with on it only an oval shield, bearing the three *fleurs-de-lis,* the Royal Bourbon cognisance, and the name of the corps—its new name, revived from Army Lists of the Old Monarchy, a name long since forgotten and totally unfamiliar.

The regimental numbers of the Grand Army, ennobled by glorious campaigns, immortalised by their associations of victory and brilliant feats of arms, instinct with a renown acquired on a hundred battlefields all over Europe, were at the same time done away with by a stroke of the War Minister's pen. That proved the most unpopular measure of all; the cruellest of blows to the *esprit de corps* and pride of the former soldiers of Napoleon. It was felt as a gratuitous insult; it was perhaps the most deeply resented injury of all. In future, in place of their treasured regimental numbers, the various corps of the Army, horse and foot, were to be known by departmental or territorial names—meaningless to nine soldiers out of ten, and without traditions—or else by the names of royal princes and princesses, and titled personages, remembered only, some of them, as having fled on the battlefield before the national armies.

Bercheney and Chamborant Hussars, Orléans Dragoons and *Chasseurs*, Regiments d'Artois, de Berri, d'Armagnac, d'Angoulême, de Monsieur, d'Anjou, and so forth—what traditions had designations such as these to compare with, to mention in the same breath with, the traditions immortally associated with the numbers, familiar as house-hold words wherever French soldiers met together, of the dragoon and *chasseur* regiments which Murat had led at Austerlitz, of the dashing hussars of Lassalle, of the *cuirassiers* whose resistless onset had swept the field at Jena, of the horsemen at the sight of whose sabres before their gates Prussian fortresses had surrendered at discretion? It came with a sense of personal degradation, as a sort of desecration on the men of regiments like the 75th of the Line, or the 32nd, the 9th Light Infantry or the 84th, or the 85th, or "*Le terrible 57me*"—to be labelled and hear themselves officially addressed on parade as "Beauvoisis" or "Auxerre" or "Nivernais," by the name of some prosaic locality, or the style of some ancient aristocrat, their titular colonel. (*See note following.*)

> *Note:*—To the army, Louis XVIII. was only a king imposed on them by their enemies; by the triumphant enemies of France, the European Coalition. He was merely the "*protégé* of foreign bayonets," placed over them by the English and Prussians; "*l'émigré rentré en croupe derrière un cosaque!*" To the soldiers he only personified defeat and disaster; and the memories that they gloried in had been of set purpose obliterated by him and his creatures. The very charter under which he had assumed authority was dated the 19th year of his reign, as though Napoleon had never been. He had proscribed their Eagle standards before which all Europe had trembled. By his ordinances he had abolished and insulted the memory of their victories. In addition he had disbanded and turned adrift their officers, and had left them to starve, without the pay that was their due, in wretchedness and rags.
>
> Fuel was added to the fires of disaffection in the ranks by the tales that went round of every barrack-room of personal ill-usage of and affronts to officers who had won the respect of all on campaign, and before the enemy under fire. *Ci-devant* colonels and captains in long-forgotten corps of the old-time Royal Army were appointed at one stride lieutenant-generals and major-generals on the Active List, ousting and sending into unemployment men, whom Napoleon himself had picked out for command, whose names were household words to the Army.
>
> In almost every regiment officers who had grown grey in war-service before the enemy, who had won distinction on a hundred battlefields, were shelved; set aside for *émigrés*, who,

a quarter of a century before, had been boy subalterns in the army of the *ancien régime*, and had not set foot in France since they fled the country at the outbreak of the Revolution. These were brought back and posted wholesale as colonels and *chefs de bataillon* all through the Army, superseding and driving into poverty veterans who had raised themselves to their ranks and positions through personal merit and war-service, and had qualified step by step in the different grades. At a *levée* one day, after a review before the Duc de Berri, a grey-headed old regimental officer stepped forward, according to custom, and made a request to have granted to him for his services the Cross of St. Louis. "What have you done to deserve it?" was the Prince's reply, uttered in a cold and sneering tone. "I have served in the Army of France for twenty years, your Royal Highness!"
"Twenty years of robbery!" was the cruel and insolent answer as the Duc de Berri turned his back on the veteran. The words were repeated everywhere among the soldiers and had the worst effect. Another tale that caused deep resentment throughout the army was that of the treatment which Marshal Ney had received at Court when protesting against rudeness which had been shown by certain ladies of title to his wife one day at the Tuileries. They had openly insulted the Maréchale Ney by making sarcastic and contemptuous comments on her comparatively lowly birth.

Marshal Ney personally complained to the king, but was coldly referred to the Court Chamberlain. He laid his complaint before that functionary and was personally rebuffed "in a harsh and insolent manner "as the only reply to which the Marshal with his wife had withdrawn from Paris altogether. And more than one other officer of eminence, it was told, had in like manner been forced to cease attendance at Court. When the moment came for the reappearance of Napoleon in their midst, the Army was more than ready to receive their old leader with open arms and rally once more to the Eagles.

Napoleon announced the return of the Eagle in his first address to the army, sent off on his landing to be distributed broadcast among the soldiers.

Come and range yourselves under the banners of your chief. ...Victory shall march at the *pas de charge*: the Eagle with the national colours shall fly from steeple to steeple to the towers of Notre Dame!

The first of the regimental Eagles to make its appearance in France accompanied Napoleon from Elba and landed with him. It was the Eagle of the six hundred veterans of the Old Guard who, as the "Elba Guard," had volunteered to share Napoleon's exile, and had formed his personal escort. It figured in the historic scene at Grenoble a week after the landing, where Napoleon, on meeting the first soldiers sent to arrest his advance, by the magic of his presence and the sight of the Eagle borne behind him, so dramatically won over to his side the former 5th of the Line, the first regiment of the army to throw in its lot with Napoleon after Elba.

The Eagle that had its part on the historic occasion—with its silken tricolour flag, embroidered with silver wreaths and scrollery, and golden bees, crowns and Imperial ciphers, and inscribed "*L'Empereur Napoléon à la Garde Nationale de Ile Elba*"—is now in private possession in England. It fell by some means into the hands of a Prussian soldier at the occupation of Paris after Waterloo and was sold a few weeks later to a visitor to Paris. In the dramatic scene of the meeting of Napoleon with the 5th of the Line, General Cambronne, Commander of the Elba Guard, bore the Eagle a few paces behind Napoleon and held it up appealingly to the regiment.

The 5th of the Line, says one story, vouched for by an eyewitness, was marching out to block a narrow gorge through which ran the road Napoleon was known to be taking. At some little way off, his party was seen approaching, he himself being readily recognised by his small cocked hat and *redingote gris*. Immediately the men were formed up across the road, and, as Napoleon came nearer, they were ordered to make ready and present. They did so: the muskets came up and were levelled. Then came a pause; dead silence; an interval of breathless suspense.

Napoleon's own action decided the issue. Stepping rapidly forward, opening and throwing back his great-coat as he did so, he called aloud to the regiment: "*Soldats, voilà votre Empereur! Que celui d'entre vous qui voudra le tuer, faire feu sur lui!*" ("Soldiers, here is your Emperor! Let anyone who wishes to kill him fire on him!")

A Royalist officer hastily called out the order: "*Le voilà! donnez feu, soldats!*" But not a shot came. The next instant, with shouts of "*Vive l'Empereur!*" the soldiers lowered their muskets, broke their ranks, and rushed forward to surround Napoleon and welcome him in a frenzy of enthusiasm.

According to another story, this is what took place. Before the word "Fire!" could be given, Napoleon had stepped forward, close up to the muzzles of the levelled muskets. With a smile on his face he began in his usual colloquial, familiar way when talking to the men: "Well, soldiers of the 5th, how are you all? I am come to see you again: is there any one of you who wishes to kill me?"

Shouts came in reply of "No, no, Sire! certainly not!" The muskets went down; Napoleon passed along the ranks, inspecting the men just as of old; after that the regiment faced about, took the lead of the party, and, with Napoleon in the middle and the "Elba Guard" bringing up the rear, all marched on towards Grenoble.

There, meanwhile, events had been moving rapidly. The commandant of the garrison was an *émigré* officer, but most of the troops had been won over for Napoleon by Colonel Labédoyère, at the head of the 7th of the Line. The commandant ordered the gates to be closed, which was done; also the cannon on the ram-parts to be loaded. That order was duly obeyed; "but the men rammed home the cannon-balls first, before putting in the powder, so that the guns were useless." Labédoyère marched out with his regiment to meet Napoleon, the band playing, "and carrying the Eagle of the regiment, which had been concealed and preserved."

They met Napoleon a short distance from Grenoble and, with the 5th, led the way in, arriving after dark.

On Napoleon's approach, the populace thronged the ramparts with torches; the gates were burst open; Napoleon was borne through the town in triumph by a wild and intermingled crowd of soldiers and workpeople. (*See note following.*)

Note:—It was the action of Marshal Ney that sealed the fate of the Bourbon *régime*.

Ney had accepted the Restoration as bringing peace to exhausted France; he had given in his allegiance to the Bourbons. Angry and sick at heart as he was over the ill-treatment meted out to his brother officers, and the humiliations that the new *régime* had inflicted on the army, and sore over personal grievances of his own, he had, in spite of all, loyally held back from intriguing against the restored dynasty. Napoleon's leaving Elba, when he first heard the news, he condemned outspokenly as a crime against France.

Impulsive and headstrong by nature, he forgot his grievances, and hastened to Paris to offer his sword to the King. Napoleon, he said to the king at the interview at the Tuileries, which was immediately granted him, was a madman and deserved to be brought to Paris "like a bandit in an iron cage." So hostile witnesses at Ney's court-martial declared, though Ney himself emphatically denied using any words of the kind. His services were accepted gladly, for Ney was the most popular of all the marshals with the soldiers, and he was sent to lead the army against Napoleon. Besançon was proposed as his headquarters, and he betook himself there.

Almost at once, however, anxieties and doubts beset Ney. On taking up his command he found but few regiments available. He was promised reinforcements, but none arrived, and while he waited, no news of the rapidly altering situation reached him from Paris. Meanwhile the news came steadily in from all sides that the soldiers could not be trusted to oppose Napoleon. Ney was still loyal to the Bourbons, and he moved his troops nearer the line of advance Napoleon was taking; to Lons le Saulnier, midway between Besançon and Lyons. To officers who hinted that the soldiers would not fight if Napoleon appeared, Ney answered angrily: "They shall fight. I will take a musket and begin the firing myself! I will run my sword through the first man who hesitates!"

But events were moving too fast: the tide of Bonapartism was rising visibly on all sides. Napoleon, Ney heard, was being received everywhere with acclamation; the soldiers were said to be declaring for him by thousands. Already in every garrison the soldiers were displaying their old Eagle cap-badges and tricolour cockades. "Every soldier in the Army," relates Savary in his *Memoirs*, "had preserved his tricolour cockade and the Eagle-badge of his *shako* or cap. It was needless for any order to be given for their resumption; that had been done on the first intelligence of the Emperor's landing in France."

Everywhere too, officers who had kept back and hidden the old regimental Eagles and tricolour standards, were bringing them out openly. In regiments where the Ministerial order had been obeyed and the Eagles sent to Paris for destruction, the soldiers now took out the Bourbon arms from the white flags, substituting a tricolour shield for the royal shield with the three *fleurs-de-lis.*

Ney next began to doubt what line of conduct he ought to adopt. On one side was his oath of allegiance to the king. On the other was the prospect of a civil war which would be ruinous to France, which he, at the head of his army, had it in his power to prevent. It became borne in on him as his duty to the country in the circumstances to throw his influence on the side of his old comrades and Napoleon. His personal grievances against the Bourbons rankled in his mind, and self-interest urged him to go with the stream; but it was rather a sense of duty and patriotism, to avert a civil war, that impelled Ney to take the action that he did.

His final decision was influenced by an insidiously worded letter from Napoleon, playing on Ney's personal feelings and calling him by his old name of "the Bravest of the Brave." The letter was brought to him by two secret emissaries on the night of March 13, who urged on the marshal that his soldiers were about to abandon him, and that it was impossible for him single-handed to hope to stem the current of national feeling. That and the letter turned the scale. Ney decided to abandon the cause of the Bourbons.

Assembling his troops on parade next day, he publicly declared for Napoleon in a fiery proclamation addressed to the Army. "Officers, under-officers, and soldiers," Ney began, reading out the proclamation from on horseback in front of the assembled battalions, "the cause of the Bourbons is lost forever! The dynasty adopted by the French nation is about to re-ascend the throne. To the Emperor Napoleon, our Sovereign, alone belongs the right of reigning in our dear country." The proclamation concluded with these words:

> Soldiers, I have often led you to victory. I will now conduct you to that immortal phalanx which the Emperor Napoleon is leading towards Paris. It will arrive there within a few days, when our hopes and our happiness will be forever realised. Long live the Emperor!

The declaration came as fire to a train of gunpowder. Ney had hardly uttered a dozen words before frantic exclamations and shouts burst forth; *shakos* and caps and helmets were raised and waved on muskets and swords, amid tumultuous cries of "*Vive l'Empereur!*" "*Vive le Maréchal Ney!*" The men broke their ranks and rushed headlong round Ney, catching hold of him and kissing his hands and feet and uniform: "those not near enough kissing his embarrassed *aides de camp*." Shouted some: "We knew you would not leave us in the hands of the *émigrés!*" The marshal at the close was escorted back to his quarters amid a crowd of excited soldiers cheering frantically.

The scene there was very different. Arrived in his quarters, Ney found himself at once surrounded by a group of anxious and nervous staff-officers and *aides de camp*. Said some: "You should have informed us of it before, *M. le Marechal!* We ought not to have been made witnesses of such a spectacle!" One or two officers protested and resigned on the spot. One *aide de camp*, indeed, a former *émigré*, broke his sword in two and flung the pieces at Ney's feet, "It is easier," he exclaimed passionately, "for a man of honour to break iron than to break his word."

"You are children," was the marshal's answer. "It is necessary to do one thing or the other. What would you have me do? Can I stop the advancing sea with my hands? Can I go and hide like a coward to avoid the responsibility of events I cannot alter? Marshal Ney cannot take refuge in the dark! There is but one way to deal with the evil to take one side and avert civil war. So we shall get into our hands the man who has returned, and prevent his committing further follies. I am not going over to a man, but to my country."

Napoleon entered Paris on the night of March 20. The Eagles made their first appearance in the capital next day. They had been officially restored as the standards of the Army by an Imperial decree issued on March 18 from Lyons.

Paris saw them again first at the review of the garrison of the capital which Napoleon held within twenty-four hours of his arrival; on the Place du Carrousel, in front of the Tuileries. There too the Imperial Guard, reconstituted that same morning, made their public reappearance. In the midst of the brilliant scene, as Napoleon was ending the address of personal thanks for their loyalty that he made to the assembled troops in dramatic style, suddenly General Cambronne marched on to the parade at the head of the Elba Six Hundred, with drums beating and escorting the former Eagles of the Guard. Drawing up in line ceremoniously, the "Elba Guard" halted before Napoleon, saluting and dipping the Eagles forward. A frantic roar of enthusiastic cheering greeted the salute of the Eagles.

Napoleon took instant advantage of the first pause as the cheering subsided. Pointing to the veterans just arrived, and standing with the Eagles ranged in front of them, held on high at arm's-length by their bearers, he again addressed the assembled troops.

> They bring back to you the Eagles which are to serve as your rallying-point. In giving them to the Guard, I give them to the whole Army. Treason and misfortune have cast over them a veil of mourning; but they now reappear resplendent in their old glory. Swear to me, soldiers, that these Eagles shall always be found where the welfare of the nation calls them, and those who would invade our land again shall not be able to endure their glance!

"We swear it! We swear it!" was the answer that came back amid tumultuous shouts from every side.

The Eagles restored by proclamation as the standards of the army, and the regiments reconstituted by their old numbers, to the unbounded gratification of the soldiers everywhere, another Imperial proclamation announced that Napoleon would once again personally distribute new Eagles to the regiments. The ceremony of the Field of Mars of ten years before would be repeated. The Emperor, with his own hand, would present each Eagle to a regimental deputation, which would specially attend in Paris to receive it. To give the utmost possible *éclat* also to the proceedings on the occasion, just as the former presentation of the Eagles had been made an integral feature of the Coronation celebration, so now the forthcoming distribution would take place at the same time that Napoleon renewed his Imperial oath of fidelity to the Constitution, as reshaped by the "*Acte Additionel*," which had been drafted to comply with the political exigencies of the moment.

The date provisionally fixed was towards the end of May. By that time the returns of the *Plébiscite* voting, to authorise the re-establishment of the Empire, would be known. The historic event takes its name of the "*Champ de Mai*" from the date proposed for it, although, in actual fact, the ceremony took place on June 1. The place appointed was where the former distribution of the Eagles had been made, the Field of Mars, the wide open space in front of the Military School, and the display was to be on no less *grandiose* scale than its predecessor.

Immense wooden stands were erected all round the Field of Mars, with tiers of benches, to seat, it was calculated, as many as two hundred thousand people. In front of the Military School was set up an Imperial throne, under a canopy of crimson silk, and elevated on a gorgeously decorated platform. Napoleon was to take his new Imperial oath from the throne, and there-upon formally attach his signature to the "*Acte Additional.*" There was to be a religious service also, and for that an altar was erected at one side of the throne, raised on steps and draped in red damask, picked out with gold. The balconies and stands all round were draped and hung with tricolour flags, festooned amid gilded Eagles, and heraldic insignia, and emblematic figures meant to typify the prosperity and glory awaiting France under the returned Imperial *régime*.

As on the previous occasion, all the celebrities of France were invited, and had their allotted places on the stands nearest the throne. As before, too, the central arena was packed with a dense array of troops; the deputations called up to receive the Eagles, the massed battalions of the Imperial Guard, and detachments of all the regiments of the garrison of Paris. It was a radiantly fine summer's day, and the display offered a spectacle of surpassing brilliance. Says one of the officers: "The sun flashing on 50,000 bayonets seemed to make the vast space sparkle!"

A hundred cannon fired from the Esplanade of the Invalides ushered in the day of the "*Champ de Mai*" Again, at ten o'clock, the artillery thundered forth as Napoleon quitted the Tuileries in State to take his way to the Field of Mars, "amid prodigious crowds of spectators applauding enthusiastically," along the Champs Elysées and across the Pont d'Jéna.

Nine of the marshals who had cast in their lot with the returned Emperor rode on either side of Napoleon's coach: Davout, Minister of War, who had not yet sworn allegiance to the Bourbons; Soult, the newly appointed Chief of the Staff of the Army; Serrurier, Governor of the Invalides; Brune and Jourdan; Moncey and Mortier; Suchet and Grouchy. Ney was absent; Napoleon had refused to see him. Ney's widely reported speech to Louis XVIII., that he would "bring the bandit to Paris in an iron cage," had not been forgiven. Murat was in disgrace for his recent blundering move in Northern Italy, which had vitally affected Napoleon's plans. His desertion during the closing campaign, when Napoleon was at bay after Leipsic, moreover, was beyond condonation.

Of others who had been at Napoleon's side on the Field of Mars ten years before, Lefebvre and Masséna professed to be too old and infirm for service in the field, although Masséna was still nominally on the Active List, and had been in command for King Louis at Toulon. He was due in Paris to meet Napoleon, but his fidelity was more than doubtful: "gorged with wealth, Masséna thought only of preserving it." Augereau kept in the background, Napoleon refusing to have more to do with him. Berthier, on that very morning, was lying dead at Bamberg in Bavaria; whether victim of an accident or suicide has never been made clear. Lannes and Bessières were in their graves, fallen on the field of battle.

Bernadotte, King of Sweden, was actively on the side of the enemy. Marmont, Oudinot, Macdonald, and Victor, marshals of later creation, had left France in company with the Bourbon princes. Old Kellerman and Perignon, "Honorary Marshals" of 1804, had not come forward again, remaining in seclusion; nor had St. Cyr, "the man of ice," another marshal since the Field of Mars, who was staying at home with studied indifference, "occupying himself on his estate with his hay crops and playing the fiddle."

Napoleon was accompanied in the State coach by three of his brothers—Lucien, Joseph, and Jerome. This time there was of course no Empress present. Josephine was dead: Marie Louise was holding back elsewhere. None of the Bonaparte princesses appeared in the procession. The only one attending the *"Champ de Mai"* came as a spectator: Hortense Beauharnais, the daughter of Josephine and wife of Louis Bonaparte. She had gone on in advance to the Military School and was seated among the exalted personages awaiting Napoleon there; accompanied by her two boys (one the future Third Napoleon, the "Man of Sedan"). She seemed most interested, as we are told, in the sketch-book she brought with her to draw a picture of the scene.

Napoleon alighted in the First Court of the Military School, being acclaimed on all sides as he made his appearance with vociferous shouts of "*Vive l'Empereur!*" Preceded by palace *grandees* and court officials, who had alighted from their carriages in advance and formed up to receive him, he entered the building and passed on through to take his seat on the throne.

> He had the air of being in pain and anxious, (*describes an onlooker.*) He descended slowly from his carriage while a hundred drums beat '*Au Champ.*' Then, advancing quickly, returning the salutes of the assemblage at either side with bows, he proceeded to the throne, and sat down, gazing round at the people in their

dense masses as he did so. Jerome and Joseph seated themselves on the right; Lucien on the left; all three clad in white satin with black velvet hats with white plumes. Napoleon himself had on his Imperial mantle of ermine and purple velvet embroidered with golden bees.

For a time the thundering cannon salutes and acclamations of the people that hailed Napoleon's appearance on the dais were deafening. Bowing repeatedly on every side, he took his seat on the throne, while all present stood and remained uncovered. The guns then ceased, the music of the bands and the drummings and trumpetings of the battalions died away into silence. On that the ceremony of the day opened with the celebration of High Mass by the Archbishop of Tours.

The religious portion of the pageant, we are told, "seemed to arouse no interest in Napoleon. His opera-glass wandered all the time over the immense multitude before him." His attention was not recalled until the Mass was over, when the delegates from the Electoral College, marshalled by the Master of the Ceremonies, ascended the platform, and ranged themselves before the throne. A Deputy stepped forward, and after deep obeisance, in a loud resonant voice read an address teeming with sentiments of patriotic attachment and expressing inviolable fidelity towards the Emperor personally.

Napoleon seemed to listen with interest, "marking his approbation with nods and smiles." The deputy ceased speaking amidst rapturous applause, and then Arch-Chancellor Cambacérès, resplendent in a gorgeous orange-yellow robe, stood forward in front of Napoleon to notify officially the popular acceptance of the new national Constitution. He declared the total of the votes given in the *Plébiscite* to show a clear million in favour of the restoration of the Empire. There was a flourish of trumpets, and forthwith the chief herald proclaimed that the "Additional Act to the Constitution of the Empire" had been agreed to by the French people.

Again from all round thundered out an artillery salute, and the whole assembly rose to their feet and cheered. A small gilded table was brought forward and placed before Napoleon, who, the Arch-Chancellor holding the parchment open, and Joseph Bonaparte presenting the pen, publicly ratified the act with his formal signature. The air resounded once more with the cannon firing and noisy acclamations on all sides.

Napoleon rose, when at length the cheering ceased, to address the assembly with one of his most impassioned dramatic harangues.

Emperor, Consul, Soldier, I hold everything from the people! In prosperity and in adversity; in the field, in the council; in power, in exile, France has been the sole and constant object of my thoughts and actions!

So he began. He closed in the same vein:

Frenchmen! my will is that of my people; my rights are theirs; my honour, my glory, my happiness, can never be separated from the honour, glory, and happiness of France!

Again came the outburst of rapturous applause. It subsided, and the Archbishop of Bourges, as Grand Almoner of the Empire, came forward. Kneeling before Napoleon he presented the *Book of the Gospels,* on which Napoleon solemnly took the Imperial Oath to observe the new Constitution. There only remained for Arch-Chancellor Cambacérès and the principal officers of State to take their oaths of allegiance to the Constitution and the Emperor, and after that a solemn *Te Deum* closed the political ceremony.

It was now the turn of the Eagles and the army. The civilian personages withdrew from the steps of the throne; the electoral deputations fell back; leaving a clear open space in front. Immediately, as if by magic, the Eagles suddenly appeared; long rows of them flashing and glittering in the brilliant sunshine. They were brought forward in procession, advancing in massed rows "resplendent and dazzling like gold."

Carnot, Minister of the Interior, the "Organiser of Victory" of the Armies of the Revolution, headed the procession, "clad in a Spanish white dress of great magnificence," carrying the First Eagle of the National Guard of Paris. Next him came Marshal Davout, Minister of War, carrying the Eagle of the 1st Regiment of the Line, and then Admiral Decrès, Minister of Marine (as representing the French Navy), carrying the Eagle of Napoleon's 1st Regiment of Marines. General Count Friant (he fell at Waterloo), as colonel-in-chief, bore the Eagle of the Imperial Guard. Other officers of exalted rank bore other Eagles.

Napoleon's demeanour, hitherto, for most of the time, formal and apathetic, altered instantaneously at the appearance of the Eagles. "He sprang from the throne, and, casting aside his purple mantle, rushed forward to meet his Eagles"; amid a sudden hush that seemed to fall over the whole assembly at the sight. Then the momentary silence was broken. An enthusiastic shout went up as the Emperor, pressing forward impetuously, as though electrified with sudden energy, took up his station immediately in front of the array of soldiers, the *élite* of the veterans of the old Grand Army left alive, as they stood there formed up in an immense *phalanx*.

To the sound of martial music the regimental deputations forthwith moved up and advanced to pass before him. Napoleon, with a gesture of deep reverence, took each Eagle into his own hands from the officer who had been carrying it, and then delivered it with stately formality to its future regimental bearer as the deputations in turn filed past him.

He had a word for the men of every corps as each set of ten officers and men drew up before him. To some he said, glancing at the number of their regiment on their *shakos*, "I remember you well. You are my old companions of Italy!" or, "You are my comrades of Egypt!" and so on. Others he reminded of past days of distinction. "You were with me at Arcola!" he said to one group, or "at Rivoli!" "at Austerlitz!" "at Friedland!" to others, as might be—his words, we are told, "inspiring the men with deep emotion." For each of the National Guard deputations he had also their little speech. To one detachment for instance, as it came up, he said: "You are my old companions from the Rhine; you have been the foremost, the most courageous, the most unfortunate in our disasters; but I remember all!"

The last Eagle presented, Napoleon called on the soldiers to take the Army Oath of fidelity to the Standard, using his customary Eagle oration formula.

> Soldiers of the National Guard of the Empire! Soldiers of my Imperial Guard! Soldiers of the Line on land and sea! I entrust to your hands the Imperial Eagle! You swear here to defend it at the cost of your life's blood against the enemies of the nation. You swear that it will always be your guiding sign, your rallying point!

Some of those nearest interrupted Napoleon with shouts of "We swear!"

He went on: "You swear never to acknowledge any other standard!"

The shouts of "We swear!" again broke in vociferously.
Napoleon again went on:

> You, Soldiers of the National Guard of Paris, swear never to permit the foreigner to desecrate again the capital of the Great

Nation! To your courage I commit it!

Cries of "We swear!" repeated continuously amidst a tumult of clamour, once more burst forth.

Napoleon continued and concluded, turning to his favourite *pretorians*:

> Soldiers of the Imperial Guard, swear to surpass yourselves in the campaign which is now about to open, to die round your Eagles rather than permit foreigners to dictate terms to your country!

He ceased after that, and once again the air vibrated with shouts of "We swear! We swear!" and ejaculations of "*Vive l'Empereur!*" from the soldiers and the throng of onlookers cramming the stands around.[1]

The military *finale* of the day was the march past of the assembled troops before the Emperor, in slow time, headed by the Eagles. Says one of the spectators:

> Nothing could have been more imposing, than this concluding display in the magnificent pageant. Amid the crash of military music, the blaze of martial decoration, the glitter of innumerable arms, 50,000 men passed by. The immense concourse of beholders, their prolonged shouts and cheers, the occasion, the man, the mighty events which hung in suspense, all concurred to excite feelings and reflections which only such a scene could have produced.

On the other hand, we have this from a colder critic of the scene:

> The display was without heart, and theatrical; the vows of the soldiers were made without warmth. There was but little real enthusiasm: the shouts were not those of future victors of another Austerlitz and Wagram, and the Emperor knew it!

Which are we to believe?

According to Savary, who was close beside him, Napoleon, for his part, was satisfied with the enthusiasm of the soldiers.

The Emperor left the Field of Mars confident that he might rely on the sentiments then manifested towards him, and from

---

1. The silken standard flags attached below the Eagles were plainer in design than the flags of 1804 and 1808. They were of the ordinary pattern of the national banner, three vertical bands of colour, edged with golden fringe. Lettered in gold on the white central band of the flag was the Imperial dedication, worded similarly to the inscription on the older flags, and on the reverse the names of the battles in which the corps had taken part—"Austerlitz," "Jena," etc.

that moment his only care was to meet the storm that was forming in Belgium.

The new Eagles left Paris that night with their escorts. Each, on its arrival where its regiment was stationed, was received with elaborate ceremony, and formally presented on parade to the assembled officers and men; a religious service being held in addition in some cases, at which all were sworn individually to give their lives in its defence. This, for instance, is what took place with one regiment, the 22nd of the Line, stationed with the advanced division of Grouchy's Army Corps on the Belgian frontier at Couvins, near Rocroy, in the Ardennes. One of the officers describes:

> The new Eagle, all fresh from the *gilder's* shop, was solemnly blessed in the church of Couvins; then each soldier, touching it with his hand, swore individually to defend it to the death. After the religious service the regiment formed in square, and the colonel delivered an address, in which he recalled the old glories of the 22nd of the Line, and expressed his conviction that the regiment would worthily uphold the old-time fame of the corps in the coming campaign. The glowing language was received with great emotion, and as of happy augury for the future. [2]

---

2. Napoleon left Paris for the front on the early morning of June 12, after spending several hours in his cabinet, issuing orders and making arrangements for the carrying on of the Government in his absence. Caulaincourt, acting for the time being as Foreign Minister, was with Napoleon until the last moment, and witnessed his departure. "The clock struck three, and daylight was beginning to appear. 'Farewell, Caulaincourt!' said the Emperor, holding out his hand to me, 'Farewell! We must conquer or die!' With hurried steps he passed through the apartments, his mind being evidently fully taken up with melancholy thoughts. On reaching the foot of the staircase, he cast a lingering look round him, and then threw himself into his carriage and drove away."

CHAPTER 13: AT WATERLOO
"Ave Caesar! Morituri te Salutant!"

The Eagles figure in four episodes in the story of Waterloo.

They had their part at the outset in that intensely dramatic display on the morning of the battle, when, before the eyes of Wellington's soldiers, drawn up with muskets loaded and bayonets fixed, and guns in position ready to open fire, Napoleon passed his army in review; the last parade of the Last Army on the day of its last battle. Said Napoleon himself afterwards, in words that are in keeping with the resplendent spectacle: "The earth seemed proud to bear so many brave men!" ("*La terre paraissait orgueilleuse de porter tant de braves!*")

It was a little after nine in the morning that the Last Army of Napoleon moved out from its bivouacs of the night before to take up its station for the battle. This is how a British hussar, who was looking on, describes the opening of the wonderful show:

> Marching in eleven columns they came up to the front and deployed with rapidity, precision, and fine scenic effect. The drums beat, the bands played, the trumpets sounded. The light troops in front pressed forward, and the rattle of musketry was followed by the retreat of our horsemen and foot soldiers. Light wreaths of smoke curled upwards into the misty air, and through this thin veil the dense dark columns of the French infantry and the gay and gleaming squadrons of French horse were seen moving into their positions. Before them was the open valley, yet green with the heavy crops; behind them dark fringes of wood, and a thick curtain of dreary cloud.
>
> The French bands struck up so that we could distinctly hear them. Not long after, the enemy's skirmishers, backed by their supports, were thrown out; extending as they advanced, they

spread over the whole space before them. Now and then they saluted our ears with well-known music, the whistling of musket-balls. Their columns, preceded by mounted officers to take up the alignments, soon began to appear; the bayonets flashing over dark masses at different points, accompanied by the rattling of drums and the clang of trumpets.

They took post, their infantry in front, in two lines, 60 yards apart, flanked by lancers with their fluttering flags. In rear of the centre of the infantry wings were the *cuirassiers*, also in two lines. In rear of the *cuirassiers*, on the right, the lancers and *chasseurs* of the Imperial Guard, in their splendid but gaudy uniforms: the former clad in scarlet; the latter, like hussars, in rifle-green, fur-trimmed *pelisse*, gold lace, bearskin cap. In rear of the *cuirassiers*, on the left, were the horse-grenadiers and dragoons of the Imperial Guard, with their dazzling arms.

Immediately in rear of the centre was the reserve, composed of the 6th Corps, in columns; on the left, and on the right of the Genappe road, were two divisions of light cavalry. In rear of the whole was the infantry of the Imperial Guard in columns, a dense dark mass, which, with the 6th Corps and cavalry, were flanked by their numerous artillery. Nearly 72,000 men, and 246 guns, ranged with matches lighted, gave an awful presage of the approaching conflict.

Napoleon rode out to watch them as they deployed into position. He took his stand at the point where the columns reached the field and wheeled off to right and left to form up in readiness for the signal that should launch their massed ranks forward across the intervening valley against the British position in front. Marshal Soult, chief of the General Staff, rode close behind Napoleon on one side; Marshal Ney, in charge of the main attack that day, was on the other. In rear followed in glittering array the cavalcade of staff officers, with, dragged along after them, tied by a rope to a dragoon orderly, Napoleon's Waterloo guide, the inn-keeper De Coster.

Hardly had Napoleon himself ever witnessed before the like of the tremendous display of enthusiasm that greeted his presence on the field on the morning of that final day.

The drums beat; the trumpets sounded; the bands struck up '*Veillons au salut de l'Empire.*' As they passed Napoleon the standard-bearers drooped the Eagles; the cavalrymen waved their sabres; the infantrymen held on high their shakos on their bayonets. The roar of cheers dominated and drowned the beat of the drums and the blare of the trumpets. The '*Vive l'Empereurs!*' followed with such vehemence and such rapidity that no commands could be heard. And what rendered the scene all the more solemn, all the more moving, was the fact that before us, a thousand paces away perhaps, we could see distinctly the dull red line ("*la ligne rouge sombre*") of the English Army.

So one French officer (Captain Martin of the 45th of the Line) describes. Another, a veteran of Count d'Erlon's First Army Corps, says:

The shouts of "*Vive l'Empereur!*" rose more vehemently, louder and longer than I ever heard before, for our men were determined that they should be heard among the brick-red lines which fringed the crest of Mont Saint-Jean.

It was for the Eagles the counterpart of the Day of the Field of Mars, the culminating act of homage to Napoleon from the soldiers of the Grand Army. If we may use the words of Lamartine:

The sight of him, was for some a recompense for their death, for others an incitement to victory! One heart beat between these men and the Emperor. In such a moment they shared the same soul and the same cause! When all is risked for one man, it is in him his followers live and die. The army was Napoleon! Never before was it so entirely Napoleon as now. He was repudiated by Europe, and his army had adopted him with idolatry; it voluntarily made itself the great martyr of his glory. At such a moment he must have felt himself more than man, more than a sovereign.

His subjects only bowed to his power, Europe to his genius; but his army bent in homage to the past, the present, and the future, and welcomed victory or defeat, the throne or death with its chief. It was deter-mined on everything, even on the sacrifice of itself, to restore him his Empire, or to render his last fall illustrious. Accomplices at Grenoble, Pretorians at Paris, victims at Waterloo: such a sentiment in the generals and officers of Napoleon had in it nothing that was not in conformity with the habits and even the vices of humanity. His cause was their cause, his crime their crime, his power their power, his glory their glory.

But the devotion of those 80,000 soldiers was more virtuous, for it was more disinterested. Who would know their names? Who would pay them for the shedding of their blood? The plain before them would not even preserve their bones! To have inspired such a devotion was the greatness of Napoleon; to evince it even to madness was the greatness of his Army!

They knew, too, not a few of them, the stamp of men they were about to meet. Never before that day, of course, had Napoleon met British soldiers on the battlefield; but there were others present who had, and a good many of them. Many a French regiment at Waterloo had old scores of their own to settle, past days to avenge. The 8th of the Line, the fate of whose "Eagle with the Golden Wreath" at Barrosa has been recorded, were on the field, and dipped their glittering new Eagle, received at the "*Champ de Mai*," in salute as they passed Napoleon that morning. So too did the 82nd, whose former battalion Eagles from Martinique are at Chelsea now; the 13th of the Line and the 51st, who lost their regimental Eagles in the Retiro arsenal of Madrid; the 28th, who met their fate, and lost their Eagle under the bullets of the British 28th in the Pyrenees. Others were there who had fought against Wellington in Spain, and, more fortunate, had preserved their Eagles.

Among these were the 47th, who on the battlefield at Barrosa lost and regained their Eagle; and the 105th, mindful yet of their terrible Salamanca experience of what dragoon swords in strong hands could do. The 105th were destined, soldiers and Eagle alike, to undergo a fate more fearful still, ere the sun should set that day.

Two of the regiments that paraded before Napoleon to meet the soldiers of Wellington had met under fire the sailors of Nelson at Trafalgar: the 2nd of the Line, now in Jerome Bonaparte's division of Reille's Army Corps, and the 16th, serving with the Sixth Corps. A third regiment, the 70th, which did duty as marines at Trafalgar, was with Grouchy, not many miles away; as was the 22nd of the Line, whose Eagle, taken at Salamanca, is at Chelsea Hospital, and the 34th, whose drum-major's staff is to this day a prized trophy of the British 34th (now the First Battalion of the Border Regiment), won in Spain, when, as it so befell, two regiments bearing the same number crossed bayonets on the battlefield.[3]

3. Trafalgar, on the French side, it may be added by the way, had a distinguished representative at Waterloo in the person of the officer at the head of the Artillery of the Imperial Guard, General Drouot. He had fought against Nelson as a major of artillery doing duty in the French fleet. His ship was one of the few that escaped into Cadiz after the battle, whence he was recalled to join the Grand Army in the Jena campaign. Drouot was the officer who, during the retreat from Moscow—where he brought the artillery of the Guard through without losing a gun—"washed his face and shaved in the open air, affixing his looking-glass to a gun-carriage, every day, regardless of the thermometer!"

The famous 84th of the Line were at Waterloo, with their proud legend, "*Un centre dix*," restored at the "*Champ de Mai*," flaunting proudly on their new silken flag as the Eagle bent in salute to Napoleon; also, the hardly less widely renowned 46th, the corps of the First Grenadier of France, La Tour d'Auvergne, whose name was called at the head of the list at that morning's roll-call and answered with the customary answer, "Dead on the Field of Honour"; also, too, Napoleon's former-time favourite, the 75th, mindful still on that last day of their glorious youth when "*Le 75me arrive et bât l'ennemi*"—a motto that an earlier colonel of the corps had proposed once to replace on the flag by "*Veni, Vidi, Vici.*"

The Old Guard paraded in their fighting kit, with, as usual, in their knapsacks their full-dress uniforms, carried in readiness to be put on for Napoleon's triumphal entry into Brussels.

Drouet d'Erlon rode past at the head of the First Army Corps; Count of the Empire in virtue of his rank as a general; once upon a time the little son of the postmaster at Varennes, where Louis Seize and Marie Antoinette so pitifully ended their attempted flight, harsh old Drouet, ex-sergeant of Condé dragoons, from whom he inherited his talent for soldiering. General Reille led past the Second Corps. He, curiously, had had something of a naval past. He had hardly forgotten that other battle-day morning, when he galloped on to the field of Austerlitz, and reported himself to the Emperor as having come direct from Cadiz, put ashore from the doomed French fleet of Admiral Villeneuve just a week before it sailed to fight Trafalgar.

Both Reille and his men, above all others, were burning with excitement and eagerness that day to get at the enemy. They had missed taking part either at Ligny or Quatre Bras, through contradictory orders which had kept them marching and counter-marching between the two battlefields; unable to reach either in time. Smarting under the reproach that they had been useless in the campaign, though the pick of the Line was in their ranks, the men one and all were burning to retrieve their reputation.

Count Lobau—he took his name from the island in the Danube which played so vital a part in the Battle of Aspern—was at the head of the Sixth Corps, the third of Napoleon's grand divisions of the army at Waterloo. Formerly General Mouton, Napoleon renamed him when he made him a Count for his skill and heroism at Aspern. "*Mon Mouton*," said Napoleon of him once as he watched the general in action, "*est un lion.*"

Napoleon himself was in the highest spirits, full of pride and confidence. In that mood had he announced his intention of holding the review. There was no need to hurry, he said; Blücher and Wellington had been driven apart. The parade would pass the time while waiting for the soaked ground to get dry, and make it easier for the guns to move from point to point. And there was also this. The spectacle would have assuredly a disquieting effect on the Dutch and Belgians in Wellington's army. Many of the men in front of him had served with the Eagles In former days: all stood nervously in awe, it was notorious, of the mighty name and reputation of Napoleon. Hesitating, as some were known to be, between their fears and their patriotism, the influence of the imposing spectacle might well—believed Napoleon—turn the scale and induce them to come over.

This was Napoleon's plan for the battle, as outlined that morning to his brother Jerome. First would be the general preparation for attack by a tremendous cannonade all along the line from massed batteries. On that, the two army corps of D'Erlon and Reille would advance simultaneously and assault in front, supported by cavalry charges of *cuirassiers*. Then, if the English had not yet been beaten, would follow the final assault, the crushing blow that it would be impossible to resist; to be delivered by the remaining army corps of Lobau and the Young Guard, supported by the Middle Guard and the Old Guard. So Napoleon planned to fight and win at Waterloo.

Of the ultimate issue of the day he flattered himself there could be no two opinions. "At the last I have them, these English!" ("*Enfin je les tiens, ces Anglais!*") he exclaimed jubilantly as he reconnoitred Wellington's position in the early morning. At breakfast with the two marshals, Soult and Ney, he declared that the odds were 90 to 10 in his favour. "Wellington," he said to Ney, "has thrown the dice, and the game is with us."

He turned fiercely on Soult, who, knowing the mettle of the British soldier from experience, had entreated him to recall Grouchy's 30,000 men from watching the Prussians near Wavre.

"You think because Wellington has defeated you, that he must be a very great general! I tell you he is a bad general, and the English are but poor troops! This, for us, will only be an affair of a *dejeuner*—a picnic!"

"I hope so," was all that Soult said in reply.

At that moment Reille and General Foy, experienced Peninsular veterans both, whose opinions should have had weight, were announced. Said Reille, in reply to Napoleon's asking what he thought: "If well placed, as Wellington knows how to draw up his men, and if attacked in front, the English infantry is invincible, by reason of its calm tenacity and the superiority of its fire. Before coming to close quarters with the bayonet we must expect to see half the assaulting troops out of action."

Interposed Foy: "Wellington never shows his troops, but if he is yonder, I must warn your Majesty that the English infantry in close com-bat is the very devil!" ("*L'infanterie Anglaise en duel c'est le diable!*")

Napoleon lost his temper. With an exclamation of angry incredulity he rose hastily from the breakfast table, and the party broke up.

He spent a great part of the day watching the battle from a little mound, a short distance from the farm of Rossomme; mostly pacing to and fro, his hands behind his back; at times violently taking snuff, occasionally gesticulating excitedly. Nearby was a kitchen table from the farmhouse, covered with maps weighted down with stones, with a chair placed on some straw, on which at intervals he rested. Soult kept ever near at hand, and the staff remained a little in rear. It was not until the afternoon was well advanced that Napoleon got again on horseback.

As related by the guide De Coster in conversation with an English questioner a few months after Waterloo, this is what passed:

"He had frequent communications with his *aides de camp* during the day?"

"Every moment."

"And when they reported what was going on?"

"His orders were always '*Avancez!*'"

"Did he eat or drink during the day?"

"No!"

"Did he take snuff?"

"In abundance."

"Did he talk much?"

"Never, except when he gave orders."

"What was the general character of his countenance during the day?"

"*Riante!*—till the last charge failed."

"How did he look then?"

"*Blanc-mort!*"

"Did he say '*Sauve qui peut*'?"

"No! When he saw the English infantry rush forward, and the cavalry in the intermediate spaces coming down the hill, he said: 'A present *il est fini. Sauvons-nous!*'" (*See note following.*)

Note:—Napoleon it may be of general interest to add—passed the whole of the day, between the review in the forenoon and late in the afternoon when he rode forward to witness the Guard start for the last charge, on the ridge of high ground near Rossomme. So the memoirs of the officers of his staff unanimously record. At no time was he near the so-called "observatory," in regard to which there has recently been a controversy, based on the publication of a letter by the eminent surgeon, Sir Charles Bell, who was at Waterloo, and rendered very valuable service to the wounded. This is the story as told in his letter by Dr. Bell:

> About half a mile of ascent brought us to the position of Bonaparte. This is the highest ground in the Pays Bas. I climbed up one of the pillars of the scaffolding, as I was wont to do after birds' nests.... We got a ladder from the farm-court; it reached near the first platform. I mounted and climbed with some difficulty; none of the rest would venture.... The view was magnificent. I was only one-third up the machine, yet it was a giddy height. Here Bonaparte stood surveying the field.
>
> This position of Bonaparte is most excellent; the machine had been placed by the side of the road, but he ordered it to be shifted. The shifting of this scaffolding shows sufficiently the power of confidence and the resolution of the man. It is about sixty feet in height. I climbed upon it about four times the length of my body, by exact measurement, and this was only the first stage. I was filled with admiration for a man of his habit of life who could stand perched on a height of sixty-five feet above everything, and contemplate, see, and manage such a scene.

Mention of the scaffold-platform is also made by Sir Walter Scott, who rode over the field in August 1815. Sir Walter gives this version, in a letter to the Duke of Buccleuch:

> The story of his (Napoleon's) having an observatory erected for him is a mistake. There is such a thing, and he repaired to it during the action; but it was built or

erected some months before, for the purpose of a trigonometrical survey of the country, by the King of the Netherlands."

Thomas Kelly, an enterprising London publisher, went further, He had a picture of the erection drawn, and brought it out as a popular print in October 1815, under the title of *Bonaparte's Observatory to view the Battle of Waterloo.* The print shows a three-tiered structure, apparently quite lately constructed, with three platforms, and ladders leading from one platform to the other. Napoleon himself is depicted on top, his spy-glass at his eye, and with two staff officers in attendance.

There certainly was a structure of the kind on the field. Such a thing, in a dilapidated condition, is to be seen in miniature on the Siborne model of the battlefield at the Royal United Service Institution. It is made to scale, and in its essential features bears out Dr. Bell's description. It stands close to the "wood of Callois "by the Nivelle road, rather more than a mile to the south of Hougoumont. It has only one platform, whence it would overlook the trees and give a good view of the battle.

On the other hand, in addition to the silence of all Napoleon's officers on the subject, we have this plain statement from Frances Lady Shelley, an intimate friend of the Duke of Wellington, who was in Paris during the occupation after the battle and was also taken over the battlefield by the Duke of Richmond some three months after Waterloo. It appears in her recently published *Diary*, and may be taken as settling the fate of the story of "this towering and massive perch," "that wonderful scaffold," "that huge scaffolding," "part of Napoleon's equipment at Waterloo," as a modern historical writer calls it.

This is what Lady Shelley wrote at the time:

> Throughout the battle of Waterloo Napoleon remained on a mound, within cannon shot, but beyond the range of musketry fire. He certainly was not in the observatory after the battle began; nor could he have from that spot directed the movements of his troops. That observatory was built for topographical reasons by a former Governor of the Netherlands something like a century ago.

How Wellington's Trophies Were Won

It was in Napoleon's second grand attack that our two Waterloo

Eagle-trophies, the most famous spoils ever won by the British Army, came into Wellington's hands.

The first attack began about half-past eleven, when Reille's corps, on the French left, made its opening effort against Hougoumont. Intended by Napoleon at the outset rather as a feint to mislead Wellington into fixing his attention on that side, the stubborn defence of Hougoumont involved the Second Corps in a struggle that kept it fully occupied for the whole day; unable to take part or be of use elsewhere.

The second grand attack took place shortly after two in the afternoon, when Marshal Ney made his tremendous onslaught with thirty-three battalions of Drouet d'Erlon's First Army Corps on the left-centre of the British position, to the east of the Charleroi road, where Picton's men held the ground.

The launching of Ney's attack just then came about as the result of Napoleon's sudden and disquieting discovery that the Prussians were approaching. It was to have opened an hour earlier, but, because of that, had been held back at the last moment. Napoleon, while looking round with the idea that Grouchy's troops might be in sight in that quarter, made the discovery with his own eyes. Those round him, indeed, at first doubted what the dark object—which appeared in the hazy atmosphere like a shadow on the high ground near Mont Saint-Lambert, some six miles off to the north-east—really was.

Soult at first could make out nothing; then he was positive it was a column of troops—probably Grouchy's. The staff, scanning the suspicious neighbourhood with their telescopes, asserted that what the Emperor saw was only a wood. The arrival of some hussars with a Prussian prisoner, whom they had just captured while trying to get round with a despatch from Bülow to Wellington to announce the approach of the Prussian Fourth Corps, settled the question.

Napoleon paced backwards and forwards for a minute, taking pinches of snuff incessantly. Then he ordered off his Light Cavalry to reconnoitre; dictated to Soult an urgent message recalling Grouchy; and sent off an *aide de camp* to tell Lobau to wheel the Sixth Corps to the right, facing towards Saint-Lambert. After that he gave Ney orders to open his attack.

Ney took in hand his work forthwith, and at once a terrific cannonade opened. Eighty French field-guns, a third of Napoleon's artillery on the field, began firing together from the plateau in front of La Belle Alliance; storming furiously with shot and shell to break down the British resistance, and clear the way for the onset of the charging columns. Without slackening an instant the guns thundered incessantly for nearly an hour; getting back from the British artillery in reply a fire that was at least as vigorous and no less effective.

Then Ney gave the word to advance.

Immediately the French infantry were on the move, They went forward massed in four divisions; in four solid columns of from four to five thousand men each, advancing *en échelon* from the left, with intervals between of about four hundred paces. Eight battalions made up each column, except that of the second division, which had nine. The battalions stood drawn up in lines, three deep, with a front of two hundred files. They were packed closely, one behind the other; with intervals between, from front to rear, of only five paces.

So closely were they wedged together, that there was barely room between the battalions for the company officers. Two brigadiers, Quiot and Bourgeois, led the left column, General Allix, their chief, being elsewhere; General Donzelot, a keen soldier and universally popular as the best hearted and most genial of good fellows, headed the second column; Marcognet, a grim, hard-bitten veteran, a prime favourite with Marshal Ney for his dogged determination in action, had the third; General Durutte was in charge of the fourth, away to the right.

With their battalion-drums jauntily rattling out the *pas de charge*, amid excited cries and loud exultant shouts of "*En avant!*" "*Vive l'Empereur!*" the columns stepped off. Ahead of them raced forward at a run swarming crowds of *tirailleurs*; extending fan-wise as they went, spreading out widely across the front in skirmishing array. The four massed columns surged quickly forward and over the edge of the plateau down the slope on to the space of shallow valley between the armies. As they did so, from the moment they crossed the crest-line and dipped below, a fierce hurricane of fire beat in their faces. Round-shot and shrapnel swept the columns through and through, tearing long bloody lanes through the densely packed masses of men.

Marshal Ney accompanied the first column for some part of the way, riding by the side of Drouet d'Erlon.

As they crossed the intervening ground below, the death-dealing British guns fired down on them incessantly, but in spite of all, they stout-heartedly moved forward, without checking their pace. It was terribly toilsome work in places: now they had to plough laboriously over sodden and slippery ground; now to trample their way through cornfields with standing grain-crops nearly breast-high, or, where trodden down, tangling round the men's feet.

Quiot's brigade turned off to attack La Haye Sainte, but the rest of the division, Bourgeois' men and the three other columns, held on their way, moving in dense phalanxes of gleaming bayonets up the slopes.

The second column, Donzelot's, reached the top a little in advance of the others, and was met by Kempt's brigade of Picton's troops, which charged it and forced it to yield ground.

A moment later Marcognet's column reached the British line, coming up over the crest of the hill immediately in front of Picton's Highland Brigade.

Received with a furious outburst of musketry from all along the extended British line, Marcognet's leading files were thrown into some confusion by the hail of bullets. They were, however, veterans, and though their ranks were shaken, they still pressed on, amid a tumult of fierce cries and shouts of "*Vive l'Empereur!*" and the wild clash and rattle of their drums.

But they got no farther. The British brigadier on the spot, Sir Dennis Pack, called on the nearest Highland regiment, the 92nd, to charge them with the bayonet. A moment after that, all unexpectedly, the cavalry of the Union Brigade were on them.

The Highlanders dashed forward with exultant cheers and levelled bayonets, taking the French volley that met them without firing back a shot. They did not, however, get up to the French, nor actually cross steel on steel. As the Highlanders got within a dozen yards the column suddenly stopped short, and some of the men in front seemed suddenly to be panic-stricken. A moment before all were madly yelling out: "Forward!" "Victory!" Now they began to turn their backs in disorder.

It was not, though, at the sight of the bayonets. They had seen and heard something else. The thundering beat of approaching horse-hoofs shook the ground.

With a trampling turmoil of horse-hoofs the cavalrymen of the British Union Brigade burst on the scene, galloping forward from their former post in rear of Picton's infantry. The Scots Greys were on the left; the Inniskillings in the centre; the Royal Dragoons on the right.

Marcognet's men heard their approach, and the next moment saw the horsemen coming at them. The unexpected sight startled and staggered them; and some of those in the front line gave way. The alarm

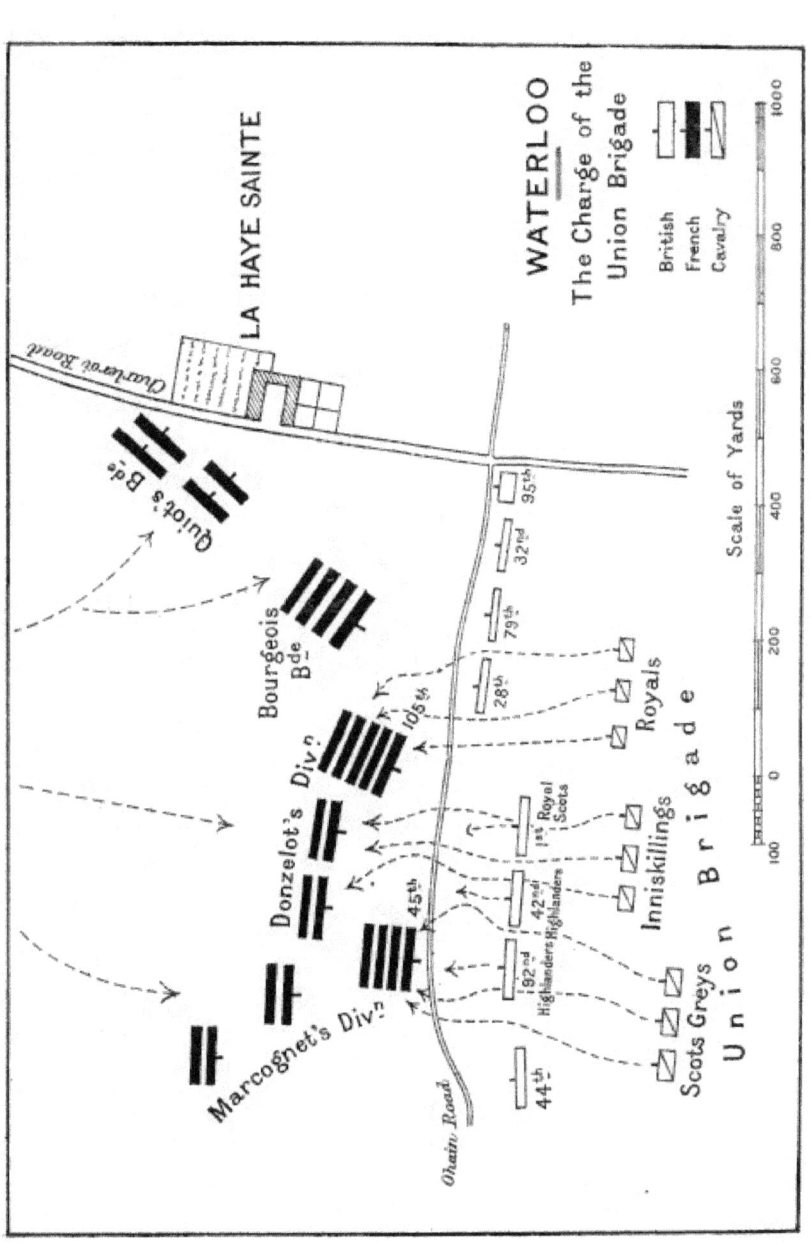

spread at once, as most of the rest realised what was approaching. The whole column swayed to and fro violently. Then it lost cohesion and began to roll back in mingled ranks downhill.

A moment later the Greys were among them. "The smoke in which the head of the French column was enshrouded had not cleared away when the Greys dashed into the mass. An officer describes:

> Highlanders and Greys charged together, while shrill and wild from the Highland ranks sounded the mountain pipe, mingled with shouts of 'Scotland forever!'

So The men of the 92nd seized hold of the stirrup-leathers of the horsemen, and charged with them. Captain Siborne describes:

> All rushed forward, leaving none but the disabled in their rear. The dragoons, having the advantage of the descent, appeared to mow down the mass, which, bending under the pressure, quickly spread itself outwards in all directions. Yet in that mass were many gallant spirits who could not be brought to yield without a struggle; and these fought bravely to the death.

Says someone on the French side:

> We heard a shout of 'Attention! Cavalry!' Almost at the same instant a crowd of red dragoons mounted on grey horses swept down upon us like the wind. Those who had straggled were cut to pieces without mercy. They did not fall upon our columns to ride through and break us up—we were too deep and massive for that; but they came down between the divisions, slashing right and left with their sabres and spurring their horses into the flanks of the columns to cut them in two. Though they did not succeed in this, they killed great numbers and threw us into confusion.

The foremost French battalion of Marcognet's column was the 45th of the Line, one of Napoleon's favourite corps, recruited in the capital, and always spoken of by him as *"Mes braves Enfants de Paris."* Said he of them indeed once, when pointing them out to the Russian Envoy at the grand review of June 1810:

> Mark those soldiers, Prince: that is my 45th—my brave children of Paris! If ever cartridges are burned between my brother the Emperor of Russia and me, I will show him the efficiency of my 45th. It was they who stormed your Russian batteries at Austerlitz. They are scamps (*"des vauriens"*) off duty, but lions on campaign; you should see their dash, their intrepidity; above all,

their cheerfulness under fire!

Small men—"ideal *voltigeurs*" Napoleon also called the 45th they stood a poor chance against the stalwart swordsmen of the Scots Greys.

It was they who were to yield up the first of our British Eagle-trophies of Waterloo. The prize fell to a non-commissioned officer of the Greys, Sergeant Charles Ewart, a Kilmarnock man, who achieved the feat of taking it single-handed. Ewart, an athletic fellow of splendid physique and herculean strength, six feet four in his stockings, and a notable *sabreur*, was plunging through the struggling press of infantry, slashing out to right and left, when he caught sight of the Eagle of the 45th, with its gorgeous new silken flag, bearing the glittering inscription in letters of gold—"Austerlitz, Jena, Friedland, Essling, Wagram." It was being hurried away to the rear for safety in the middle of a small band of devoted men who surrounded it, and were fighting hard with their bayonets to keep the British off. Sergeant Ewart saw that and rode straight for the Eagle-bearer. Parrying the bayonet-thrusts at him as he got up, he cut down the French officer who carried the Eagle, and then had a fight with two others. These, first one and then the other, were killed or disabled by the sergeant, who in the end carried off the splendid trophy triumphantly.

Ewart himself, in a letter to his father, tells his own story of the taking of the Eagle:

> He and I had a hard contest for it. He thrust for my groin; I parried it off and cut him through the head, after which I was attacked by one of their lancers, who threw his lance at me, but missed the mark by my throwing it off with my sword, at my right side. Then I cut him from the chin upwards, which went through his teeth. Next I was attacked by a foot-soldier, who, after firing at me, charged me with his bayonet; but he very soon lost the combat, for I parried it and cut him down through the head. That finished the contest for the Eagle.

Napoleon was watching the progress of the fight through his glasses. He witnessed the charge of the Scots Greys—unaware, of course, that it was his pet "*Enfants de Paris*" who were undergoing their fate. "*Qu'ils sont terribles ces chevaux gris!*" was the exclamation that, according to the guide De Coster, fell from Napoleon's lips at the sight. The Greys cut his unlucky 45th to pieces, and had overthrown the rest of Marcognet's Division in three minutes. "In three minutes," says a

The fight for the standard
Sergeant Ewart of the Scots Greys taking the Eagle of the 45th at Waterloo..

British officer in the charge, "the column was totally overthrown and numbers of them taken prisoners."

Sabring their way through the remnants of the 45th, and leaving the prisoners to be secured by the Highlanders, the Greys then charged the supporting regiment, the 25th of the Line. These, "lost in amazement at the suddenness and wildness of the charge and its terrific effect on their comrades on the higher ground in front," were caught in the act of trying to form square. Some of them fired a few shots at the dragoons, but the impetus of the first charge carried the Greys in among them with a rush, driving in the foremost ranks and making the rest of the column in rear roll back and break up. In panic and despair they threw down their muskets and, according to a British officer, "surrendered in crowds." The Eagle of the 25th, however, was saved. It was carried safely off the field, and is now one of the Napoleonic relics at the Invalides.

Ewart was at once sent to Brussels with the trophy, and on his arrival carried it through the crowded streets "amidst the acclamations of thousands of spectators who saw it." He was given an ensigncy in the 3rd Royal Veteran Battalion in recognition of his exploit. The sword he used at Waterloo is now among the treasures of Chelsea Hospital, and Ewart's old regiment bears embroidered on its standard a French Eagle, with the legend "Waterloo."[4]

Within a few moments of Sergeant Ewart capturing the Eagle of the 45th, an officer of the Royal Dragoons, Captain A. K. Clark (afterwards Sir A. K. Clark-Kennedy) took, also in hand-to-hand fight, the other Eagle sent home by Wellington from Waterloo—that of the 105th of the Line, the leading regiment of Bourgeois' Brigade.

The Royals, on the right of the Union Brigade, came down on the French left column. That, as yet, had had no enemy in front of it, and was advancing with cheers and shouts of triumph across the crest-line of the ridge. It overlapped and extended beyond the flank of what had been Picton's line, and so far had only been fired at from a distance

---

4. The *"fanion"* of the second battalion of the 45th shared the fate of the regimental Eagle. It fell to Private Wheeler of the 28th, the "Slashers," (*Slashers* also published by Leonaur), the present 1st Battalion of the Gloucestershire Regiment. The 28th, on the left of Picton's line, had, like the Highlanders, charged forward among the French, following close after the Greys. Wheeler, after a fierce fight with the bearer of the *"fanion,"* in which he was severely wounded, bayoneted the French sergeant and carried off the trophy. It disappeared in an unexplained manner some days later, during Wellington's march on Paris, while being forwarded to the Duke's headquarters.

by artillery and part of the 95th. Suddenly the French were startled by the apparition of a mass of cavalry quite near; coming on within eighty or ninety yards of them—emerging from the battle-smoke at a gallop.

The sight took them completely by surprise. The loud shouts of triumph stopped abruptly. One of the Royals describes:

> The head of the column appeared to be seized with a panic, gave us a fire which brought down about twenty men, went instantly about, and endeavoured to regain the opposite side of the hedges.

They had just crossed the Wavre road along the slope, about halfway up. It was the men of one corps, the 105th of the Line, who so turned back. They, of all in the regiments of Napoleon's army, knew what it was to be charged by cavalry. They had had one fearful experience of what cold steel in strong hands could do, and wanted no second. They were the same 105th whom Wellington's Hanoverian Dragoons, in the pursuit after Salamanca, had ridden down and slaughtered so mercilessly. Once more the fearful fate was about to overtake them- was at hand, was on them! In the ranks were many veterans who had served in the 105th in Spain before 1814, and had rejoined on Napoleon's return from Elba. The slaughter after Salamanca was a grim and horrifying memory in the regiment that every man shuddered to recall. It all came back vividly to them now, as the flashing sabres of the Royal Dragoons burst into view, making for them across the ridge. The whole regiment gave back and broke, turning for help to the supporting 28th in rear.

But they were not able to reach their refuge in time. Without drawing rein the Royals pressed home their charge. They were into the 105th in a moment, cutting them down on all sides.

In that *mêlée* the Eagle of the 105th met its fate. Captain Clark-Kennedy himself describes how that came about how he came to take the Eagle. He was in command of the centre squadron, leading through the thick of the ill-fated infantrymen.

> I did not see the Eagle and Colour (for there were two Colours, but only one with an Eagle) until we had been probably five or six minutes engaged. It must, I should think, have been originally about the centre of the column, and got uncovered from the change of direction. When I first saw it, it was perhaps about forty yards to my left, and a little in my front. The officer

who carried it, and his companions, were moving with their backs towards me, and endeavouring to force their way through the crowd.

I gave the order to my squadron, 'Right shoulders forward! Attack the Colour!' leading direct on the point myself. On reaching it I ran my sword into the officer's right side, a little above the hip-joint. He was a little to my left side, and he fell to that side, with the Eagle across my horse's head. I tried to catch it with my left hand, but could only touch the fringe of the flag; and it is probable it would have fallen to the ground, had it not been prevented by the neck of Corporal Styles' horse, who came close up on my left at the instant, and against which it fell. Corporal Styles was standard-coverer: his post was immediately behind me, and his duty to follow wherever I led.

When I first saw the Eagle, I gave the order 'Right shoulders forward! Attack the Colour!' and on running the officer through the body I called out twice together, 'Secure the Colour! Secure the Colour! It belongs to me!' This order was addressed to some men close to me, of whom Corporal Styles was one.

On taking up the Eagle I endeavoured to break the Eagle off the pole, with the intention of putting it into the breast of my coat, but I could not break it. Corporal Styles said, 'Pray, sir, do not break it,' on which I replied, 'Very well. Carry it to the rear as fast as you can. It belongs to me!'

Taking hold of the Eagle, Corporal Styles turned away. He had a fight to get through with it, and had, we are told, literally to cut his way back to safety.

Captain Clark-Kennedy, who received two wounds and had two horses killed under him, was given the C.B. He was granted later, as an augmentation to his family arms, the representation of a Napoleonic Eagle and flag; with for crest a "*demi*-dragoon holding a flag with an Eagle on it." Corporal Styles was appointed to an ensigncy in the West India Regiment. The Royal Dragoons wear the device of a Napoleonic Eagle as collar-badge, and bear an Eagle embroidered on their standard.

As with the 45th, so with the 105th—both battalions of each regiment lost their colours; the regimental Eagle and the "*fanion*" of the second battalion. The "*fanion*" of the 105th, described as "a dark blue silken flag, with on it the words '*105me Régiment d'Infanterie de Ligne*,'" came into British possession in a manner that is not clear. It was not taken in fight by the Royals. Was it picked up on the field after the battle by some camp-follower and sold? Its existence and whereabouts remained unknown until some twenty-four years afterwards. As it happened, curiously, General Clark-Kennedy, as he then was, himself lighted upon it by chance, hanging in the hall of Sir Walter Scott's home at Abbotsford. How it got there, in spite of all inquiries, the general was unable to discover.

Two other Eagles, it would appear, had adventures at Waterloo.

One, according to an unconfirmed story, was taken and lost by the Inniskillings, who charged the 54th and 55th of the Line, stationed at the rear of Bourgeois' Brigade, just after the Royals attacked the leading battalion of that column. A trooper named Penfold claimed to have taken the Eagle of one of the two regiments:

> After we charged, I saw an Eagle which I rode up to, and seized hold of it. The man who bore it would not give it up, and I dragged him along by it for a considerable distance. Then the pole broke about the middle, and I carried off the Eagle. Immediately after that I saw a comrade, Hassard, in difficulties, and, giving the Eagle to a young soldier of the Inniskillings, I went to his aid. The Eagle got dropped and lost.

The second of these two Eagles is said to have been captured by the Blues, the Royal Horse Guards, and then lost in much the same way. *Wellington's Supplemental Despatches*, records:

> A private in the Blues killed a French officer and took an Eagle; but his own horse being killed, he could not keep it.

A French officer also mentions the taking of the Eagle by the Blues and its recovery. About the time that the ill-fated 45th of the Line and the 105th lost their Eagles in front of Picton's Division, another Eagle elsewhere had a narrow escape from capture, being saved by its colonel's personal act. That took place in front of Hougoumont, with the Eagle of the 1st of the Line. The regiment was in Jerome Bonaparte's Division in front of Hougoumont, and had made an attack on the outbuildings of the *château*, which the defenders had beaten off.

At the last moment, as the French assault recoiled, the Eagle-bearer and his two fellows were shot down together. The battalion fell back, leaving the Eagle lying on the ground in the open, beside its dead guardians. For the moment, apparently, the British defenders did not see the trophy thus left within their reach. Before they did so Colonel Cubières, of the 1st of the Line, discovered its loss and saw where it had fallen. He ran out by himself, picked up the Eagle, and, escaping harm of any kind, carried it back to the regiment. According to M. Thiers, "the English officers checked the fire of their men while the deed was being performed, in admiration of his courage" an interesting detail in the story if true!

The Last Attack and After: The Eagles of the Guard

In the third episode in the story of Waterloo we strike another note. How the Eagles of the Guard fared in the closing hour of the battle, when Napoleon staked his last desperate throw and lost—that final phase remains to tell.

Fourteen Eagles of the Guard were on the field. All came safely through the battle and survived the risks and perils of the night retreat that followed, to recross the frontier with the rallied remnants of the stricken host. Only three, however, are now in existence: one at the Invalides; the other two in private keeping in France, The remaining eleven were, some of them at any rate, destroyed by the officers on the final disbanding of the Grand Army, refusing to give them up to the emissaries of the Bourbon *régime* sent to receive them for conveyance to Vincennes, where as many as could be got hold of among the regimental Eagles underwent their fate by fire.

Five Eagles went forward in the great last-hope attack of the Guard against the centre of Wellington's position, the overthrow of which cost Napoleon the battle. They were the Eagles of the 3rd and 4th Grenadiers of the Guard, and of three regiments of the *Chasseurs* of the Guard, the 1st, 3rd, and 4th. All five are among those that have disappeared since Waterloo.

Close beside the Eagle of the 3rd Grenadiers it was that Marshal Ney fought so heroically, as he led in person the historic grand attack of the Imperial Guard. His fifth horse was shot under Ney in the advance, and he then drew his sword and strode forward on foot alongside the Eagle-bearer. So he led until the column reeled back and broke under the sudden attack of the British Guards across the crest-line of the slope. At that moment Ney lost his footing, and fell in the confusion. "He disappeared," says a French officer, "just at the moment that the Guard gave way. But he was up again in a moment, and with voice and gesture strove his hardest to rally them."

It was to no purpose. The great column wavered, swayed, and then fell apart in disorder. "*Mitraillée, fusillée, reduit à quinze ou seize cent hommes, la Garde recule!*" Ney was swept off his feet in the retreat, and borne backwards; carried away in the rush of the fugitives, struggling helplessly in the crowd. "Bathed in perspiration, his eyes blazing with indignation, foaming at the mouth, his uniform torn open, one of his epaulets cut away by a sabre-slash, his star of the Legion of Honour dented by a bullet, bleeding, muddy, heroic, holding a broken sword in his hand, he shouted to the men, 'See how a Marshal of France dies on the battlefield!' But it was in vain: he did not die."

Then Ney, mounting a trooper's horse, made for a regiment near, whose men were falling back in fair order, with their Eagle borne defiantly in their midst—the 8th of the Line. With them was a battalion of the 95th, also displaying their Eagle gallantly as they, too, tried to withdraw in regular formation. Ney made them face about, and put himself at their head. He appealed to them in the words he had used just before, when trying to rally the Guard: "*Suivez moi, camarades. Je vais vous montrer comment meurt un Maréchal de France sur le champ de bataille!*"

The men turned to face the enemy, with a shout of "*Vive le Maréchal Ney!*" They charged forward towards where some of the red-coats of Kempt's and Pack's infantry showed themselves in the van of the pursuers. But at the same instant some horsemen of a Prussian hussar regiment dashed at them at a gallop. The sight of the horsemen was too much for their shattered nerves. They turned their backs and ran off panic-stricken. Ney's last rallied band broke and fled, with cries of "*Sauve qui peut!*"

Yet not quite all. A small band of the men of the 8th kept round their Eagle, and retired in order, still holding it up. Chef de Bataillon Rullière, of the 95th, snatched the Eagle of that regiment from its bearer, broke the staff, and carried off the Eagle concealed under his coat.

Ney's sixth horse was shot under him as the men turned. Again getting to his feet he staggered on in the midst of the crowd of fugitives until he at last found his way into one of the rallying squares formed in rear by some of the survivors of the Guard. There now, beside the Eagle of the 4th Chasseurs of the Guard, Ney made his last stand at Waterloo—at bay, desperate. He fought in the square, "shoulder to shoulder with the rest, shooting and thrusting with a musket and bayonet he got hold of," as the square slowly made its retreat off the field, until in the darkness it broke up, and the men dispersed. The devotion of a mounted officer who met the marshal on foot, utterly worn out and by himself, and gave up his horse to him, enabled Ney in the end to reach a place of safety.

Napoleon was watching the Second Column of the Guard at the moment of its disaster. How the overwhelming catastrophe burst on his gaze, abruptly and all unexpectedly, makes one of the most dramatic of historic scenes. At that moment Napoleon was about to lead in person the reserve of the Guard, three battalions which he had retained near him throughout, to reinforce the fighting line.

While they were being marshalled for the attack—one battalion deployed, with a battalion in close column on either side—he kept his glass turned upon the conflict in which he intended to bear a part.

Suddenly his hand fell.

'*Mais ils sont mêlée!*' he ejaculated in a tone of horror, his voice hollow and quavering. He addressed his *aide de camp*, Count Flahault, who was under no illusion as to what troops were meant. The sun had just set. There was no radiance to prevent all men seeing what was going on out there in the north-west.

Immediately on that followed the general collapse: the almost instantaneous breakup of the French Army all along the line.

First the trampled corn in rear was sprinkled, then it was covered, with a confused mass of men moving south; behind and among them the sabres of Vivian's hussars and Vandeleur's dragoons rose and fell, hacking and hewing on every side.

'*La Garde recule!*' sounded like a sob in the motionless ranks of the Old Guard (the three battalions near Napoleon), and sped with astonishing swiftness to every part of the field. '*La Garde recule!*' cried the men of Allix, Donzelot, and Marcognet, and began to melt away from the vantage ground they had recently so nobly won. '*La Garde recule!*' whispered Reille's columns, still unbroken on the left. Far on the right, Durutte's battalions, suddenly confronted by the heads of Ziethen's columns, where they had been told to look for Grouchy's, caught up the word.

Next, the uneasy murmur, '*Nous sommes trahis!*' was heard for was there not treason? Had not General Bourmont and his staff, and other officers, openly gone over to the enemy? '*La Garde recule!*' Oh fatal cry! soon swelling into one still more dreadful—last tocsin of the soldier's agony—'*Sauve qui peut!*' Papelotte and La Haye were abandoned, and from the east, as already from the west, the wreck of the Last Army rolled to-

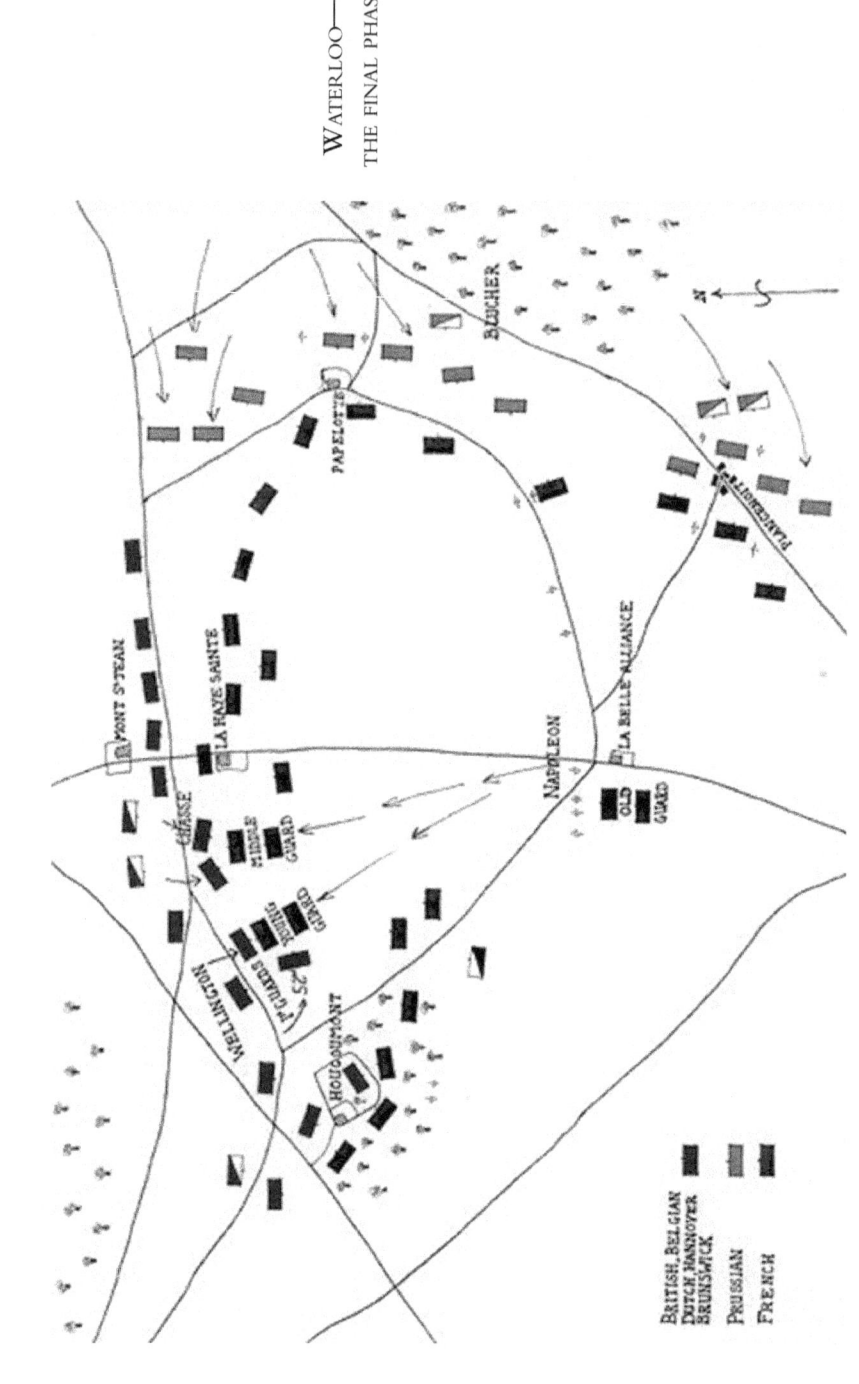

wards the Charleroi road.

The Eagle that was close beside Napoleon at that most awful moment of his life, as he saw his Guard break and fall back in confusion, is at the Invalides now. It is the Eagle of the 2nd Grenadiers of the Guard; one of the three reserve battalions that were forming up to go forward at the moment of the catastrophe.

Napoleon watched the panic begin to spread over the field for a brief moment. Then he roused himself to try to meet the impending crash. First he formed the Guard battalions nearest him into square. Then he sent off his last remaining gallopers, in the futile hope that it might be possible to rally the men of the nearest divisions to him before they had time to scatter. But the effort was hopeless: it was beyond possibility to stem the raging torrent of frantic soldiers, now in full flight on every side, racing past in the direction of Jemmapes. The lie that he had sent round just before the Guard started on its charge, that Grouchy had arrived, recoiled on his own head. The panic-stricken soldiers would not be stopped.

They had been told that Grouchy had arrived. They had found instead Ziethen's terrible Prussians. Now they would listen to nothing. The fugitives streamed past, rushing on and bellowing as they went that they had been betrayed and that all was lost!

After that Napoleon rode into the nearest square, and took shelter in its midst. It was that of the Second Battalion of the 2nd Chasseurs of the Guard. The square moved off at once towards La Belle Alliance, and, turning there into the Charleroi road, took its way back towards Rossomme, half a mile in rear, where the two battalions of the 1st and 2nd Grenadiers of the Old Guard had remained all day.

At Rossomme Napoleon passed to the square of the First Battalion of the 1st Grenadiers of the Old Guard. The two battalions of the Guard there had already formed in squares of their own accord, with their Eagles held on high in their midst. They were joined by the 1st Chasseurs of the Guard, coming up from Caillou, a short distance in rear. The three squares held their ground firmly, beating off the headmost of the Prussian attacks. They remained halted until, on some of the Prussian artillery nearing the place, Napoleon himself gave the order to move away in retreat.

At a slow step, the drums rolling out the stately "Grenadier's March," sullen and defiant, the Old Guard, with Napoleon in the midst of the square of the 1st Grenadiers, set forth on their last journey. Their Eagle

The square of the Old Guard at bay after Waterloo

was still borne on high in their midst—close beside Napoleon. It is the Eagle that is now treasured in Paris by the descendants of General Petit, the commander of the grenadiers at Waterloo the Eagle of the *Adieu* of Fontainebleau; the same Eagle that led the Guard at Austerlitz and Jena, at Eylau and Friedland, at Wagram, and throughout all the horrors of the retreat from Moscow. It escorted Napoleon off the field after Waterloo.

The Grenadiers of the Guard escorted Napoleon for four miles from the battlefield, beating back repeated efforts that were made by Prussian cavalry to break up their ranks. To maintain their formation to the last was their only hope of safety; and terrible were the measures they took to safeguard themselves and keep their ranks intact. Friend or foe who attempted to get in among them was mercilessly shot down. "*Nous tirons*," describes General Petit, "*sur tout ce qui presentaient, amis et ennemis, de peur de laisser entrer les uns avec les autres.*" They took their way along the Charleroi road; the 2nd Grenadiers marching on the *chaussée* itself, the 1st Grenadiers to the left of the road. With marvellous calmness and cool courage did the veterans proceed on their way.

> Every few minutes they stopped to rectify the alignment of the faces of the square, and to keep off pursuit by means of rapid and well-sustained musketry.

Erckmann-Chatrian's soldier of the 25th, who was amongst the fugitives streaming across country on either side of the high-road, tells how he heard from afar the stately drum-beat of their march. "In the distance *La Grenadière* sounded like an alarm-bell in the midst of a conflagration. Yet, indeed, this was much more terrible—it was the last drum-beat of France! This rolling of the drums of the Old Guard sounding forth in the midst of disaster had in it something infinitely pathetic as well as terrible." (Also published by Leonaur in *The Napoleonic Novels: Volume 1-The Conscript & Waterloo.*)

And of the scene with Napoleon in the square of the Grenadiers as it tramped its way along, we have this from Thiers:

> With sombre but calm countenance, he rode in the centre of the square, his far-seeing glance as it were probing futurity and realising that more than a battle had been lost that day. He only interrupted his gloomy meditations to inquire now and again for his lieutenants, some of whom were among the wounded near him. The soldiers all round seemed stupefied by the disas-

ter. The men moved stolidly on, almost without a word to one another. Napoleon alone seemed to be able to speak; occasionally addressing a few words to the Major-General (Soult), or to his brother Jerome, who rode beside him. Now and again, when harassed by the Prussian squadrons, the square would halt, and the side that was attacked fired on the assailants, after which the sad and silent march was resumed.

Throughout the march, keeping their position at a little distance from the squares of the Grenadiers, rode the Horse-Grenadiers and the Mounted *Chasseurs* of the Guard. One of the finest displays of soldierly endurance ever made, perhaps, was that given by the Horse-Grenadiers of the Guard as the magnificent regiment left the field, "moving at a walk, in close columns and in perfect order; as if disdaining to allow itself to be contaminated by the confusion that prevailed around it." So describes a British officer who saw them ride away. They beat off all attacks and kept steadily and compactly together.

They literally walked from the field in the most orderly manner, moving majestically along, with their Eagle in their midst, as though merely marching to take up their ground for a field-day.

This, further, is what a British officer of Light Dragoons, who came up with them in the pursuit, says of their heroic demeanour:

Seeing the men of our brigade approach, they halted, formed line, and fired a volley—a rare thing for dragoons—and waited a few minutes, as much as to say, 'We are ready to receive your charge if you are so disposed'; then finding we did not advance, they again continued their slow retreat.

The Eagle of the Horse-Grenadiers has disappeared since Waterloo: that of the Mounted *Chasseurs* of the Guard is in existence, in France, in the custody of a member of the Bonaparte family. It was preserved by General Lefebvre-Desnouettes, colonel-in-chief of the regiment, who commanded the *Chasseurs* at Waterloo. Carried in safety to France, the Eagle was then taken to America, when the general, on whose head a price had been placed, escaped across the Atlantic in the autumn of 1815. He presented it later to Joseph Bonaparte, in the possession of whose representatives the Eagle is now. It still bears attached to the staff the green silk guidon-shaped flag, inscribed "*Chasseurs de la Garde*," and embroidered with gold and silver laurel-leaves, which it bore at Waterloo.

Napoleon quitted the square of Grenadiers about two miles from Jemmapes. By that time the Prussians had ceased their attacks on the Guard for easier prey elsewhere. He rode on at a little distance ahead; the battalions of the Guard at the same time re-forming into columns of march. They kept with the Emperor until the neighbourhood of Jemmapes was reached. There Napoleon and Soult and the others quitted the road, betaking themselves across the fields to make their way as best they could to Charleroi, whence Napoleon was able to continue his flight in a post-chaise.

Yet another of the Waterloo Eagles of the Guard with a story to be told of it was that of the 2nd Chasseurs—one of the Eagles that have now disappeared. How the Eagle was saved from capture, and finally brought through to safety, recalls a remarkable and dramatic incident of the battle.

The 2nd Chasseurs was one of the twelve battalions of the Young Guard detached by Napoleon late in the afternoon to assist General Lobau and the Sixth Army Corps to keep off the Prussian flank attack. Between them they saved the army from an even worse catastrophe than that which actually befell Napoleon at Waterloo—from having to surrender. For nearly an hour after the rout had become general, the Sixth Corps, and the battalions of the Young Guard assisting it, by their heroic resistance, prevented the Prussians from breaking in on the only line of retreat open to the defeated army, and enabled Napoleon to get clear away. To quote the words of a modern military writer:

> Lobau, recognised to the full that he alone interposed between the Prussians and the French line of retreat. If he failed, retreat would be cut off, and the army taken in rear as well as in front and flank; not a man would get away. The fate of the Army, the Emperor, of France, rested on Lobau at the supreme moment, and splendidly he did his duty. Dusk had given way to dark, only illuminated by the blazing ruins of Planchenoit, before Lobau retired, but by that time the rear of the flying army had cleared the point of peril, and comparative safety was assured. Still steady, and in good order, he took post on the highroad to close the line of flight and block pursuit, and the gallant remnant of the Sixth Corps and the Young Guard had to bear the full fury of the combined advance of the enemy. Nothing at Waterloo can surpass for coolness, courage, and determination the heroic resistance of Lobau.

It was in the village of Planchenoit that the 2nd Chasseurs fought side by side with the other battalions of the Guard in that quarter under the leadership of General Pelet, to whom Napoleon had specially entrusted the defence of the post. Planchenoit was defended foot by foot at the point of the bayonet against ever-increasing numbers of the Prussians. The 2nd Chasseurs were the last troops of all to quit, after contesting the village house by house, cottage by cottage, fighting the Prussians man to man among the bushes and walls of the gardens, and finally in the churchyard, where they made their last stand at bay, desperately combating among the tombstones. Fresh Prussians kept coming up to join in the attack, but the 2nd Chasseurs, their Eagle defiantly displayed in the midst of the battling throng, resisted stubbornly. When at the last they drew off, the whole of Planchenoit was a mass of flames, blazing from end to end.

There remained a rough half-mile of open ground before they could get to the Charleroi road—the line of retreat along which, by that time, a large proportion of the fugitives from the main army had got away. The 2nd Chasseurs, in rear of all, as they left their last shelter in Planchenoit and were beyond the churchyard walls, were swept down on by a furious rush of Prussian cavalry, and half the regiment was cut to pieces. The moon was rising by that time, and the Prussians had sufficient light for their deadly work.

The survivors, broken up, and thrown in irremediable disorder, could after that only run for their lives. But they still bore their Eagle among them. It was draped under a black cloth. Somebody, in some house in the village, as they were falling back to the churchyard, had, it would appear, caught up a strip of crape or black cloth, and hastily wrapped it round the Eagle to conceal it in that way from hostile eyes. The Eagle-bearer refused to break the Eagle from the staff, and hide it under his coat, as others had done elsewhere with other Eagles.

With the Eagle so covered, a small party of devoted soldiers were accompanying their standard as the survivors of the Prussian charge hastened towards the Charleroi road, when there came yet another attack from the Prussian horse, who charged among them and trampled them down as the troopers slashed mercilessly at the fugitives. At that moment the Eagle and its guardians found themselves near the General. They were isolated and cut off in the midst of the wild *mêlée*. Pelet caught sight of them, desperately striving to protect the Eagle-bearer, who was frantically clutching at the Eagle-staff as he held on to it and tried to get through.

Pelet made for the group, shouting at the top of his voice: "Rally, Chasseurs! Rally on me! Save your Eagle or die round it!" ("*A moi, Chasseurs! A moi! Sauvons l'Aigle ou mourons autour d'elle!*")

In the midst of the frenzied tumult his cry for help was somehow heard by the men ahead. They turned back in their flight and fought their way to the threatened Eagle. Others pressed round to join them, until by degrees was formed a compact body between two and three hundred in number, who with their bayonets kept the cavalry back as they fought their way towards the high-road step by step.

More than once they had to halt and face about, as the Prussian horsemen in their repeated attempts to capture the Eagle circled round them, and dashed in at them again and again, but,:

> Forming what is usually termed a rallying square, and lowering their bayonets, they succeeded in repulsing the charges of the cavalry. (At one point in the retreat) some guns were brought to bear upon them, and subsequently a brisk fire of musketry; but notwithstanding the awful sacrifice which was thus offered up in defence of their precious charge, they succeeded in reaching the main line of retreat, and saved alike the Eagle and the Honour of the Regiment.

★★★★★

The Eagles of the Guard all came safely through the turmoil and horrors of the night of the rout after Waterloo. And—it seems incredible, but the fact is vouched for by several officers—so did the other Eagles of the army. All at Waterloo, it is declared, were brought back to France, except the two taken from the ill-fated 45th and the 105th of the Line by the Scots Greys and the Royals. Those two only remained as trophies in the hands of the victors. General Charras, whose good faith we have no right to impugn, declares the fact in explicit language, and another officer relates how, on the day after the battle, when the rallied remains of the army assembled at Phillippeville and Maubeuge, "the soldiers wept tears of joy at learning how many of their Eagles had been saved."

Says General Charras, describing how the Eagles were saved that night:

> Two standards had been lost on the battlefield. There was none other lost. In the crowd of disbanded horsemen and foot-soldiers, marching and running pell-mell, some still armed, others having thrown away or broken their sabres and guns under the

impulse of rage, of despair, of terror, there were to be seen, by the pale light of the moon, little groups of officers of every grade, and of soldiers, spontaneously collected round the standard of each regiment, and advancing sabre in hand, bayonet on the gun, resolute and imperturbable in the midst of the general disorder.

'*Place au drapeau!*' cried they when the rout arrested their march, and this cry always sufficed to cause the very men who had become deaf to every word of command and to all discipline to stand aside before them and open a passage. They had often to endure peril, they had often to repulse the enemy's attacks, but they saved their conquered flags from the attempts and hands of the conqueror.

Grouchy also saved all his Eagles—although one had its adventures in the attack on Wavre, and was nearly lost to the Prussians. The story this time is not exactly creditable to some of those concerned; but the regiment in question, it must be said, had but few old soldiers in its ranks, having been made up almost entirely of recently levied and half-trained conscripts. Also, it had just previously been very roughly handled by the Prussians on the battlefield of Ligny. There, indeed, it had been charged by cavalry, and had suffered severely. The unfortunate regiment was the 70th of the Line.

In Grouchy's fighting at Wavre they were in Vandamme's Division, which had orders to carry the bridge over the Dyle and storm the town, held by the Prussians in considerable force. To give the 70th a chance of getting their revenge for Ligny, and winning back the old good name of the regiment, Vandamme specially chose them for the post of honour in the attack; appointing the 70th to lead the van in the preliminary storming of the bridge. They led the attack, dashing forward bravely enough at the outset, and got halfway across. Then they stopped short, their ranks decimated by the furious fire with which the Prussians received them from the houses on the opposite bank, hesitated, went on a few paces, stopped again, and finally ran back in panic.

The sight of the sudden rout maddened their leader, Colonel Maury. Stooping from his charger, he snatched hold of the Eagle from its bearer, and held it up before the men. "What! you scoundrels! You dishonoured me two days ago; you are again disgracing me today! Forward! Follow me!" ("*Comment, canaille! Vous m'avez deshonoré avant-hier, et vous recidiviez aujourdhui! En avant! Suivez moi!*") Brandishing the Eagle the colonel turned his horse to ride back across the bridge. The drums beat the charge: the regiment followed. But all was to no purpose. As fate willed it, the gallant colonel fell, shot dead before he could get across, and at the sight of his fall panic again seized the regiment. They ran wildly back again, leaving the dead colonel's body and the Eagle lying halfway across the bridge.

The Eagle was rescued and brought back by the men of another regiment. Had it not been for the sudden rush forward of the leading company of the 22nd of the Line, the regiment supporting the 70th in the attack, the Eagle would have been taken. Several Prussian soldiers had indeed already run forward to pick it up, and their leader was in the act of doing so when the foremost of the rescuers arrived, beat back the Prussians, and recovered the fallen Eagle.

The failure of this one regiment at Wavre is the only recorded instance of bad behaviour before the enemy in the Waterloo campaign. And for it too, in view of the composition of the regiment in question, some allowance may surely be made.

THE EAGLES ANNOUNCE VICTORY TO LONDON

The last of the four episodes is supplemental: the story of how Wellington's Eagle-trophies themselves first announced Waterloo to London.

The two Eagles were sent to England immediately after the battle, together with Wellington's Waterloo despatch, by Major the Hon. Henry Percy, of the 11th Light Dragoons, who was almost the only member of Wellington's staff who went through the battle unwounded. He arrived in London, displaying the Eagles from his post-chaise as he travelled through the streets, on the stroke of eleven o'clock on the night of Wednesday, June 21.

Up to then not a word had come from Wellington: not a word of reliable news as to what had happened had reached England. Rumours of an early check to the French had arrived, from unofficial sources, during the previous day, but nothing more had been heard, and all London was on tenterhooks of suspense.

The battle was fought on Sunday the 18th. But no news of it, or in regard to it, of any kind reached England during either Monday or Tuesday. There was no intelligence from the seat of war at all. On the Wednesday morning the *Times* announced vaguely that Napoleon had struck the first blow unsuccessfully. A Mr. Sutton, of Colchester, it said, the owner of packet-boats running between Harwich and

Ostend, had forwarded a message to the effect that there had been fighting on the 15th and 16th and skirmishing on the 17th, and that a fresh battle was beginning on the morning of the 18th. His informant at Brussels had sent that news.

There was no more news until Wednesday afternoon, when the *Sun* came out with a special edition stating that the Government had received no despatches, but that:

> A gentleman who left Ghent on Monday, and two others from Brussels, brought word that Sunday's battle had been successful.

All London was in the streets until between ten and eleven that night, in a state of eager expectation; but repeated inquiries at the Horse Guards, at the War Office, and at the Mansion House only met with the answer—"No news yet."

It was just as the crowds were dispersing, tired of waiting, and taking it as certain that nothing could be known until the morning, as the clocks were on the stroke of eleven, that Major Percy arrived in London. His niece, Lady Bagot, in whose words the story may best be told says:

> He left the Duchess of Richmond's ball on the night before the battle, and had no time to change his dress, or even his shoes, before going into action. When he received orders to go to England with the despatches, he posted to Antwerp, and there took the first sailing boat he could find to convey him to Dover, where he landed in the afternoon. He found that a report of the victory had preceded him there. The Rothschilds had chartered a fast sloop to lie off Antwerp, and bring the first news of the battle to the English shore—news which was to be used for Stock Exchange purposes.
>
> My uncle's confirmation of the rumour of a great victory was received with the greatest relief and enthusiasm. At that time the hotel-keeper at Dover, a certain Mr. Wright, had the monopoly of the posting arrangements between that port and London. He immediately placed his best horses at my uncle's disposal, and despatched an express to order fresh relays all along the road. Besides the despatches my uncle took the two captured Eagles of the Imperial Guard with him. These, being too large to go into the carriage, were placed so as to stick out of the windows, one on each side. In this manner he drove straight to the Horse

Guards, where he learnt that the commander-in-chief, at that time the Duke of York, was dining out. He next proceeded to Lord Castlereagh's, and was told that he and the Duke of York were both dining with a lady in St. James's Square. To this house he drove, and there learnt that the Prince Regent was also of the dinner-party.

Requesting to be shown immediately into the dining-room, he entered that apartment bearing the despatches and the Eagles with him. He was covered with dust and mud, and, though unwounded himself, bore the marks of battle upon his coat. The dessert was being placed upon the table when he entered, and as soon as the Prince Regent saw him he commanded the ladies to leave the room. The Prince Regent then held out his hand, saying, 'Welcome, Colonel Percy!' 'Go down on one knee,' said the Duke of York to my uncle, 'and kiss hands for the step you have obtained.' Before the despatch could be read, my uncle was besieged with inquiries of various prominent officers engaged, and had to answer 'Dead' or 'Severely wounded' so often that the Prince Regent burst into tears. The Duke of York, though greatly moved, was more composed.

By this time my uncle was exhausted from fatigue, and begged the Prince's permission to go to his father's house in Portman Square. The crowd was so great in St. James's Square, that he had the greatest difficulty in getting through it and reaching my grandfather's house, which was soon surrounded by anxious multitudes begging for news of relations and friends. My uncle told them that the victory was complete, but that the number killed and wounded was very large. He told them that he would answer more questions next morning.

The Eagles themselves in fact announced the victory in London. People in the streets saw the chaise as it passed on its way with its horses at a gallop, racing at full speed along the Old Kent Road, across Westminster Bridge, and through Parliament Street to Whitehall, "the gleaming lamps showing a French Eagle and the French flags projecting from each window."

The news spread like wild-fire, and before Colonel Percy could reach the house where the Prince Regent was dining—Mrs. Boehm's, in St. James's Square—South London was flocking over Westminster Bridge to Whitehall. The West End heard the news immediately afterwards, and everybody hurried out again into the streets.

It became quickly known where the chaise had gone after leaving the Horse Guards, and promptly an ever-increasing crowd hurried off there. Before the despatch had been read an enormous mass of people had assembled in St. James's Square, outside the house. They were in time to hear the cheering by the company inside the house that greeted the reading of the despatch; the cheers were instantly echoed back, accompanied by an outburst of vociferous shouting followed by a tremendous chorus of "God save the King!"

The windows of the dining-room were open, and a moment later the two Eagles with their tricolour flags were thrust through. They were held up, with candles at either side, to show them plainly, so that all might know that the victory had been decisive.

For a few minutes dustmen's bells and watchmen's rattles were sprung all over London. Liquor was produced at many a street-corner, and toasts were drunk to Wellington and confusion to Bonaparte.[5]

The closing scene took place on Thursday, January 18, 1816 on the

---

5. The news of Waterloo reached Paris just twenty-four hours earlier than it reached London—during the night of Tuesday, June 20. How it was broken to the French capital forms a story little less dramatic than the other story of how the news of Waterloo arrived in London. In Paris they had had news of the successful opening of the campaign. On the 18th, just as Napoleon was holding his last review, before Waterloo opened, the "triumphal battery" of the Invalides was firing a *feu de joie* in honour of victory over Blücher at Ligny. On Monday and Tuesday, the 19th and 20th, Napoleon's Ligny Bulletin, with details, was published in the *Moniteur*. When the *cafés* closed that evening, there was as yet no word of Waterloo. But at that same moment the news was arriving—in a private message to Carnot, the Minister of the Interior. What had happened leaked out first at his house.

"On that evening," describes M. Edgar Quinet, "several persons were assembled at the house of M. Carnot, and they vainly asked him for news. To evade these importunate questions, Carnot went to a card-table and sat down with three of his friends. He from whom I have this story sat opposite the Minister. By chance he raised his eyes and looked at Carnot; he saw his countenance, serious, furrowed, with tears pouring down it. The cards were thrown up; the players rose. 'The battle is lost!' exclaimed Carnot, who could contain himself no longer." The news spread through Paris like wild-fire. It was not believed at first; the catastrophe was too stunning, too terrible. To that succeeded a gloomy stupor (*une morne stupeur*). "They had not long to wait. All was known next morning. The astounding news of the rout of the army in Belgium, and the still more astounding news of the arrival of Napoleon in Paris, were spread through the great city almost simultaneously, and stirred to the depths its restless and volatile population. Twice before had Napoleon suddenly returned to Paris—from Moscow, from Leipsic—and each time alone, without an army. Thus had he again presented himself."

"General Thanksgiving Day for the Restoration of Peace." The two Eagles were on that day publicly paraded at the Horse Guards and laid up in the Chapel Royal, Whitehall, with ceremonies similar to those that attended the reception of the Barrosa and Salamanca trophies. Again the battalions of the Brigade of Guards in England, with their bands "in State clothing," turned out to take part in the display, the Eagles, as before, being made to march round the square and do formal obeisance to the British flag by being prostrated in the dust before the Colour of the King's Guard of the day, at which sight, as on the former occasions, both the troops and the crowd of spectators "instantaneously gave three loud huzzas with the most enthusiastic feeling."

The Duke of York, as commander-in-chief, presided this time at the parade. Two sergeants of the Grenadier and Third Guards who had been wounded at Waterloo were selected to carry the Eagles; escorted by a picked company of eighty-four officers and men "drawn from among the heroic defenders of Hougoumont on the field of battle." Lifeguardsmen and Blues just arrived from the Army of Occupation, in France, assisted the Foot Guards on parade.

The escort entered the Chapel Royal by the two doors in equal divisions, the band playing and marching up to the steps of the Communion Table, where they filed off to right and left. As soon as the band had ceased, the two sergeants bearing the Eagles approached the Altar and fixed upon it their consecrated banners. Both the Chaplain-General to the Forces (Arch-deacon Owen) and the Bishop of London, with two Royal Chaplains ("the Rev. Mr. Jones and the Rev. Mr. Howlett"), officiated in the service; the Bishop preaching a special sermon, with for his text Psalm 20. verses 7 and 8:

Some trust in chariots and some in horses:
but we will remember the name of the Lord our God.
They are brought down and fallen:
but we are risen and stand upright

After the customary blessing, the band played 'God save the King!' the whole congregation standing. Among those who attended were a considerable number of persons of fashion and distinction in public life, the Dukes of Gloucester and York, and the Earl of Liverpool, and several officers of the army and navy, with many elegant and distinguished females.

CHAPTER 14

After the Downfall

The remnant of the Waterloo army, as mustered and officially reported to Paris on July 1, 1815, after it had been withdrawn by convention with the Allies beyond the Loire, numbered some 23,000 of all arms.[1] The soldiers had their Eagles with them. The Eagles were still the standards of the army, although all was over with Napoleon, and he had set out on his flight from Malmaison to the coast near Rochfort to find the *Bellerophon* awaiting him there.

The last occasion on which an Eagle of Napoleon's Army had its part on parade was one day, near the Loire, with a regiment not at Waterloo. It was when the news of Napoleon's abdication reached its colonel. He was Colonel Bugeaud of the 14th of the Line, in after years the famous Marshal who gained Algeria for France. As it happened, the 14th had not long received their Eagle from the "*Champ de Mai*." It had been brought by the deputation of the regiment sent to Paris to receive it at the hands of the Emperor, but had not yet been formally presented on parade, owing to the regiment being on the march from the south-eastern frontier of France.

The 14th joined the rallied remnants of the Waterloo army to the

---

1 The Campaign of the Hundred Days, it has been estimated, from first to last cost Napoleon in round numbers, in killed, wounded, and prisoners taken in the field:
Ligny (Killed and wounded) ... 10,000
Quatre-Bras (Killed and wounded) .. 4,300
Waterloo (Killed and wounded) ... 29,500
(Prisoners unwounded) ... 7,500
Wavre (Killed and wounded) ... 1,800
Lesser actions (Killed and wounded) .. 2,100
Total .. 55,200
Out of the 126,000 men with whom Napoleon took the field, he lost some 43 per cent, of hia army in the week between June 15 and 22.

south of the Loire, and there Colonel Bugeaud made the presentation of the Eagle. For the occasion he made use of the Napoleonic formula of address at such ceremonies, but with a variation to suit the altered situation. He took the opportunity to remind the regiment that, if the chief had fallen, they yet owed allegiance to their country. The colonel began:

> Soldiers of the 14th, here is your Eagle. It is in the name of the nation that I present it to you. If the Emperor, as it is stated, is no longer our Sovereign, France remains. It is France who confides this Eagle to you as your standard; it is ever to be your talisman of victory. Swear that as long as a soldier of the 14th exists no enemy's hand shall touch it!

"We swear it!" responded the soldiers all together, and then the officers stepped forward in front of the ranks, waving their swords and again shouting, "We swear it!"

The end for the Eagles of Napoleon came on August 3, 1815. On that day the Ministerial decree was promulgated, abolishing them and the tricolour flag, and disbanding the entire Army. The white Bourbon flag was restored once more, with a new form of Army organisation, which substituted "Departmental Legions" in the place of regiments. As in the year before, it was notified that all Eagles were to be sent to the Artillery *dépôt* at Vincennes for destruction there, according to law—the metal of the Eagles to be melted down, their silken tricolour flags to be burned.

The date of the final disbandment was fixed for September 30, and in almost every case there was a pathetic scene when the hour came for the soldiers to take their last farewell of their Eagles.

> On the day of the disbandment, (*describes one officer, speaking of his own regiment,*) we all paraded, and the roll was called for the last time. Then the Eagle was passed solemnly down along the line, the band playing a funeral march. The officers and soldiers, all in tears, after saluting it, embraced and kissed the Eagle. It was then escorted back to the colonel's quarters to be packed up in a box and forwarded, according to the official instructions, by carrier to the Ministry of War, thence to go to Vincennes.

In a few cases, where the senior officers knew that they had nothing to hope for in the way of consideration from the new *régime*, the Eagles were publicly broken up at the last parade by the colonels themselves, with a blacksmith's hammer or pioneer's hatchet, and the

La Revue des Morts.

silken tricolour flags cut to pieces, after which the metal fragments, together with the shreds of the flags, were distributed as keepsakes among officers and men. That being done, all silently dispersed, never to reassemble. In some other cases, as had happened a twelvemonth previously, the Eagles disappeared before the last parade—the officers in the various regiments having arranged for one of themselves to retain the Eagle of the corps privately, either by agreement or after drawing lots.

It was in this way that what Napoleonic Eagles and flags are now at the Invalides came to be there. They were kept hidden by their possessors until after the Revolution of July, 1830, and then, on the formation of the present collection of standards and trophies being officially sanctioned, most of those at present exhibited were brought to light and presented, either by those who had been treasuring them in secret, or by their heirs and families.

Three Waterloo Eagles are at the Invalides: those of the 2nd Grenadiers of the Guard, and of the 25th and 26th of the Line; these last two of the regiments in the columns charged by the Scots Greys and the Royals. In addition to the Eagles, there are at the Invalides several standards that saw service on the battlefield under Napoleon and survived the vicissitudes of war: seven flags of infantry, and as many of artillery, one *cuirassier* standard, and five other cavalry standards. Most of these originally bore Eagles on their staves, but those Eagles are now wanting.[2]

---

2. Five Eagles were on show in London in the autumn of 1815, in the so-called "Waterloo Museum," having been acquired somehow on the occupation of Paris. Two were described as the Eagles of the 5th of the Line and of the Seamen of the Guard, and two as National Guard Eagles—all four having been presented at the *Champ de Mai*. The fifth purported to be the Eagle of the "Elba Guard." None of the five had ever been in action.

ALSO FROM LEONAUR
AVAILABLE IN SOFTCOVER OR HARDCOVER WITH DUST JACKET

THE 9TH—THE KING'S (LIVERPOOL REGIMENT) IN THE GREAT WAR 1914 - 1918 by Enos H. G. Roberts—Mersey to mud—war and Liverpool men.

THE GAMBARDIER by Mark Severn—The experiences of a battery of Heavy artillery on the Western Front during the First World War.

FROM MESSINES TO THIRD YPRES by Thomas Floyd—A personal account of the First World War on the Western front by a 2/5th Lancashire Fusilier.

THE IRISH GUARDS IN THE GREAT WAR - VOLUME 1 by Rudyard Kipling—Edited and Compiled from Their Diaries and Papers—The First Battalion.

THE IRISH GUARDS IN THE GREAT WAR - VOLUME 1 by Rudyard Kipling—Edited and Compiled from Their Diaries and Papers—The Second Battalion.

ARMOURED CARS IN EDEN by K. Roosevelt—An American President's son serving in Rolls Royce armoured cars with the British in Mesopatamia & with the American Artillery in France during the First World War.

CHASSEUR OF 1914 by Marcel Dupont—Experiences of the twilight of the French Light Cavalry by a young officer during the early battles of the great war in Europe.

TROOP HORSE & TRENCH by R.A. Lloyd—The experiences of a British Lifeguardsman of the household cavalry fighting on the western front during the First World War 1914-18.

THE EAST AFRICAN MOUNTED RIFLES by C.J. Wilson—Experiences of the campaign in the East African bush during the First World War.

THE LONG PATROL by George Berrie—A Novel of Light Horsemen from Gallipoli to the Palestine campaign of the First World War.

THE FIGHTING CAMELIERS by Frank Reid—The exploits of the Imperial Camel Corps in the desert and Palestine campaigns of the First World War.

STEEL CHARIOTS IN THE DESERT by S. C. Rolls—The first world war experiences of a Rolls Royce armoured car driver with the Duke of Westminster in Libya and in Arabia with T.E. Lawrence.

WITH THE IMPERIAL CAMEL CORPS IN THE GREAT WAR by Geoffrey Inchbald—The story of a serving officer with the British 2nd battalion against the Senussi and during the Palestine campaign.

AVAILABLE ONLINE AT **www.leonaur.com**
AND FROM ALL GOOD BOOK STORES

www.ingramcontent.com/pod-product-compliance
Lightning Source LLC
Chambersburg PA
CBHW031622160426
43196CB00006B/237